# DRIVE NACHO DRIVE

### A Journey
### from the American Dream
### to the End of the World

Brad Van Orden
Sheena Van Orden

First published in 2013

Copyright © Brad Van Orden, 2013
All rights reserved

ISBN (Print): 978-0-9897665-0-0
ISBN (Kindle): 978-0-9897665-2-4
ISBN (Nook): 978-0-9897665-1-7

*To Mike McKay*

*for teaching us that there isn't a moment to waste*

# Contents

Drive Nacho Drive

# Part 1

# In a Past Life

At 4:30 I dizzily stumbled out of bed. My skis waited in the car, and as I passed the table by the front door I grabbed the breakfast I'd set out the night before. By 4:45 I was coaxing my eyes open as I barreled through the snow, NPR on the radio, banana in hand, waking up to news of skiers lost in avalanches in California. Unseasonably high snowfall this year. At 6:00 I climbed steadily upward in the dark, the cold mountain air burning my lungs with each breath, the ski slopes illuminated only by the snow's reflection of the stars in the night sky. Through my headphones I was immersed in a podcast about traveling the world. This was part of the ritual.

After an hour of hiking in the dark, imagining travel to faraway places, I reached the top of the mountain. 7:00 – just in time for the rising sun to cast a shadow of the San Francisco peaks all the way across the high desert to the Grand Canyon, barely visible below the horizon. As I put away my climbing skins, pulled on my jacket, and kicked my telemark boots back into my bindings, I couldn't shake the silly grin from my face. With a nudge of my ski pole I sent myself sailing down the mountain I'd just climbed, crouching into each turn and springing up again, laying down the day's first tracks. At the "headwall," half way down the mountain, I picked up enough speed to scare myself. *Yep, still alive!* I still couldn't get that silly grin off of my face.

By 8:00 I was back in the car heading down the mountain, just in time for an 8:30 meeting at work. There's just something about being in the mountains.

On our first morning in the Colombian Andes I awoke to an unfamiliar crispness in the air. Having spent the last five months in Central America we were getting used to stifling heat and humidity. We crawled out of our down sleeping bags and put the coffee on. It was going to be a long day.

James and Lauren emerged from their truck bundled up like New York City hobos. Overnight their front tire had gone flat, causing their truck to tilt steeply to one side, so James had spent the night crushing Lauren against the fender well. Another night in the life of a homeless person, I guess. Sheena and I had slept like babies in Nacho's pop top roof tent, but the cold was a firm reminder that we had reached the Andes.

We donned our packs, bid ado to our new friend Jeni — the tiny red-cheeked girl who lived in the rock hut next to our camp — and set off toward the towering, snow-capped peaks to the Southeast. The double track dirt road ended shortly beyond our camp, and gave way to a small singletrack leading up the valley toward *Pan de Azucar* and *El Pulpito del Diablo*, looming above.

The trail rose higher and higher over mountains of shale, and before long we found ourselves scrambling over boulders up a steep rock fall towards the first pass: *Paso de Cusiri*. If all went well we would complete two 15,000' passes before descending to the *Laguna de la Plaza*, a high glacial lake at 13,780 feet, where we would camp. We were told the hike would take about seven hours, but by the fourth hour dark clouds had moved in and cloaked the pass like a woolen shawl. The trail wound upwards in a series of steep switchbacks straight into the cloud.

In the early afternoon we reached the top of *Paso de Cusiri*, and in doing so found ourselves in the middle of a snowstorm. A mixture of snow and rain pelted us like horizontal pellets from an invisible army of pellet gun–toting boy scouts. We hid behind the wooden plank summit sign, which announced that we'd arrived at the inhospitable elevation of 14,469'. We assessed the situation, running out from behind the sign to look beyond the pass to see what lay in store for us. The trail disappeared into a carpet of dark clouds and whipping wind and snow.

"Onward and downward?" I asked, hoping for dissenters.

"Uh…It's decision time, guys," James said. Seeing the out, we had a short discussion and decided to throw in the towel and head back down in the direction we'd just come. We weren't prepared for blizzard conditions, and some of the team were already experiencing numb fingers and toes. Nothing says "killjoy" like frostbite. Or pulmonary edema.

When we reached the rock fall on the way down, the entire section had been turned into a freezing cold waterfall. I had a split second daydream of me waking up dead, wrapped in my soggy sleeping bag at the bottom of a raging, icy cascade, and silently lauded our decision to turn back.

The following day, after having returned safely, albeit very cold and very tired, we picked up camp and moved to *Hacienda La Esperanza*. Marco, a stereotypical woolen poncho–wearing Colombian cowboy, cooked us dinner in his kitchen and showed off his antiques and old photos. Outside the weather was drizzling and gray.

In the morning we awoke, threw our things together and departed camp through fields reminiscent of Switzerland, interspersed with rocky spires jutting up through the grass while long haired dairy cows moseyed about.

We hiked through a glacial valley laced with streams before climbing upwards over a series of rocky plateaus. On our right, an enormous rock wall separated us from the sprawling mountains and the tiny towns we'd driven through to get here; Onzaga, Covarachia, Soatá, and El Cocuy. To our left, glacier-capped peaks shimmered above the rocky terrain, taunting me with their 17,000 foot untracked powder bowls.

After five hours of uphill slogging we reached our destination for the night: *La Cueva del Hombre*. I had asked Marco why it was called The Man Cave before we set off from La Esperanza.

"Long ago, ducks would stop at the lake for a rest from their migration, and the men would shoot them. The men would sleep in the cave after they shot the ducks, so it is called *La Cueva del Hombre*. The ducks don't come any more." I noted that Marco should make up a more titillating story about how the Man Cave got its name.

We all set up our tents within the cave, and then Sheena and I then set off for a hike up to the lake to have a look around while James and Lauren took a nap. We bundled up and bounced out from under the overhang feeling light without our packs.

The trip from the cave to the lake took a damn, dirty long time, but once we crested the ridge and the landscape spread out in front of us, we lost our breath. *Pulmonary edema? Nope!* The mountain to the left was capped by a massive bowl of untouched snow from top to bottom, where the glacier spilled over the edge of a vast chasm; a crashing calamity of building-sized ice chunks paused in suspended animation. On the opposite side of the basin, another glacier spilled down from the top of a 17,000 foot peak, terminating at the edge of a colossal sheer rock wall. The ice composing the second glacier bore a map of its ancient history in dirty veins crisscrossing its surface, and diving into its depths. Between the walls of the basin were a series of small lakes fed by the runoff from both glaciers. All we could do was stare in awe, a mixture of blood and adrenaline coursing through our veins.

"So, how was it?" James peered out of his tent as we ducked back into the cave, having just awoken from his slumber.

I was at a loss for words. "It was…I felt like my heart was going to explode."

As evening rolled around, we concocted a feast of broken up lasagna noodles with canned tuna in olive oil, and soon the shadows engulfed our cave and a harsh chill pressed the warm air into the valley below. We all huddled into our tent and passed the evening playing the travel-size board game, *Trouble*.

The feeling as we unzipped our tent in the morning to discover the ground covered in snow was a stew of surprise, nostalgia, and regret. The continued snowfall and resulting accumulation meant that there would be no more excursions to the glacial lakes. It also meant that, since we didn't know how much snow was forecasted to fall, we would have to make a mad dash for lower elevation. We hastily drank our morning coffee and packed our things. James and Lauren, both having lost their gloves, fashioned mittens out of wool socks, and we all pulled plastic bags over our feet before slipping them into our shoes – poor man's Gore-Tex.

Hiking in the snow is about as close as we can get to a state of total serenity. The snowflakes absorb any stray sounds and create a supernatural silence, while the muffled crunch of snow under our feet composes a rhythmic soundtrack to our movement. As we silently descended through the snowy landscape my mind wandered to our winter camping trips to Durango, filling our tent with good friends and sleeping in the snow near the ski hill. I reflected on my regular hikes up Agassiz Peak before work, the shadow of the peaks stretching across the desert, and the rewarding turns. I thought about our dear friend Mike who had perished in an avalanche while backcountry skiing near his home in California. I had heard about it on NPR while heading up to the mountain before work, but never imagined that it could have been my friend who was lost. I remembered the discussion that Sheena and I had on the way home from his funeral, which ultimately led to us quitting our jobs and setting off on this very trip.

I liked that it was snowing; It put a silly grin on my face. There's just something about being in the mountains.

In the early afternoon I had raced home in my 1979 GMC van. It was the first motorized vehicle that I'd ever bought, and I had spent a great number of evenings transforming it into what I had considered the ultimate roving bachelor pad for traveling to mountain bike races. Couch, entertainment center made of particle board, old school tube television, VCR, and two subwoofers. For some reason I had highlighted the interior with strips of foam covered in zebra-striped fabric. I suppose I should be forgiven, seeing as how I was a senior in high school and just coming to terms with my bad fashion and interior decorating sense.

It was Friday, and I had a mountain bike race in two days just a few miles from my house, so today's ride would be an easy spin into town and back, maybe fifteen or twenty miles. I threw on a pair of shorts and a blue long sleeved shirt, hopped on my bike, and headed out the driveway. I still remember what I was wearing twelve years later, because it turned out to be an important day. I also remember that I had a goatee, because Sheena later told me that she thought it made me look like a creepy old man. But I'm getting ahead of myself.

As my ride wound down and I spun out the final couple of miles before home, I passed by the race venue where I noticed the trailer for the Wolf Creek Bicycles team, which was run by my friend Jerry. I figured I'd swing by and give Jerry a hard time before carrying on home.

When I arrived at the trailer, Jerry was nowhere to be found and the only soul to be seen was a brown haired girl sitting in front of the trailer sketching something in colored pencils. I parked my bike and walked over in my stretchy spandex shorts, and asked if I could have a seat. The girl looked up at me, a creepy old man with a goatee, wearing stretchy spandex shorts.

"Uh, sure," she said, not wanting to be rude. "I'm Sheena."

I took a seat and watched her draw for a few minutes as she waited for me to get bored and leave. We chatted for a while and started to hit it off, and by the end of our conversation I had asked her if she wanted to come back to my place and share in my ritualistic pre-race carbo-loading dinner of spaghetti. Of course, being in high school, it would be prepared by and eaten with my mom. She opened the trailer door, peered in and asked her dad if it would be okay. Ernie peered out of the trailer with the intense, wide eyes of a natural born killer and gave me a long, intimidating stare down. He begrudgingly agreed, and a half an hour later I returned with my creepy molester van to pick her up.

The following weekend happened to be the weekend of my senior prom. I had spent considerable time and energy planning it out, and to top it off I had even fooled a perfectly normal girl into actually coming with me to the dance. I had arranged for my racing buddy, Brandon, to drive up from Phoenix in the morning to do a mountain

9

bike ride. I had found him a date as well, so we would all drive together back to north Phoenix for dinner, before driving back to Prescott for prom, whereupon Brandon could drive back home to Phoenix. It was the plan of a stupid person, but I had spent considerable time and energy coming up with it.

When Brandon arrived, we took to the trails. Being that we were racing buddies, there was a high degree of one-upmanship going on, and we were both riding a little bit faster and trying a little bit harder than either of us was willing to lead on. The ride culminated in a three mile downhill trail, which descended some fairly rough terrain with somewhat serious consequences for mistakes. We made it down the first set of twenty or so steep log stairs designed to divert runoff, past the drop off from the elevated tree root onto the thin trail above an arroyo, and around several tight, exposed corners. As we approached the hairiest part of the trail, a descent down the side of a dry waterfall, I thought it best to warn Brandon.

"Brandon," I yelled, "this part is really gnarly, so slow down and stay left!"

I had yelled these instructions over my shoulder as we both drifted at high speed around the rocky corner coming into the section, and just then my right foot clipped a rock, sending me out of control directly toward the waterfall. The last thing I remember before blacking out is slamming my front wheel into a log and becoming airborne.

"Where am I?"

"You're in the forest."

"Where am I?"

"Dude, you're in the forest."

"Uhh…Where am I?"

"Jesus man, you're in the forest!"

"Where am…what are you doing here? You live in Phoenix."

"I'm in town to go riding with you. We were mountain biking and you crashed. You've asked me where you are like twenty times now."

"We're mountain biking? Well then where's my bike, and how the hell did we get all the way out here? I can't believe you're in town."

"Yeah, today is your prom. I'm going there with you."

I could believe that he was in town because I could actually see him, but prom? I'm a science guy, and if I can't observe it or prove it through deductive experimentation, I find it very hard to place much credence in it. But what if? My first feeling was one of fear; I would need a date. I had no time to prepare. How was I expected to prepare for prom when I had only found about it now?

"You've been out cold for ten minutes, dude. I was starting to freak out because I didn't know how to get out of here to find help. Jesus, man, when you hit that log your whole body went limp and your arms went behind your back. You flew through the air like a ragdoll and slammed face first right into these rocks! I thought you were dead."

I looked around and took inventory of my surroundings. I couldn't remember a single thing from the entire day. My bike sat upright, leaned neatly against a rock at the bottom of the waterfall. When my rear wheel had hit the log, the force of the impact flattened out my titanium seat rails, snapping my seat in half in the center. My chin had a pretty bad gash and the bone felt cracked. My teeth had cut through my lips, and one of my upper teeth had broken off. I had lacerations all around my mouth and nose, but my helmet didn't have a scratch on it.

A couple of hours later I sat at my kitchen table while my mom picked gravel out of my face with tweezers and a Q-tip.

"Are you sure you don't want to go to the doctor? What if you have a concussion? And I really think this one needs stitches," she said.

"No, I'll be fine. We can just bandage it up and deal with it later." It was getting hard to speak because my lips were beginning to swell, closing off my mouth. And she was right, I had a Class III concussion. Just then the phone rang. It was Katie, my prom date.

"Oh hi," I muffled, "sorry I haven't been in touch. I was in a terrible bike accident. My mom is picking rocks out of my face right now…yes, it's very painful…no, I'm not going to the doctor, we're still on for tonight. I'll pick you up around five, I'm taking you to dinner at Uncle Louie Pizza in Cave Creek."

"Ooh...yeah, about that," she said, "I wanted to let you know that I was invited to have dinner with a group of my choir friends."

"What? What do you mean you're going with your choir friends? We have a double date lined up, and my friend is already in town."

"yeah, I wish I could, but I kind of told them I'd come with them. See you at prom?"

I hung up the phone and stared blankly ahead. I heard the tinkle of gravel as my mom plunked it into the glass bowl, but all I could feel was the kind of pain and rejection that usually only exists in a high schooler's worst nightmare involving terrible outcomes to highly public social situations.

My mom finished picking the rocks from my face, doused my wounds in hydrogen peroxide, and then wrapped my entire face in white bandages to keep my wounds closed in lieu of stitches. Below my eyes, the only thing visible were my swollen lips poking out of my mess of white bandages. As I reviewed her handy work in the mirror, I remembered. Sheena, the girl from last weekend, she lives in Cave Creek, and only a couple of miles from Uncle Louie Pizza! I dialed her up and asked if she had dinner plans.

"No, why? And why does it sound like you're speaking through a straw?" It was a date.

When we arrived in Cave Creek I got out of Brandon's truck, made a sad attempt to wipe the wrinkles out of my tuxedo, and then walked to Sheena's door. When the door opened, Sheena and her mom both peered out, and then recoiled in disgust.

"I thought, who is this guy? This isn't the same guy I met at the bike race," Sheena would later tell me.

We arrived at Uncle Louie Pizza and ordered. By now my lips had completely sealed shut from the swelling, and it would be impossible to eat. Starving, I politely parted my lips with two of my fingers and asked the waitress in simplified, halting English if they could possibly put a couple of slices of the Blue Bomber in a blender with some milk so I could drink my dinner. The waitress blinked a long blink and seemed to fight the urge to wretch, and then kindly informed me that they didn't have a blender.

The evening would continue to unfold in a most unpleasant fashion. The trip back to Flagstaff was awkward and silent — Brandon and his date didn't seem to have much in common — while I remained crammed into the extended cab folding child's seat, rendered completely silent by swollen lips, and trying not to fall asleep for fear of slipping into a coma.

Prior to arriving at prom, Brandon dropped me off at my house where I switched cars, and then drove to prom all alone in the DeLorean. This seems like the right time in the story to mention that I had asked for, and been granted permission, to drive my grandpa's DeLorean. I had imagined my date being very impressed by my bitchin' Back to the Future car, but as this was to be one of the worst days of my life, I was destined by fate to drive to prom all alone in the DeLorean, and then be asked by the parking lot attendant to park it many minutes' walk from the actual prom, rendering the entire public display completely futile.

The night would only get worse; my date would spend the entire night hanging out with her choir friends instead of me; Brandon's date would leave him the moment they arrived at the dance, preferring the company of others to his exclusive company; Brandon would get bored and inform me that things weren't working out as planned, and that he was driving home. The icing on the cake would come later, when it would emerge that most of my high school classmates had split their vote amongst the popular Prom King nominees, and I, who was nominated as a sort of joke by my friend Carissa, would seize the bulk of the nerd vote, securing for me the highest number of votes and thus the title of Prom King.

I was horrified. I stood in front of a sea of my peers, each looking at me with sad eyes like those of people who have just witnessed the tragic clubbing of a baby seal by a heartless hunter. I waited for the bucket of pig's blood to land on my head.

I left early, and as I tried to stealthily slip from my front door to my bedroom carrying my ornate blue and gold crown, my mom asked how it went.

I painfully parted my lips with two fingers and mumbled, "I don't want to talk about it!"

Sheena and I got to know each other over the ensuing weeks, and by the time the National Championship mountain bike race in Big Bear, California rolled around, we were a couple. As a surprise, I made her a mixed CD, which I delivered to her on our drive from Big Bear to Flagstaff. When we arrived and parked under a big pine tree, she told me that a proper mixed CD needed proper cover art, so I grabbed a permanent marker and transformed the CD into a car tire. Across the sidewall I wrote the word *Goodyear*.

And it was a good year.

I moved from my home in Prescott to Flagstaff, to start my studies at Northern Arizona University. Sheena, being a year behind me, stayed in Cave Creek to finish off High School. Throughout the year we met whenever we could. We camped together at bike races on the weekends, she bought an old BMW and used it to drive to Flagstaff when she could, and on occasion I would surprise her by riding my road bike to her house unannounced. The trip was 130 miles, so I would typically collapse in exhaustion on her bed, where I would remain until she went to work at Barro's Pizza, and could revive me with slices of pepperoni with ranch dressing.

When she graduated from high school, she moved in with me in Flagstaff, replacing Brandon — yes, the same Brandon — as my roommate. And my roommate she would remain.

In college I bought a cruiser bike from one of Flagstaff's mountain bike pioneers. The frame was from a 1970's road bike, and I outfitted it with a pair of rusty blue handlebars and old chrome fenders. I named it Clarence, because every old and beloved vehicle deserves a name, and used it to commute to my classes. Sheena's grandmother gave her an old bike, which she aptly named Peach on account of the color.

Sheena and I lived in an apartment complex in the woods in between North and South Campus, and we rode our cruisers through the hilly campus like untiring San Francisco bicycle messengers. In the snow I would slide wildly around corners while Sheena rode more carefully, laughing and scalding me not to hurt myself. On days when our classes were near one another, Sheena would sit on my rusty blue handlebars and I would ferry her from class to class. Sometimes she would lean back against my arms, straighten her legs, and point her toes rigidly forward like a needle point, a move that I called "The Torpedo," and we would ride as fast as we could spearing the air like the pointed mast of a Spanish Galleon.

By the time I was a Junior at university, I had been racing as a professional mountain bike racer for a few years. It should be noted that in most cases, being a professional at something implies that one makes enough money at it so as to be considered a profession. It is not so in all professional sports, and particularly in professional mountain bike racing. Most professional racers, with the exception of a select few, have other jobs. I fit into this second category, and while I was out on the bike for 15–30 hours per week, logging ten or fifteen thousand miles per year, I subsisted primarily off of money that was supposed to be used for college expenses. To move to the next level as a cyclist, there were few things that worked better than moving to Europe.

And so, when Sheena was 19 and I was 20 years old, we moved to Europe. Once we had the idea, it didn't take much coaxing for us to start putting one foot in front of the other, and by the time the summer wound down, we were on a plane to Europe with two suitcases and four bikes packed into enormous boxes. We settled into a small townhouse with a mold problem overlooking the Bristol Channel on the south coast of Wales, unpacked our bikes, and signed up for classes at the University of Wales in Swansea.

For a year we explored Wales on our bikes, and did so in a constant state of disbelief in what we saw. The network of narrow, seldom-trafficked roads in Wales are extensive, crisscrossing the countryside and mountains like spaghetti thrown onto a map. From our house we could ride north into the rolling canyons of the Brecon Beacons, turn left and traverse a meandering stream flanked by moss-laden trees, and then pass castles and sheep pastures before climbing the eerie Black Mountains, and then descending back to our home by the sea. Or we could ride east through Port Talbott, turn inland and ride through the Afan Forest and into the mountains, passing traditional stone villages before ascending a mountain pass, and riding across sweeping valleys before looping back through hills dotted with medieval coal mining towns. For the first time we became keenly aware that there really is a whole world out there to discover, and that the most rewarding parts are often subtle, only to be uncovered piece by piece after embedding oneself into a place and letting it reveal its secrets over time.

Sheena and I graduated from NAU on the same day in 2006. A few weeks later we boarded a plane for Europe, paid for with the very last of our student loan money, determined to discover a little bit more of the continent before settling down into our careers. On June 2nd, exactly five years after we became a couple, and after having hiked to a mountaintop overlooking Lake Como in Italy, I proposed to Sheena. To my great relief, and sparing us from a long and awkward hike down the mountain, she accepted my proposition.

Sheena had landed a job as a Credit Manager for a bank, a job which she grew to despise with a steamy passion. Her job was to sell lines of credit to anyone and everyone that called her, regardless of whether they should have been taking out more lines of credit. I gently teased her and called her a loan shark to lighten the mood most days when she would return home in tears, owing to how much she hated her job.

I had started a software company for the renewable energy industry during my final year at university, but it wasn't self sufficient by the time of my graduation. I got a job as a mechanical engineer in the Medical Products Division of W.L. Gore & Associates, better known as Gore-Tex, where I went to work designing catheter delivery systems for atrial septal defect occcluders. In layman's terms, I designed fancy straws that could be inserted into patients' legs and guided into the heart, through which really fancy and really expensive umbrella-like objects could be deployed, plugging unwanted holes in the heart's atrial septum.

Each afternoon I returned home from work, and then went to work writing software until Sheena would come home. I would stop for an hour to comfort her with regard to her bad day at work, and then we'd eat dinner before I retired to my computer for further software development.

One day, things improved immensely. This happened on account of Sheena being hired by Gore-Tex, just like me, to do worthwhile work that she very much enjoyed, and henceforth ended her ritual of hating her job. We carried on, worked hard, and moved into a relatively large house in downtown Flagstaff. We got married, honeymooned, and each year we took a two week vacation to Europe.

Eventually my software company started picking up, owing much to the fact that I finally finished tweaking the code and started focusing on selling it, a necessary business transition that most engineers find gut wrenching and endlessly nerve wracking. I hired a network guy and together we nursed the company along, helping it find its feet. Soon, I got a call from the CEO of a wind turbine company, and he wondered if I'd mind if he bought my company.

When I got the call I was opening a gate for my grandpa on Mingus Mountain, where he had built a cabin. I had heard about this new CEO—he was a "turnaround guy." Companies that needed that extra push would hire him, and he would come in with a new management team and bring the company to the next level. When he arrived on the scene, the newspapers reported that he had big plans to go public with the wind turbine company. He reiterated this to me on the phone.

"Tell you what," he began. "I like what you've created, and I think it would help us take this thing to the next level. I'll buy your company, but under one condition: you come with it." He then confidently spelled out the steps he'd be taking over the next 18 months, which would culminate in him taking the company public.

When I hung up the phone I was ecstatic. We were one year into the two-year execution of our savings plan for our big trip, but if I played my cards right this would put an end to all of that. We were home free!

A couple of days later we sat down to negotiate. I was asked to stay with the company for at least two years, but was able to talk it down to one. For my company, my partner and I would receive some cash and some stock in the wind turbine company. With a fair level of confidence that the 25 year old company would soon go public, we opted for less cash and a majority stock agreement. If things went well, we'd be rolling in it in a short 18 months.

It was a risk and we knew it, but the potential reward was huge. As a gesture of good will, I gave half of my cash to one of our early investors who had taken a chance on us, because you should take care of the people who take care of you.

The day after I got the call from the wind turbine company's CEO asking me if I'd sell my company I walked into work at Gore-Tex with sweaty palms. It was time for our morning stand up meeting, in which each team member would disseminate their day's work plan to the rest of the team. By random chance I was to go last. Each person talked about what testing they'd be doing that day, which ISO standards they'd be reviewing, and the like. When it was my turn, I made it quick.

"Today I'll be quitting my job. I haven't thought much beyond that point. That's all I have."

A couple of months later, tax time rolled around. As it turns out, our agreement was rather unique in the world of business acquisitions, and our tax man determined that we should pay taxes on the value of our stock as though it were cash income, which ate up nearly all of the money I had left from the acquisition. All of a sudden my stock held much more importance than it had before. We would indeed have to finish executing our savings plan, but we'd keep our fingers crossed that one day in about 18 months we'd find ourselves bloody rich.

Given Murphy's law, combined with the fact that renewable energy is a politically volatile industry, it will come as no surprise that the wind turbine company failed to go public. And not only did it fail to go public, but the CEO was fired, replaced by another CEO who was soon fired, to be replaced by a board of directors who relocated the company, missed the mark on a big new product offering, and then abruptly went out of business, rendering my stock valueless.

It all goes to show that the world behaves in strange ways, and that nothing is certain. The only certainties are those things which we can control, and we can't control all that many things outside of our own will and determination.

With each passing year, our lives bore a closer and closer resemblance to the ever-promoted American Dream. We were both working professionals, the living was easy, and we were occupying a relatively nice house with four bedrooms. Just like the song, there were even two cats in the yard. But after several years passed, we started to realize that time seemed to be passing more quickly than ever before. We would think back to events that had happened two or three years prior, and they seemed like they had happened last month. We knew that something needed to change, that we would have to do something interesting and adventurous to shake things up. But we didn't know what. And Sheena's biological clock was ticking, so we'd need to do something soon, before we had a really good excuse not to do anything. Children or some such.

Initially we had the wild idea that we should move to Germany. It was at a time when both of us were working for Gore-Tex, and they had a location just outside of Munich. Sheena immediately gravitated toward the idea, and we started preparing. I started taking German lessons on the BBC website, and we investigated living costs and good neighborhoods. I researched bus schedules for getting from Munich to the Alps to go skiing. I decided to fill out an *Associate Development Plan* at work, in which I formally declared my desire to transfer to Munich, and then had it signed by leadership. I would later find out that these plans are filed away and have no real importance or authority,. But I didn't know this, and in the end it didn't matter.

It didn't matter because after a few months we got used to the idea of moving to Munich, and it no longer seemed like a the big pre-children adventure that we had hoped for; we would simply be doing the same thing in a different location. We quietly filed the idea away and I eventually stopped taking my German lessons.

Mike's funeral was held in his high school auditorium. Outside snow covered the ground, accumulation from the recent storm that had dumped record depths on the Sierra Nevada range. It was this very storm that had tempted Mike and a fellow ski patroller into the backcountry only a few days prior, into Government Canyon, where he would drop in and trigger the avalanche that would take his life. Ski patrollers had later scoured the canyon with their avalanche probes and shovels looking for Mike's skis, but were only able to recover one, and it leaned against the wall behind the podium where Mike's friends and family would spend the evening recounting all of the things he'd accomplished, and all of the lives he had touched in his 23 years. He had certainly left a big impression on us, and we still couldn't believe that he was gone.

On the way home from the funeral, driving past Big Bear Lake where Sheena and I had begun our relationship together, we had the discussion that we felt compelled to have when a young life is lost. Are we really living each day, or are we taking them for granted? We had wanted to do something big and memorable before we had kids, but we had procrastinated about it. If we were going to do something, we'd need to be more proactive. We'd need to think of something and just do it. But what to do?

A year later I was standing at my desk when Steve walked by my window. Steve is a happy guy who drives a Volkswagen van. As he passed I blurted out the first thing that came into my head:

"Hey Steve, let's drive your hippie bus to Tierra del Fuego."

He paused for a second, and then without blinking said "I don't think so" and continued on his way. A minute later he sent me a link to an article about a couple who drove their VW camper van through the

Americas and Africa. I took one look at the article's title, and quickly sent it on to Sheena, along with the question "Want to do this?" She immediately responded with "Yes!"

That evening we decided that we would buy a Volkswagen camper van, save a bunch of money, and drive around the world. We would call the van Ignacio because Ignacio is a dignified name, and because every old and beloved vehicle deserves a name. It would be "Nacho" for short. We scribbled out a savings plan and set the wheels in motion. On the fifth day of December, on opposite sides of town, Sheena and I each walked into our respective places of work and quit our jobs.

Sheena posted a quote on our refrigerator that said "Those who wish for the weekend are wishing their lives away." We may have taken the quote more literally than its author intended, but we wanted to be damn sure that we weren't wishing our lives away.

# Part 2

# Wanderlust

# 1

*Arizona, United States — December, by Brad*

The other day I went to lunch with my company's CEO. He looked down into his Chicken Korma, and then up at me. "I think you should see a shrink," he said. It was obvious what he thought of our idea to drive Nacho around the world. "I'll even pay for it. Just lay on the couch for an hour, and let's see what happens." We'd received a wide variety of responses to the news of our leaving, but this one was unique, suggesting that our desire to live meant that we must be crazy.

The response from Sheena's coworkers fell to the opposite extreme. She gathered them all together in a common area between the office cubicles and told them all at the same time, which resulted in the entire accounting department breaking into tears simultaneously. The following day one of her coworkers wrote her a poem about our trip and laminated it. It occurred to me that a graduate student in sociology would do well to write a thesis about the varying reactions to shocking news among different office professionals.

I do enjoy observing the responses that people have to the news of our trip; a person's reaction is telling of their experiences and outlook on life. If they've never traveled, they tend not to see the point in our decision. The young and well traveled tend to be enthusiastic and encouraging. Those who have done something like this before become nostalgic and evangelistic in their encouragement for us to get underway. Members of my grandfather's generation have the most predictable and consistent response: their eyes relax and seem to focus on some distant object, they nod their heads, and say something to the tune of "Do it now before it's too late." My actual grandfather had this same response, but then followed it up with, "But you'll never make it through the Middle East because they'll set your car on fire." Thanks Grandpa.

Some people don't like what we're doing, or perhaps they find it infuriating that young people are doing these things when they themselves have not found the courage or means to do so. Coupled with the anonymity that the internet affords, we've received some downright spiteful feedback, like this from "Donalie" in Florida. We have no idea who she is.

> "...considering all the people who don't have a car of any age to live in or the gas to go from one town to another, I don't give a hoot. I guess you just don't get it, Brad...There are much more important things to do than to go traveling for years. The one good thing is that they quit their jobs, hopefully opening up jobs for people who need and want to work. I wish them well but I don't admire them."

I haven't been able to figure out what must have been so bad about her life to give her this kind of outlook. We tend to find the advice of people who have been in our shoes more motivating and relevant. The letter we received from a guy named Todd was more encouraging.

> "Reminds me of the trip I took in a different mode of transport. After college I fitted out my 26ft sloop and headed over the horizon to points south from Morro Bay, CA. I was gone for the better part of the year, cruising the coast all the way down to Zihuatanejo and back, solo. Of course I had my mask, fins, and sling, not to mention a quiver of boards. Otherwise, I didn't have a clue. Literally. See, I had not sailed at all before this, and had acquired my knowledge from books. Oh the horror I put my mother through... Sorry mom, I love you.
>
> What I got was an adventure of the grandest sorts; what 23 year old wouldn't? I loved Baja – my favorite place by far. So many good right hand point breaks, lobster, and amazing sunsets and sunrises. Eventually warmer water called, and I ended up posting up at an anchorage in Puerto Vallarta. It was heaven. Good anchorage, good wave, little town... Of course the people are super kind and friendly as well. You will have more of the same.

*One thing I found out was that exploring and riding waves from a boat is a very romantic idea, but very difficult. A boat can get you into some places where a car cannot, but for the most part, all of the good breaks down the coast are reachable by 4 wheels. And guess what? There is no rocking or creaking when the swell is up. No worry of dragging anchor into the impact zone or out to sea. No wondering if you're going to find that sandbar that shifts with the rain and tide.*

*Sorry for the ramble/reliving the past, but I've done what you've done. Pinched the pennies, scrapped and saved. Gone against the flow of the norm to do something that leaves most people with more questions, even after you've answered them all. I told my then girlfriend and now wife (I can't believe she married me after this story I am about to tell) that I couldn't take her out to a nice dinner, because that meant another week in Mexico. Mind you, this is one of the last times I would see her before jumping over the border. The family pressure and guilt can be heavy at times, and seems strange and misplaced because in the end, you're fulfilling and living out your dreams. Just keep telling them you love them! And hey, with Skype, wireless, Facetime, etc, the world is a lot smaller in many regards.*

*Finally, I met so many older couples who reveled in what I was doing. I specifically remember Peter from Canada who said, "You've got it figured out Todd. Take off now while you can. While your body is still young, while your mind and perspective are still fresh. While you're open to everything." While I still don't think I have it figured out (I mean, I bought a Vanagon…) my trip, my experiences – the people and places I visited and met – will be with me for a lifetime. In the end, that's what it's all about."*

I prefer to think that our experience will be more in line with Todd's. I hope that our trip helps us to understand people better by experiencing their cultures, seeing how they live, and seeing how and why they do things differently than we do. I doubt that any shrink could provide this kind of insight, so I think we'll stick with the plan.

# 2

*Arizona, United States — December, by Brad*

When I was a kid, the purse strings were tight. I recall often eating one of my mom's signature dishes: "Tuna and Crackers"; spread saltine crackers out on your plate, cover them with a creamy tuna concoction, and then eat it. If my mom taught me one thing, it was that you never breathe with your mouth open when it's freezing cold out. If she taught me one thing relevant to this discussion, it was how to be frugal.

Throughout this process, people have asked us how we're able to afford to pick up and drive around the world when we're so young. Trust fund? Ponzi scheme? Nope, just good old fashioned penny pinching. It's actually not so hard. The toughest part is making the "all or nothing" decision to actually do it.

We decided to do this trip right before leaving on vacation to Spain. We scribbled out our savings plan before we left, but perfected it on a long hike in the Alpujarras mountains. By that time we had realized that we were in the midst of a vacation on which we were wasting money that should have been going into the Nacho Fund. By the end of our hike we had outlined our plan. We identified the expensive aspects of our life, and created an attack plan to kill (or severely maim) each one. I now bequeath to you our savings plan so that we may get this out of the way once and for all.

## Nacho Fund Expedient Growth Step 1: Move into someone's pantry

When we first got ourselves into this mess, we were renting a house in downtown Flagstaff, Arizona. We had 1,800 square feet with a sizeable yard, and it was pretty expensive. We set out to find something smaller. What we found was something MUCH smaller. We named our mini chateau *The Dollhouse*.

The Dollhouse is roughly 420 square feet, and is half the price of our old place. It used to be a Mormon family's food pantry. Seriously.

The Dollhouse is 10 minutes from downtown on a shared property with two other young couples. It has a garden, chickens, horseshoe pit, campfire ring, and an outdoor dining area in an aspen grove. Its small size forced us to spend a lot more time outside. You know, playing horseshoes, lighting fires, and falling off of the roof while shoveling snow from atop our sagging abode.

## Nacho Fund Expedient Growth Step 2: Ride more bike

It's pretty easy to spend a couple hundred dollars per month on gas if you're not careful. We decided to ride bikes to work instead of driving whenever possible. Like so many aspects of this plan, we liked to make a game out of it; "Okay, we're only allowed to fill up once this month. You in?"

I know, sometimes you just don't feel like riding bikes. "It's freezing and my kidneys ache!" Okay, crybaby. For those days we have our Vespa, Cicilia. She's a 1963 VBB 150, and gets somewhere around 75mpg. If you fart within 10 feet of this thing it'll take you to the store. So efficient. So sensible. So...feminine?

Just so that people don't make the mistake of thinking that I take myself seriously on little Cicilia, I wear a cute pearly white helmet that matches her paint job. I may look dainty, but I still give a nod and pound the air with a clenched fist when Harley riders pass me.

**Nacho Fund Expedient Growth Step 3: Stop eating like Donald Trump. Or some other rich guy.**

As a present to ourselves when we graduated and got good jobs, we allowed ourselves to spend freely on groceries. It's important to eat well. Turns out spending freely doesn't necessarily equate to eating well. It just equates to spending freely.

We had these little dinosaur-like beasts (chickens) running all over the place, so we let them pull their weight by feeding us. We ate one of them early on, but decided that eating their eggs was a better investment.

We also inherited a nice organic garden with the property. Sheena took to the garden like Batman to rogue justice, seasonally eliminating our produce bill.

When the garden wasn't producing, we joined a co-op called Bountiful Baskets. For $15 every two weeks we took home two laundry baskets full of fresh fruits and vegetables. If we were vegetarians we'd be home free, if not a little chronically tired.

Last, but not least, Sheena started making bread. Now, instead of paying $4/loaf for the good stuff, we paid $0.25/loaf for the great stuff. Little things. They add up.

**Nacho Fund Expedient Growth Step 4: Stop paying people to make dinner for us.**

Like every American, we were spending a large proportion of our income on eating out. We started by cutting back to once per week, but by the end we were down to once every two weeks. Now our restaurant bills are down around $100/month. When you only get to eat out twice per month, you must make it count, so thanks to our friends at the Himalayan Grill for feeding us just about every week for the last two and a half years.

## Nacho Fund Expedient Growth Step 5: Stop buying so much crap.

As consumers we get a lot of stuff pushed our way, and start to believe that we need it; cars, clothes, electronics, toilet paper. Well, one of those things is important. How else are you supposed to play video games with your friends?

We started by affording ourselves the luxury of spending $300 per month on anything that wasn't rent, food, or gas. It sounds easy, but I challenge you to try it. Not easy. After a while we got used to it, so we continually reduced it until we got it to $100, which is where it's been for almost two years. Strangely we don't even notice any more. It doesn't feel like we're sacrificing.

One way we minimized our spending was by entertaining ourselves in ways that didn't cost money. We used Netflix and consciously spent more time with friends at home rather than going out. We started a dinner club, where four couples would take turns hosting dinner, and started a beer tasting group with a bunch of friends.

## The verdict

We were ultimately able to reduce our spending by more than half. This allowed us to put all of my paychecks into savings while we lived off of Sheena's. In the end it only took us about two and a half years to reach our goal. You heard correctly: two and a half years of saving will allow us to buy three years of freedom.

The other interesting outcome of this ordeal is that we found ourselves enjoying life much more at the end than we did when we started. Everything we did to save money made our life immediately better in some way. We ate better, spent more time in the sun and with good friends, and distanced ourselves from the consumerism cycle. Simplify.

# 3

*Leaving Arizona — December, by Brad*

When I was in college, I remember a bike ride from Flagstaff to Sedona with my friend Mike, during which we descending the Mogollon Rim into Oak Creek Canyon, whereupon we caught up to a minivan. Being a college student, and thus having bad judgment, I took the initiative to fly past the minivan in the oncoming lane as we approached the blind corner of a switchback. By the time Mike passed him, the aggressive soccer dad had time to roll down his window and brandish a threat.

"If I catch you, I'm gonna kill you!"

Knowing that death by minivan would soon arrive, we queasily sprinted for our lives and ducked into a campground before the angry soccer dad could catch and kill us. Sometimes we look at all of the evidence and do stupid things anyway.

And so it came to be that we found ourselves moving out of the Dollhouse, rendering ourselves homeless with twelve inches of snow on the ground. Sheena and I, having looked at all of the evidence and decided that there wasn't anything we could do about it, reluctantly transferred boxes through the snow to the barn, hauled many of our belongings off to the thrift store, and frequently got Nacho stuck in the snow as we repeatedly traveled back and forth on the disheveled snowy back road to our house. But as the snow falls at home, the deserts of Northern Mexico are entering their prime season, so December it is. When all was finished, we sat in the middle of our empty floor and celebrated our completion by eating leftover cake from my company's Christmas party.

A few nights prior our good friend Nathan stopped by the Dollhouse. Nathan is an engineer and avid outdoorsman, but if he will be known for one thing 100 years from now, it will be for his skill as a beer brewer. Over the summer he brewed a Coffee Vanilla Stout that still haunts Sheena in her dreams, causing her voice to rise by an octave whenever she talks about it. On this visit to the Dollhouse he was slinging his latest brew, World Wide Quadrupel, a limited edition brew made to mark the occasion of our departure. He dropped off several bottles, which will be done conditioning in January, so we'll get to start enjoying them somewhere in Mexico. Until then Nacho's toilet paper storage cabinet has been repurposed as a beer cabinet. Priorities.

After loading up the van we hit the road, and as we rolled out of town I hit the button on our GPS tracker and added the first point to our trip map and officially said goodbye to Flagstaff.

I had envisioned our departure this way: we would wake up from a long night of peaceful sleep, say goodbye to Sheena's family, and roll out of town. In reality, the days leading up to our departure were a frantic scramble. The morning of the departure was a sleep deprived sprint. We woke up at Sheena's parents' house at 6:00 and finished two more van projects before packing up. After a while the packing of the van became too much, so we just threw everything into boxes and set them on the floor. We can deal with this later.

The goal for the first day of our trip was to arrive in Puerto Peñasco, Mexico, and to enjoy celebratory margaritas and tacos on the beach. An hour after leaving the plan was adjusted, and we decided to see a group of my childhood friends in Tucson for dinner. No problem, we could still be rugged overlanders in Tucson, we'd just camp inside of Nacho in my friend Shannon's driveway. Extreme. As it turns out, our great around-the-world road trip is turning out to be full of unexpected twists; Sheena and I woke up this morning on an air mattress on Shannon's floor, after which Shannon decided to make us breakfast and coffee. Shortly thereafter I tweaked my back while typing on the computer, which prompted our friend Leah, a massage therapist, to give both of us massages, painting a completely different picture of just how rugged we thought we were.

Today I stood outside of Nacho changing my shirt, and it dawned on me: we're homeless. Driving south toward the Mexican border we began to feel queasy. Everything seemed to be moving so fast, like we were going along with a situation over which we no longer had control; sort of like being gained on by a minivan-driving soccer dad with a death wish.

# Part 3

# Drive Nacho Drive

# 4

*Puerto Peñasco, Mexico — January, by Brad*

During the same trip on which I proposed to Sheena we visited the Greek island of Santorini. We had heard that the most amazing sunset in the world could be seen from the town of Oia, high on the edge of the caldera of the island's blown out volcanic center. We made our way to Oia one evening and took our place on the cliff's edge. As the sun plunged slowly into the sea, we kept waiting for the sky to ignite in the most beautiful sunset we'd ever seen, but it never happened and the sunset from Oia went down in history as the 128th best sunset I'd ever seen.

When we finally left Arizona, we reached the Mexican border at Sonoyta just as the sun reached the horizon. We crossed over, and a few minutes later the sky exploded into flames like a cheap polyester suit, creating a rainbow of color that filled the sky. There really isn't anything like a desert sunset, and hardly a better visual display to welcome us into our new vagabonding life.

In crossing the border so late in the day, we violated our first self-imposed rule of Mexican travel: no driving after dark. Given the delays in our trip thus far, and the relative safety of the road to Puerto Peñasco, we decided that it was okay just this once. Don't get me wrong, when I say "safety" I'm not talking about *banditos* and *narcotraficantes* with guns. I'm talking about cows. As soon as the sun goes down, the country's livestock takes to the roads.

Sheena napped in the passenger seat, and when she awoke at the outskirts of Puerto Peñasco, she was wielding some fierce hunger-induced anger; a term we've come to call *hanger*. We stopped at the first sign of a street side taco stand for fear that she would get any hangrier.

If there were to be an embodiment of heaven on Earth, it would be the Mexican taco stand. The one we found was fronted by a piece of plywood with the words *Tacos al Pastor* spray painted on it. We sat in the ubiquitous plastic lawn furniture that graces every taco stand in Mexico, and ordered several tacos and quesadillas. From a rotating spit of meat and pineapple a taco guru crafted our dinner with his well practiced hands; fresh flour tortillas filled with roasted pork, cilantro, onions, and fresh guacamole, a plate of limes and grilled and salted green onions, an assortment of salsas, and bowls of radishes and cucumbers. We washed it down with a bottle of sangria flavored soda called *Topo Chico*, paid our $10 bill, and were on our way. The Mexican taco stand: pretty much the best thing ever.

Puerto Peñasco, or "Rocky Point" to Americans, is a small resort town at the northern end of the Sea of Cortez. As the closest bit of ocean to Arizona, it's quite popular with the college crowd during Spring Break. January isn't a hopping time of year here, as evidenced by beachfront resorts all along the water front with empty parking lots. We drove Nacho northward past all of the resorts along Bahia de la Cholla until the road turned to dirt. We continued on until we came to Puerto Peñasco's northern outpost; a small bar and restaurant called *Wrecked at the Reef.* For $5 per night we could camp on the beach in peace, a good distance from the concrete resort jungle.

Reaching the sea filled us with an overwhelming sense of joy, and we've been riding a wave of endorphins ever since. When we arrived, I went down to the water's edge and sat for a while. *This is your new life.* No matter how often I remind myself, I still can't believe that we're doing this. We opted to simplify our lives to save money, and our lives got so much better. Now we're on this adventure and our lives have gotten magnitudes better. Can it get any better than this? I guess time will tell.

Yesterday I put on the snorkeling gear and headed out with the spear gun to see if I could catch us dinner. My visualizations of being an underwater fish-dominating Rambo went unrealized, as I only spotted a couple of small fish hanging out by the reef. Next time you dirty rats, next time. This morning before leaving Puerto Peñasco for Baja's Pacific coast, Sheena headed out on the paddleboard. After scooting around Bahia de la Cholla, her streak of never having fallen off the thing remains intact.

As I write this, the sound of crashing waves fills Nacho's interior. In the morning we'll wake up without aid of an alarm clock when the sun warms our little home. We'll roll out of bed to the sight of enormous waves crashing on the Baja coast. We'll sip our coffee and eat breakfast outdoors before going snorkeling. Or fishing. Or surfing. Holy hell, this is our new life.

# 5

*La Fonda, Baja California, Mexico — January, by Brad*

By 4:00 in the afternoon, as the sun approached the Pacific horizon, we figured Tommy, Dan, and Sunday were in the clink. The last we'd heard from them was the previous day in a quick email stating that they would meet us at Tommy's beach house near Tijuana between noon and 1:00. We bought some tamales from a guy in a beat up minivan and hunkered down on the deck of the beach house to wait. We knew something unexpected would happen on account of Sunday being in the car. Strange things are always happening to him; he's been run over by a drunk driver while on a date, sandwiched between two semi trucks, attacked by a vicious dog while on a business trip to American Samoa; the list goes on and on. Like a magnet for calamity, Sunday had surely done something to get the whole group put away at the US-Mexican border.

The previous day we had made the unexpectedly long journey from Puerto Peñasco to the Pacific Ocean. At the first military checkpoint we got out of Nacho and let one of the soldiers in, while another soldier approached us. "I'm so sorry for the inconvenience, this is a routine checkpoint to inspect for weapons and drugs. It'll only take a minute." We told him we were happy to stop, and that the weather was perfect for a quick stretch.

"Yes, the weather is great now, but in the summer we suffer in our army uniforms," he said.

We told him about our Baja trip last summer, and about the heat we had encountered.

"So you're going to Ensenada now? It's not far. You'll be there in four and a half hours," he said. We made our way across the barren desert at the Northern tip of the Sea of Cortez before turning North, where we began skirting the US border. After Mexicali we climbed high into the mountains just as the sun set, breaking our "no driving after dark" rule for the second time. We descended from the mountains into Tijuana in the dark. After what seemed like an eternity we arrived at the surf spot known as K58, South of Tijuana. Driving time: nine hours.

We awoke to waves that sounded like turbo jet props. Row after row of fifteen to twenty foot faces pounded the shore, smothering my intentions of surf practice that day. Instead, I pulled out my tackle box and proceeded to build a rig that I could use for surf fishing while Sheena went to take photographs. I've never used a proper surf rod, but got one for this trip and am anxious to try my hand. Between my underwater Rambo getup and my atom bomb – like surf fishing rig, I hope to be feeding on homemade fish tacos on a regular basis. I spent the morning practicing my surf cast, which, as it turns out, I also suck at. I'm an Arizona boy, and in Arizona we don't have water.

At nearly 5:00, after we ate tamales from the clunker minivan, after Sheena went for a run, and after I walked around the beach aimlessly like a crazy person for what seemed like an eternity, Tommy and the boys finally showed up. Contrary to tradition, nothing outrageous had happened as a result of Sunday's presence. No semi truck accident, no attack dogs, no clink. Tommy had simply forgotten his keys at home, and only realized it when they were nearly to Mexico. We had such a rough time sitting on the patio watching the ocean while we waited, we decided we would never forgive him.

We built a campfire on the beach and grilled up steaks, asparagus, and sweet potatoes. The boys broke out a box of microbrews for an impromptu beer sampling. We sat in the hot tub, and then went for a nighttime ocean swim. Sheena made hot chocolate, and I wondered why it took us so long to decide to do this. So far living in a van isn't half bad.

The next day we decided it was time to tempt fate. The waves had let up slightly since we had first arrived, but it still wasn't pretty. Tommy's house sits in the middle of a long beach break, so at any time there are about five rows of progressively bigger waves standing between the beach and the calm water beyond the breakers. *All we have to do*, we thought, *is use our weak arms to propel ourselves past all five rows of those enormous, violent waves, and we'll be home free.* Sheena and Tommy were the first to make the attempt in the tandem sea kayak.

I watched with concern as they broke through the first two sets of waves. They paddled fast and Sheena's arms shot up in the air as they crashed through each wave. I watched with fear as they paddled through the third and fourth rows of waves. The kayak became almost vertical on the wave face, Sheena's arms flailed, and the boat sailed through the air as it broke through the wave crest, crashing back into the water. I heard an audible squeal and knew it was Sheena starting to mentally break up. As they reached the fifth row of waves, I watched the boat become vertical, Sheena was ejected, Tommy flew in the opposite direction, and the boat was tumbled all the way back to shore, without passengers.

After Sheena and Tommy's ill-fated attempt, I threw my better judgment to the wind and got in the boat with Tommy. It went much in the same way as it did with Sheena. On the fifth wave, I heard Tommy's usually casual voice turn serious.

"This is going to hurt…a lot!"

The boat shot up the face of an enormous wave, but as it became airborne I remained in my seat. Tommy was long overboard as the boat sailed backwards, upside down, into the crush of the crashing wave. I remained seated as the weight of the boat drilled me upside down into the churning whitewater blender. As the boat folded me in half, I returned my lunch to mother nature. I imagined this was how Sunday felt when he got sandwiched between those two semi trucks. Our boat was gone, so we swam to shore while continuously getting pummeled by more waves.

This evening we steamed some fresh clams that Tommy collected and ate them on the patio. Then we said goodbye to our friends and they pointed the car northward. Dan is headed back to Oregon to fight fires. Sunday is headed back to Rhode Island to write mapping software, and Tommy goes back to work as a mechanical engineer on his family's California dairy farm. In the morning, Sheena and I will leave the driveway, turn right, and drive, drive, drive.

# 6

*Baja California, Mexico — January, by Brad*

If you stop putting effort into your hygiene, you eventually look like a hobo after a bar fight. And if you put up stop signs and add lines to a Mexican road, the population will eventually learn to ignore them. Our driving habits, like my attention to my appearance, are deteriorating.

Over the last few days we've been doing a lot of driving. We're eager to get past the Baja peninsula, not because we don't like Baja, but because we've already visited the region this year and are eager to find our way southward to places yet unvisited. Tomorrow we'll be off to Mazatlán by ferry, and that will signal the beginning of unmarked territory for us. Besides swamp ass and hemorrhoids, all of the week's driving has given us a new appreciation for Mexican long haul truckers, and has caused my attention to traffic laws to become more, shall we say, relaxed.

We made a long push in a single day from Bahia de los Angeles, through Geurrero Negro, and across the peninsula to the Sea of Cortez. We rolled right on through the French mining town of Santa Rosalia and into Mulege for an early taco dinner. Over the last week we've kind of overdone it on street tacos, and ended up ingesting way too much *carne asada* and pork. The resulting acid reflux reminded us that we really ought to diversify. This is Baja California, and the fish taco is king, so in Mulege we ate *tacos de camarón y pescado*.

We carried on and finally came to a stopping point at Bahia Concepcion. Usually this bay is calm and warm, so we figured we'd stay for a couple of days to relax. We made our way down a rocky road to a small cove and pulled up to a *palapa* on the beach. I still hadn't landed any fish, so I planned to do some surf fishing off of a small island near our campsite.

As luck would have it, we woke up to high winds and cloudy skies from a storm that was rolling across the peninsula. I decided that instead of fishing, it would be a great idea to go paddle boarding. The winds were strong like bull, so I ended up paddling to the island and exploring it on foot. Sheena gave the paddle board a try and ended up falling off for the first time ever after being swiped by a rogue wind gust. The water was only waist deep, but I still basked in the sweet satisfaction at seeing her plunge into the chilly water, ending her eight month streak of not falling off. We rounded out the day with shark tacos and the first bottle of Nathan's World Wide Quadrupel, which were both great, and made the decision to cut our losses and push on the next day.

When we awoke our minds were already on the road before we emerged from the van to find calm weather and a glassy smooth bay. All signs said *Stay Put*, but so early in the trip we haven't been able to shake our sense of urgency. Urgency to do what, I'm not sure. We lifted anchor and set off on the tortuous road once again on our push to get through the desolation of Baja California.

Our goal was to make it to Loreto, our favorite town on the peninsula, for breakfast before heading on to La Paz. We rounded a bend on one of the mountainous sections of road along a ravine and came across a full sized 18 wheeler that had tried to take the corner too fast. Its back end had skittered off the side of the road and both rear axles were suspended over the edge of a cliff. Its young driver sat on the side of the road with a shocked look on his face while a tow truck driver assessed the daunting work in front of him. I asked Sheena to take a picture but her pity for the driver made her unable to press the button. Like watching a hobo lose a bar fight and then taking his picture, it's hard to kick someone when they're down. No matter the entertainment value.

We made a quick stop at Loreto for breakfast of eggs, cactus, and *chilaquiles* and continued on. Really putting the "Drive" in Drive Nacho Drive. By evening we made it to La Paz, the capital and cultural center of the state. Cabo San Lucas may be the cruise ship, tourism, and college spring break drinking capital, but La Paz is a real city with real history and culture. After a dinner of stuffed potatoes and beans we parked and spent the evening strolling along the waterfront *malecón*. Entire families walked up and down the boardwalk late into the night, kids rode their bikes and rollerblades, a group of young people took turns dancing to a radio, and a young girl in sparkly red shoes pushed a stroller with a doll in it. Unbelievable. You know, the fact that Paris isn't the only place left where people still rollerblade. The happiness of La Paz's people wore off on us and we decided then and there that we would eventually settle down in a place where our children can enjoy the kind of community and outdoor living that we found in La Paz.

After a regretful night spent camping on the beach at Pichilingue next to a truck pumping polka music into the wee hours of the morning we bought our ferry tickets for Mazatlán, ate our breakfast sitting in folding chairs on a white sand beach, and then pointed Nacho south toward Cabo Pulmo. We passed a man grazing his goat on a leash in the median of a busy roadway, we emptied the contents of our library on the floor after hitting one of Mexico's ubiquitous *topes* too fast, and I rolled through stop sign after stop sign in 2nd gear. Later on we rolled through a stop sign in front of a cop. I didn't care. He didn't care. The lines and signs are just remnants of good intentions ignored.

# 7

*La Ribera, Baja California Sur, Mexico — January, by Brad*

When I was about 10 years old, I was hiking with my dad and brothers in Sedona when we decided to duck a fence to find a shortcut to some Indian ruins. A few minutes later a strung out crazy person jumped out from behind a bush wielding a sawed off shotgun. He had a string of shotgun shells around his neck and he kept the gun aimed directly at us. He had crazy in his eyes. After a half an hour of pleading, he let us go. I had this in mind as I ducked the fence and started walking into the bushes at the property that we assumed belonged to a friend of a friend in La Ribera near Baja's southern tip.

We had left La Paz on Sunday morning, heading South. We didn't know where we were going, only that there was a couple from the states trying to build some kind of permaculture farm near La Ribera. A bit of Google stalking led us to *Biosfera Buena Fortuna*, where we figured we'd find someone who knew them. We drove there and found a young American guy pruning a tree, so we asked him where we might find Tiffanie.

"I think she lives toward town a little. Look for a gate with a Buddhist symbol on it."

"What do you mean by 'Buddhist symbol'," I asked.

"I'm not really sure." he said. He was like Yoda, but more cryptic.

Back in Nacho, we headed toward town and found a gate with a strange symbol on it. Buddhism probably has strange symbols, so we figured we must be in the right place. Bingo bango. The gate was locked and there was no house in sight, just trees, shrubs, and a dirt track winding into the foliage.

After squeezing through the barbed wire fence I walked down the track past banana and mesquite trees. I noticed a child's bare footprints in the dust. After a while I came across a huge thatched palapa, under which two men and two women were building a deck, while two little girls played. No guns, no crazy people.

We spent two days in La Ribera with these folks; Tiffanie and Troy moved here a week ago with their 3 year old daughter, Anjali, from Corvallis, Oregon. They brought along their friends Tiffany and Josh, with their 3 year old daughter, Stella, to help get the property ready for living. Due to computer issues we didn't tell them we were coming, but they all welcomed our arrival – and my trespassing – with open arms. It was as if we'd known each other for years.

Tiffanie runs a food blog and was generous enough to cook for us all weekend in her open-air kitchen. We contributed cornbread cooked in our Dutch oven in the campfire, and passed around a bottle of World Wide Quadrupel. Each night we ate dinner under the *palapa*, and then sat around the campfire. Outdoor living: it doesn't suck as much as you thought.

On our second day we made our way to the beach for a bit of recreation. I still hadn't caught a fish, and was determined to finally satisfy my primordial predatory desires by landing The Big One. They say to visualize yourself succeeding to find success, so I tried. I imagined casting my bait 300 yards into the dark undergrowth of a fish infested kelp forest. I imagined a 60 pound roosterfish taking my hook, and myself bravely fighting until the fish became tired enough for me to haul it ashore, where I would plunge my dive knife into its head like a Spartan warrior. I wouldn't even show any emotion, even though it would be very emotional for even the hardest of war hardened killers. I would wipe my bloody hands on a whole bunch of Kleenex tissues and then take a photo with my kill. I would leave the bloody Kleenex tissues right there on the beach so that future beachgoers would wonder what kind of terror must have happened in that spot. It would be a story they would pass on to their grandchildren. "I tell you, grandchildren, there was more blood on that tissue than on all of Normandy's beaches. It must have been one hell of a nosebleed."

Try as I might, I couldn't seem to cast more than 40 yards. I stood there on the shore for what seemed like an hour, my pale white torso turning a splotchy red from the sun. I didn't have a fishing rod holder, so I held it with my hand, slouched over, burning. An obnoxious retired American guy walked over, beer in one hand, a cigarette in the other, and the bulbous potbelly of a malnourished famine child protruding from his frail body.

"I like your fishing pole holder! Ha! You know what your problem is? You have too much bait! Haha! I knew it when I saw you casting! Ha!" Great, I thought, I can't run away or else I'll dislodge my bait from this fish infested kelp forest. The man was yelling every word in my ear. Must be drunk. Or senile.

"You know what else you're doing wrong!? You're standing there in your shorts with those f-ing Hanes underwear! Ha! You need to jerk those f-ing pants off and put a f-ing beer in one hand. Ha! You know what else you're doing wrong!? You need to take off that f-ing watch! Ha ha ha!" Damn it all, and here I forgot my Tazer *and* my pepper spray back in Nacho. I'd just have to wait until he got bored and left.

In the end I didn't catch any fish. Turned out I wasn't casting into a fish infested kelp forest after all. My later paddle boarding expedition proved that in fact I was casting into 5 feet of water with a smooth sandy bottom. Thank goodness we're near civilization or we'd have starved to death long ago.

On Tuesday morning we loaded up Nacho and said farewell to our new friends. Josh and Troy, both emergency room doctors, found it hard to believe that we were traveling without a first aid kit, so Josh unloaded all of his supplies on us. Now we're basically a traveling medical clinic; we have an EpiPen, antibiotics, splints, various pills, and a flesh stapler. Yes, a flesh stapler. The way Josh put it, "I love these things. In the amount of time it takes for the patient to scream out one full breath of air, you can have the whole wound closed up." He said it with such nonchalance, so matter of factly, and with just a hint of crazy in his eyes.

# 8

*Mazatlán, Mexico — January, by Brad*

Sitting on the dilapidated concrete dock at the Pichilingue ferry port in La Paz I glimpsed the name of the ferry we'd soon be boarding. *Mazatlán Star.* More intriguing was the name under it which had been painted over, illegible and in French, but clearly identifying the ship as being originally from Montpellier. A ship broken in under the sunny skies of the French Riviera. The idea of traveling over sparkling blue Pacific waters aboard a majestic French vessel was to me the epitome of romance. A man with a machine gun blew his whistle, pointed at me, and I drove Nacho into the fairy tale ship's nether regions, descending two levels to the very bottom of the hull, or whatever, and parked. Nacho would spend the next 16 hours driving under the sea.

Once aboard the ship, we found our way to the sixth floor where we had reserved a three bed cabin. We paid a total of $263 for the tickets, which included under the sea parking for Nacho, the three bed cabin, dinner, and breakfast. Not a bad deal if you ask me. What it didn't include was electricity for charging our computer, as Nacho still didn't have an inverter. No, when the ship arrived from France nobody bothered to replace the outlets, so it required continental European plugs. Furthermore, the electricity was 220V instead of 110V. Welcome to Mexico, I guess.

Our entertainment options aboard the ship were fairly limited, as this was no cruise. In fact, the Customs agent in La Paz reminded us of that. Due to some mislabeling on our Mexican street map, we were unsure as to whether the ship would go directly to Mazatlán or if it would first stop in Cabo San Lucas to pick up more passengers. When I asked the Customs agent if the ship was stopping at Cabo, he gave me a half smile and said, "No sir, this isn't a cruise." So no pool? No cabaret shows? In the end we found that we could either hang out in our cabin, or we could go to the cafeteria where they served food, drinks, and had an endless stream of American films dubbed in Spanish.

Just after shoving off from La Paz we hit up the cafeteria for our free dinner; we had our choice of barbecued chicken or fish in some kind of sauce. We ate chicken, watched *Wall Street* in Spanish, and then went to bed at 8:00 due to sheer boredom.

In the morning we awoke and hurriedly made our way to the cafeteria for free breakfast time. Nothing gets us going like Mexican breakfast. Sheena staked our claim at a table by the window and I stood in line for food. Our choices this morning were *salchicha* (cut up hot dogs), or *huevos con salchicha* (eggs with cut up hot dogs). Come on, that's not a choice! *Huevos con salchicha* please! The tired looking "chef" with the scraggly beard filled our two plates with giant mounds of the egg/hot dog concoction and I returned to the table. My hot dog and egg euphoria quickly turned to nausea as I took the first bite. Fish. What we saw was a wonderful medley of processed meat and the ovulation byproducts of a flightless bird, but what we tasted was fish. Fish, as in last night's *other* dinner option.

We disembarked in Mazatlán at 10:30 in the morning, our bellies full of fishy eggs, ready to start the arduous search for our friend Santiago's house. Due to our inverter failure we still didn't have a computer, and thus no ability to tell Santiago when we would be arriving, or whether we had actually made it onto the ship. As we left the ship yard, who else would be walking across the street in front of us than Santiago. He gave us a quick wave, hopped in his Mercedes, and zipped out into traffic along the peninsular road toward the center of town.

"So, how was the ferry?" Santiago asked, once inside of his apartment in the town's historic center.

"Not too bad. Slept most of the time. We had the worst breakfast though. They didn't wash the pan that they used to cook the fish from the night before, and then used it to cook the eggs for breakfast. Most disgusting thing I've ever tasted."

He gave an understanding nod and the corner of his mouth rose in a half smile. "Welcome to Mexico."

# 9

*Mazatlán, Mexico — January, by Brad*

"You will stay in my house in Mazatlán, and you will stay for at least one week."

And that was that. I first met Santiago in 2001 when he was running a Mexican mountain bike race team. He sponsored me and a few other riders to come to Mexico to race in the *Copa Jumex*. A couple of hours into the race, my head was pounding from the heat and in my hallucinations I was swimming laps in a pool of ice cold Gatorade. The nail in the coffin came when a young rider in cutoff jean shorts and tennis shoes passed me and left me in the dust. The shame. For old times' sake, Santiago invited us on the Saturday group mountain bike ride in Mazatlán.

"Sheena, you and I will rent bikes. Brad, you will ride my bike." A pretty generous offer, considering that his bike used to be Todd Wells' race bike. If you don't know Todd, he is a two time Olympian and US national champion. However, in a sick twist of fate we were unable to find any cycling shoes and pedals to borrow. This time Sheena and I would be riding in tennis shoes. Total. Freds.

As it turned out, Santiago's rental bike was a bit dated and far too small for him. He stuck it out for the first half of the ride, but then pulled the plug.

Regardless of the bike situation, the group was charged up about getting to show us their local trail. In 2000 there was a UCI mountain bike World Cup held here, and everyone in the group mentioned it at some point. It had become a point of pride. *The world came here to ride on our trail.* We found this pride, coupled with generosity, everywhere we looked.

With Santiago as our guide we traveled all over the city to meet people and eat well during our one week stay. He would walk in front of us as we honed in on the best street carts. "See that one? It is packed with Mexicans. That is how you know it will be good." After discovering Sheena's unhealthy obsession with *Pastel de Tres Leches,* a cake made with three varieties of milk, he made it his personal mission to bring us to every establishment with good Tres Leches. By the end of our stay, she had earned the nickname *Sheena Tres Leches.* Probably not the kind of nickname a girl strives for, but it has meaning and was well earned. Now she runs every day in an effort to return to having only one chin.

A couple of days into our stay, Sheena mentioned to Santiago that her tooth had been developing an ache. Without another word, he picked up the phone and got her a dentist appointment for that evening. When we arrived at the dentist, he spent about 30 minutes with her, did a complete cleaning, took x-rays, and told her how to get rid of the ache. When it was time to go, we asked him how much we owed him. He just waved his hand in the air, and said with a smile, "Don't worry about it! Just have a good trip and be safe!"

During our stay we made friends with Chacho and his brother Ulises. They've lived in Mazatlán all their lives, and still live in their family home in the historic center. During our hike to the lighthouse, Chacho learned of Sheena's Tres Leches problem.

"My aunt makes the best Tres Leches in Mexico." It was the kind of pride we'd come to expect in Mazatlán, but sounded like a big fish story. I once had a Mexican guy tell me that he made the best enchiladas, but that ended with me waking myself up in the middle of the night by projectile vomiting out the side of my bed. We just left it at that.

Throughout the week we attended two of Santiago's city league basketball games. Going to the games was a good way for us to get together with locals; we met Jorge, who works at the Pacifico brewery, and Papas, whose family runs a taco stand on a street corner in one of the neighborhoods.

One evening we stopped at Papas' taco stand and sat down in front of the giant grill. The cook, one of Papas' family members, threw down a plate and tossed several kinds of meat onto it for us to eat while we waited. Two terra cotta cazuelas sat atop the flames filled with *tripa* and *carne asada*. A woman stood to the side making fresh tortillas for each order. After so much meat, *ceviche*, and *horchata*, we slipped into a heavenly food coma. I've said it once and I'll say it again. Mexican taco stands: pretty much the best thing ever. As we left, Papas told us to stop by his house on our way out of town to say goodbye.

On our penultimate day Chacho invited us to the beach to fly his kite, an experience that solidified the fact that neither Sheena or I would ever succeed at kite surfing. Before he went home he invited us for a going away get together. "You guys come over for coffee tonight. I have a surprise for you."

When we got to Chacho's house that evening he seemed to be smiling more widely than usual. "I will be right back." He disappeared into the kitchen and came back with two cups of coffee and a *Pastel de Tres Leches*. "I told my aunt that you love Tres Leches, so she made you this cake." Think about that. When was the last time you went that far out of your way for someone you just met? As with so many people we've met on our trip so far, Chacho is a real class act. And by the way he was right. It was hands down the best Tres Leches in Mexico.

The next day we packed up Nacho for the trip south. From the lap of luxury back to the van of luxury. As we packed, a young kid with a skateboard walked by and stopped when he looked in our van. "It's our home" I said. We got to talking and I told him about our trip. After a while he wished us luck on our trip and continued on his way. Pretty inquisitive and mature for such a young guy, I thought.

After a short while the word had gotten out amongst the neighborhood's ten to thirteen year old demographic. Throughout the afternoon kids would walk up and wish us luck on our travels. Nothing malicious or predatory, just good old fashioned nice. And here I had gone and given up on that particular demographic all together. Egg on my face.

The night before our departure we swung by Papas' modest house just down the street from his taco stand. He came out and we talked about our trip for a while, and then he told us he had something for us. He ran inside and emerged with a plastic bag full of *carnitas*. Every morning at 4:00, he told us, he slaughters a pig for his taco stand, and he had set aside some of the meat from that day's pig for us to take on the road. And just like that, we were humbled. Again.

# 10

*San Blas, Mexico — January, by Brad*

I had been standing on the beach for an hour, the bungee cord holding my dive knife to my leg cutting off the circulation to my foot. The sand flies of San Blas dined gluttonously on my flesh as I stood with my fishing pole in hand, line extending into the surf. It had been over three weeks since we reached the ocean, and I still hadn't caught a fish. The only thing saving us from starvation every day had been the miracle of commerce. I was clearly no fisherman. That is, until I felt the ever so light tug on my line.

*Could it be?* I wondered. I waited with my eyes concentrated on the tip of my rod. Yes, something was tugging on my line. I had all but decided that this ocean was completely devoid of life until this, the tug of my line, proof that life does exist in the ocean. The scientists are right!

I quickly reacquainted myself with the functionality of my reel, as I was until this point unpracticed in reeling anything in. With each feeble twist of the reel I pulled the sure-to-be behemoth sea monster of a fish closer to shore. Closer to our Dutch oven, which would be especially retrieved from Nacho's cabinet just for the occasion of this abundant fish dinner. As it neared shore, the ocean exploded as if a giant wave were crashing ashore. Moments later, as I reeled the fish onto the beach, I realized that the commotion was indeed a wave crashing ashore. My fish was lacking. Flaccid. Its four inches of length was matched in anticlimax only by its half inch of girth. My throat began to close up with the swell of tears at my ongoing failure as a fisherman, but I held it back. Just because everyone else catches big fish doesn't mean I have to. *Come on Brad*, I thought, *don't ride the bandwagon.*

Moments after I finished chopping up the tiny green fish into bait for future failed fishing ventures, I heard a squeal of joy wafting up from the beach. I looked up and saw Sheena very rapidly flapping one hand at me in a motion that I assumed was intended to make me come to her. As I approached, I saw a tiny rock next to her feet having a seizure. Upon further scrutiny, I realized that the tiny rock was actually a baby sea turtle instinctively, slowly, making its way from its nest to the ocean. The hyperventilation and the look of utter bliss on her face. The genuine satisfaction and eye-popping joy. This must be how it feels to catch a fish.

After two nights of beach camping in San Blas, the witnessing of the miracle of life, the surfing, and the reminder of my perpetual failure as a fisherman, we pointed south. Everyone we had encountered had spoken highly of Sayulita, a small and quirky expat surf town where the jungle-covered mountains meet the ocean just north of Puerto Vallarta.

We pulled into Sayulita, a compact town with cobbled dirt roads and lots of color. We hadn't seen many tourists in Baja, nor had we seen many in Mazatlán after tourism's recoil due to occasional violence between drug cartels. San Blas had a few retired expats, but not many. Sayulita was a different story. Most of the signs and almost all of the voices we heard were in English. If the Americans left, the town would be gone. At first it was a put off, but then we decided to roll with it. We're far from home, so we might as well have the taste of home when we can. We proceeded to drink espresso, eat banana pancakes, and speak English. Later, I proceeded to fall off of my surfboard and shove an ice axe–like rock right into my heel. In my scramble to find my board I took three sea urchin spines in the same foot. I swore out loud, in English.

When it came time to find a campground for the night, we were told where to find it. We found the beach front property surrounded by a tall brick fence and dotted with palm trees, and inquired about the price. $35. *You must be out of your damn mind* I thought. $35 to park for the night? We cursed our American brethren and the economic fortune they'd brought on this small town, and decided to head north a few miles to the equally small, but relatively undiscovered town of San Francisco.

In San Francisco we drove down the main street until it dead ended in a very small parking lot at the beach. A small river emptied from the jungle into the bay next to where a merengue band played while people danced. Couples sat beneath palm trees and watched the sunset. We walked over to a lady who ran a small restaurant and asked her where we could park Nacho to camp. She twirled her hand in the air and said "anywhere's fine." I pointed to the van. "Right there?" She nodded her head and said something about it being a public space. The spot was pretty perfect; a thick canopy of trees overhead, the beach a few yards away, a quiet dead end with little traffic. I asked a passing police officer if it was really okay. He thought about it for a second, looking a little confused, and then said, "sure, I don't see why not."

After the sun set, all of the cars left and we had the place to ourselves. We popped the camper top and made ourselves at home. We heard some beautiful music coming from the street outside of a café a stone's throw away, so we walked over and ordered a couple of drinks. The music was wonderful; the melancholy voice of Portuguese fado, coupled with simple guitar and a hand drum. Turns out it was Argentinean folk music played by a couple from Argentina.

After a few songs we headed back to Nacho and called it a night. We paid the restaurant owner $3 to plug Nacho into her electricity for an overnight battery conditioning, pulled the curtains, and slipped away to sleep. No brick walls, no neighbors, and $32 cheaper than the alternative. Bandwagons be damned.

# 11

*Guanajuato, Mexico — February, by Brad*

On the drive to Guanajuato, Nacho developed a high frequency vibration, most likely in one of the wheels, which also manifested itself as a vibration under braking. Being that we didn't know what was wrong, we were a little on edge about the performance of our brakes. Following the directions to the campground in Guanajuato, we climbed higher and higher into the ravines above town, and within a few hundred meters of our destination, the tiny cobbled road pitched straight down at a gradient of at least 30%. We crept along at a walking pace, hoping that our brakes would hold up. In my mind I picked a few power poles that would work as emergency stops to keep us from barreling into one of the ramshackle huts that clung to the mountainside. Of course I didn't mention this to Sheena, who was already starting to freak out. Our road ended in a tee, and we turned left. The only thing that stood between us and the campground was a tight, one lane, serpentine path that wove through a close collection of buildings at a gradient of around 30%. I slowly turned the tight corner and then floored it. Nacho groaned, climbed, and slowly came to a stop. The engine died as Sheena hyperventilated on the edge of consciousness.

Several more close calls and tricky maneuvers saw us arrive safely at our campground via an alternate route that involved driving the wrong way on a tight one-way street. When we stopped Sheena punched me, I pumped my fists in the air and growled, Sheena swore "never again," and I strutted around in circles with my chest poked out. Take that, road.

When we pulled into the campground we introduced ourselves to the only other people camping there, an elderly German couple in a 2005 Land Cruiser with a camper body. They had been on the road since 2007, having shipped their rig from Hamburg to Buenos Aires, and were slowly making their way to Alaska.

"Ve tolt our son zat zere voult be no money left! Ve vill spent it all!"

That's the spirit. I know who I want to be when I grow up.

By day Guanajuato was vibrant. Service providers walked or drove the streets advertising their services by yelling or playing jingles over loudspeakers. When they heard the propane truck's jingle, residents would wave him down and refill their bottles. Every provider had his own call; the newspaper salesman, the trash man, the knife sharpener. By night, the service calls were replaced by the dogs of Guanajuato. We had noticed that each house had a chicken and a rooster in the yard, and a dog or two on the roof. At night, the dogs owned the airwaves. My lack of patience has prohibited me from actually counting, but I imagine there were over 200 barks per minute audible from our campsite all night long. In the morning the barks were joined by hundreds of roosters bringing in the new day.

The food scene continues to keep us happy and looking forward to our next meal. Over the last month in Mexico we've learned a few things about food;

1. The street cart is king. For a couple of dollars we can eat the best tasting food on the planet, prepared from scratch before our very eyes. And despite what you may have heard, they won't make you sick.

2. If Lonely Planet recommends it, it's best avoided. We've been disappointed 100% of the time. Whoever wrote the Mexico guide was not a foodie.

3. By shopping at open air markets, it's possible to get the freshest ingredients for home cooking. We've made

some damn good meals so far, and a meal never costs more than $5 to put together.

4.  The *torta ahogada* is a must-eat. A thick bread roll stuffed with onions and juicy cubes of *carnitas*, drowned in a sauce of *chiles de arbol*. Once served, it is dowsed in more tongue searing chili sauce and drizzled with fresh lime juice. When eaten, the spicy concoction coats the hands and face like a toddler after an ice cream cone, the lips burn, and the mouth waters at the thought of another one.

5.  If you can't find a street cart, find a hole in the wall instead. Locals don't go to actual restaurants, so they're touristy, less authentic, and overpriced. For some reason, I've only had upset stomach after eating in restaurants; never from street carts.

After four days of hiking, eating, and exploring, we packed up and bid farewell to the town, the roosters, the food, and the dogs of Guanajuato. I spent the last day working on Nacho, trying to fix the brakes and the vibrations, and we hit the road with our fingers crossed. Once we escaped the winding streets and made our way back onto the mountain roads, the vibration returned, and the brakes continued to shake. Yep, sounds about right. Something to do in San Miguel de Allende.

# 12

*San Miguel de Allende, Mexico — February, by Brad*

*El Golpeador* was a squat man who moved about hurriedly. He was missing half of his little finger, likely due to the rapidity with which he carried out his projects. As he approached Nacho, I could see through the pouring rain that he was carrying a bucket full of tools, none of which were intended for a rear wheel bearing replacement: a pipe wrench, a long bar, a hammer, vise grips. I got that sinking feeling, the one you get when you forget to set the emergency brake, and then watch the station wagon carrying your whole family roll backwards into fast moving traffic.

How did we get here? It all started when I failed to fix this problem in Guanajuato.

On the way to San Miguel de Allende I carried out a meticulous series of troubleshooting steps to hone in on the problem. A casual observer might have seen me swerving violently, randomly pulling the hand brake, revving the engine, slamming on the brakes, creating an aura of danger about Nacho. To the trained professional, I was troubleshooting. The Van Whisperer. The frequency of vibration was independent from engine speed, so it wasn't in the engine or transmission. Braking didn't change the sound, so it probably wasn't a CV joint. The vibration could be momentarily eliminated during hard right turns, so it probably had something to do with a wheel on the right side. The vibration couldn't be felt through the hand brake, while it could be felt in the foot brake, so it was likely in the front wheel. There we go, front right wheel. So easy a mere child could do it!

When we arrived at the campground in San Miguel de Allende we settled in amongst enormous German and Swiss overlanding rigs, sliding into a state of rig envy. We'd been inside a few of these types at the Overland Expo, and knew they were luxurious. The elaborate electrical systems, the plush interiors, the indentured servants. The only vibration these things feel while driving is caused by crushing lowly Vanagons under their enormous tires. *Yeah*, we told ourselves, *but good luck parallel parking.* Lying to ourselves is a defense mechanism.

Over the course of our stay, we found San Miguel de Allende to be charming. The people were pleasant, the streets were kept clean, and its cobbled roads and brightly colored shops made it seem quaint. The place is full of retired foreigners; Americans, Germans, British, Canadians. Whereas this would usually bother us, it actually kind of worked in San Miguel. It lacked the obnoxious English language solicitations and predatory corner-lurking salesmen. The town operated as a Mexican mountain town where foreigners happened to live. On nice days, groups of friends would meet at the tennis courts for a few games. Bulletin boards advertised Spanish emersion programs. I walked into a wine bar to ask where I could buy European beer, and toward the end of our conversation the woman asked if I spoke English. Turned out she was American too, albeit with a convincing Mexican accent, but it was never presumed that we would do business in English. This was, after all, Mexico. It was all very refreshing to know that a town like this was possible.

One afternoon we spoke to Hans, whose family operated our campground, to see if he knew of any good mechanics. The next morning, Silverio, a suspension specialist with 10 years' experience, showed up with an assistant in tow.

I told Silverio that we wanted all of our front wheel bearings replaced. He crawled under Nacho and showed me that, in addition to our wheel bearings, our steering rack had too much play, and that the bushings holding the rack to the frame were all shot. For good measure, we asked him to have the brake rotors resurfaced as well, and to replace the front brake pads. We were going to lick this problem with the "replace everything" method. To make a good situation great, we didn't even have to move Nacho from his place in the campground. Sheena, who at this time had been feeling ill for a few days, was able to sleep upstairs the whole time they worked. See? Breaking down in Mexico makes getting sick fun!

Without hesitation, the two of them started in on Nacho. Within minutes the rotors were off, they had the steering rack removed, and they were tapping the wheel bearings out. Before we knew it, they were walking into town carrying our rotors and the steering rack. By evening the rotors were machined, they had tightened up the steering, replaced the bushings, the front wheel bearings, and the front brake pads. The total cost was $102.

The next day, when the sun came up we hit the road. Shortly thereafter, terror settled upon us like a wet blanket. The sound was back, the low hum and vibration. I swerved violently a few times and grabbed the hand brake, just to be sure I wasn't dreaming.

We pulled into the next town and asked about a mechanic, which is how we became acquainted with *El Golpeador*. I took him for a ride, showed him all of the symptoms, and told him what we'd already done. He walked around a bit, looked under the car, and made his announcement.

"It's the muffler."

He said it with such confidence, in the way that a politician makes a promise. I reiterated my extensive troubleshooting results, and he decided it was indeed not the muffler, and instead must be a rear wheel bearing. It was at this point that he disappeared into his garage, and emerging through the pouring rain with his collection of incorrect tools.

*El Golpeador* first grabbed his pipe wrench, slid his long bar over the handle, and tried unsuccessfully to remove the axle lock nut. After giving up, he jacked Nacho up and removed the wheel, but that was apparently the extent of his expertise. His next move was to use his hammer to ravish, with all of his strength, Nacho's delicate brake drum.

"Stop! What are you doing!?" He looked up at me as if I were insane. "All you have to do is remove these two bolts and it'll slide off!" He pulled out his vise-grips and removed the bolts while my mood continued to darken. As I watched him remove our brake pads, it was clear he had no idea what he was doing. He proceeded to loosen the brake backing plate before realizing that he couldn't actually remove it without removing the hub lock nut. Next, he reached behind and started loosening the bolts that hold the hub housing together. Having done this job myself in the past, I knew this was a time consuming dead end road.

"What exactly are you hoping to accomplish? Once you get those bolts undone you still won't be able to get the bearings out. You need to remove the lock nut."

He tried to convince me that he could get the bearings off from the back of the stub axle. At this point I told him to stop, I got out the Bentley manual, and showed him an exploded view of the rear hub assembly. He still tried to convince me that he could do it, that he could defy the laws of the universe, that he could bend the space-time continuum. At this, I kindly asked him to put everything back together, which took considerable time, and then we left.

Dumbass. Everyone knows that Chuck Norris is the only one who can bend the space-time continuum. And so we flipped Nacho around and slowly made our way back to San Miguel de Allende to see Silverio again. The Mexican Chuck Norris.

# 13

*San Miguel de Allende, Mexico — February, by Brad*

Sitting in Nacho one evening in San Miguel de Allende, Sheena looked over at me with wanting eyes. Almost immediately I knew it was a trap.

"Bradley?" She said, sounding so sweet. "Will you do me a really big favor?" I knew I couldn't say no. When your spouse is ill, it doesn't matter that you've retired to your easy chair for the night with a Steinbeck novel and a good beer. No, it doesn't matter if your whole body feels like Jell-O from your 15 minute hot shower, or that you're already wearing your pajamas. For the last few weeks Sheena had been feeling unwell, and after adjusting her diet had failed to deliver results, I knew she was ready to pull out the big guns.

"Does it involve going to the pharmacy?"

"Ummm...yes."

These things, like pulling teeth, are best done quickly before your body has a chance to object. I grabbed my hooded sweatshirt and canvas moccasins, opened the sliding door, and headed out of the campground. I was halfway to the pharmacy before I looked down and realized what I looked like; a black hooded sweatshirt, matching oversized black sweatpants, and canvas moccasins without socks. Being that they were my pajamas, and hence never having been worn with shoes, I had never noticed the nerdy way in which the bottoms of my sweatpants didn't quite reach my shoes. Instead the leg holes swung like hula hoops around my white, sockless ankles.

I made my way, self-consciously through the passersby on their way to dinner on this, a Saturday night. I've heard that the French secretly make fun of Americans for the subset of our population that thinks it's okay to be seen in public wearing full sweatsuits. Shame on us for giving the French a reason to laugh at us. When I see this atrocity, even I turn my nose up in disgust. And how many times have I posted snide comments on Twitter about Scottsdale women and their bad habit of wearing matching sweatsuits in public? Apparently twice.

> *"Hey Scottsdale lady, what makes you think it's okay to wear your velour jogging ooutfit to the store? No wonder the French hate us."*
> — *Twitter observation, December 19, 2009*

> *"Why do older women in Scottsdale always wear monochromatic velour jogging uniforms? Thanks for presenting yourselves so artfully…"*
> — *Twitter observation, December 19, 2010*

I made my way down our street, across *Calle Zacateros*, to the Pharmacy. I hadn't really thought through how I would approach the interaction, so it ended up going down like a train wreck. I stormed in the front door and found the young female pharmacist staring down at the counter in a kind of trance.

"I need an enema."

She looked up at me, startled. She didn't say anything, her eyes gave away her uncertainty laced with fear. She didn't blink. I wanted to turn and run, but I remembered Sheena's poor little eyes looking up at me. …*a really big favor?*

"Um…do you have any of them here…for sale?"

"No." She must have been mesmerized by my matching sweatsuit. "They sell them at Farmacia Guadalajara. It's down the road." As I left I could almost feel her thumbs on her phone keypad, texting all of her friends.

The town's main street was crowded with couples dressed to the nines heading out for dinner, old ladies crouched over going wherever it is that old ladies go, and assorted laborers making their way home after a hard day's work. Beyond all of these judging eyes, Farmacia Guadalajara.

I bobbed and weaved through the foot traffic, my matching sweatsuit grazing the odd hand or old lady cane. Straight ahead, Dilshan stood in front of his Sri Lankan restaurant talking to Greg, our waiter from the night before. When he saw me, Dilshan stopped and stared, mouth slightly ajar. As I approached, he looked at my matching suit in disbelief, and then recovered.

"Heeeeey…you're back in town?"

"Yeah…uh…our car is still broken down. I'm going to the pharmacy. You know, Sheena's feeling ill." For a minute I thought he'd suggest that we stop by for dinner again, but then I remembered he had a reputation to uphold.

"I hope it wasn't from my food!"

I assured him that it wasn't, and dismissed myself with a handshake. I turned to Greg and shook his hand, only to realize that it wasn't Greg at all, but a complete stranger. It was that moment of horror that we've all felt. *Oh, you!? I didn't mean that YOU were pregnant!* Been there.

Once inside Farmacia Guadalajara, I made my way to the back where another young female pharmacist waited. As she handed me the enema kit her eyes said *feel better*, while also saying *you look like a clown*. I picked up two packs of chocolate and headed to the checkout counter. It's just something you do when buying a product like this. Chocolate seems to lessen the blow, as if to say, "yeah, I came to buy this chocolate, but these caught my eye, so I decided to casually buy them too."

There must have been something magical in that chocolate, as Sheena was feeling like a million bucks the next day. Silverio and Mario returned to our campsite and fixed Nacho once and for all with new rear driver's side wheel bearings, and we were ready to rock. One more night in San Miguel de Allende and we were poised to hit the road to Oaxaca, near where Nacho Libre was filmed. A place where people are used to seeing Americans dressed up in funny suits. What would the French think? Oh, let's stop kidding ourselves. Since when have we ever cared what the French think?

# 14

*Oaxaca, Mexico — February, by Brad*

Before we left on our trip, people used to ask us which city in Mexico we were most looking forward to. No brainer: Oaxaca. In our minds it was a quaint food lover's paradise. We imagined strolling around, sampling mole, eating at the best street carts in all of Mexico, and giving casual high fives to Rick Bayless. Everyone we asked in Mexico prior to arriving in Oaxaca had egged us on. "What's your favorite town in Mexico?" we would ask. "Oaxaca!" they would scream.

As we entered Oaxaca state, two things changed; the topes were no longer painted, making it nearly impossible to avoid the Nacho-killing road hazards, and the verb tense on the anti-litter road signs changed from the third person formal to the second person informal. "No tires basura," they said. Google Maps said the trip from San Miguel de Allende would last 9 hours, 3 minutes. A mere 19 hours and thirty minutes of driving later, we arrived in Oaxaca city and staked our claim at the campground. The first thing we saw when we got off the bus at the food market in downtown Oaxaca city, after noting the eardrum-piercing noise of the place, was a very dirty Aboriginal-looking black man lumbering out of the raw meat section of the market without any pants on.

"I don't think he's supposed to be doing that," Sheena whispered.

Apparently the road signs aren't the only thing in Oaxaca that had gone informal.

To our dismay, Oaxaca was the polar opposite of our expectations. We passed the nude-bottomed man just as we entered the market. After swallowing the vomit from that encounter, we were met with the stench of a hundred kinds of rotting meat. The tables were stacked high with parched, fly-laden, wretchedly stinking chicken, beef, pork, and sausages. It's a miracle that I didn't ralph up the rest of my breakfast. The city's apparent specialty snack is the *chapulin*, or fried grasshopper; a food that Mexican health officials agree is a serious health hazard due to its exceedingly high lead content, but don't know what to do about it. The halls of the food market are packed with baskets full of the fried heavy metal insects.

Still believing that Oaxaca would pull through for us, we made for the market's food stalls. Nothing looked very appetizing, but we wandered over the stand with the most Mexicans at it and ordered per the waiter's recommendation. The *pollo con mole* was mediocre, and the chicken soup was palatable, but boring. Dinner was no exception; we spent two thirds of our daily budget on dinner at a place overlooking the *zócalo*, or central square, but went away disappointed. On the bright side, our dinner table was situated on the second floor at an open window, which gave us a nice vantage point to watch the very picturesque *zócalo* while a band played and people strolled.

After a mere day and a half in Oaxaca city things weren't improving, so we decided to cut our losses and head out to the surrounding smaller towns. We're not big on complaining, but given our Mecca-like expectations for Oaxaca, I thought this was a worthy exception. So far we're the only people we know who have felt this way about Oaxaca. More than anything it reaffirmed our distaste for big cities.

The surrounding towns turned out to be more rewarding. First we headed out to San Martin Tilcajete, a town of just over a thousand inhabitants, where the locals specialize in carving and painting wooden figurines. Ever the figurine lover, Sheena couldn't help herself and popped for a small wooden pig. Our beer and coffee cabinet is getting empty, so Sheena has decided that a better use for it is to store various miniature animals and other artisanal doo dads in it. Until we arrive in a country with good beer, I've decided to let her go wild.

Next we made our way back into Oaxaca city to get the final installment of our hepatitis A and B vaccinations. This involved going to a hospital, where we had to procure surgical masks in order to be let inside – quite a good idea we thought – and then had a consultation with a doctor. He didn't have the right vaccinations, as hepatitis shots aren't normally given to Mexican adults, so he sent us deeper into the city where we got our shots at a vaccination specialist.

The final stop on our Oaxaca whirlwind tour was the town of Teotitlan, where the specialty is weaving. We found a B&B that would let us camp in their courtyard, use their showers, their bathrooms, and their kitchen for around $5 per night.

By day, the air was filled with the sound of a Mexican band marching through the empty streets. We saw them pass by a few times, apparently playing to nobody. Later we saw that they had made their way onto the roof of the church, where they continued playing their songs before eventually coming down to eat ice cream popsicles in the shadow of the church. The randomness of the whole ordeal seemed to be the planking equivalent of marching bands. Teotitlan was quite nice, and we ended up staying two nights. Oh, and in the interest of acquiring more local handicrafts, we bought a naturally dyed and hand woven wool rug for Nacho.

While we had tentatively planned to spend at least four days in Oaxaca, we weren't enjoying ourselves so we left. All in all Mexico has far exceeded our expectations, and there have only been a small handful of places we haven't liked. If Rick Bayless had been there to give us a high five, maybe things would have turned out differently.

# 15

*Chamula, Mexico — February, by Brad*

We pushed ourselves into the mass of bodies while the uneasy shriek produced by hundreds of horns created a feeling as though something bad were about to happen. In a large circle in the plaza in front of the church, men in elaborate traditional Mayan dress acted out a battle themed march whose phases unfolded throughout the day. The first row of men would run ahead, brandishing wooden switches, then leap into the air, bringing their switches to the ground with a loud *thwack*! The rest followed closely behind, using their horns to make the eerie shriek. A continuous stream of rockets made explosions that shook the ground. It didn't feel like any festival we'd ever been to. Looking around, we seemed to be the only white people in the entire town. Around us, thousands of Mayan descendants looked on with somber, serious faces. Nobody was smiling. We felt uneasy.

A young Mayan man came over to us, looked up to me, and asked me something. I couldn't catch everything due to his thick Tzotzil accent, but he seemed to want to bring us somewhere. I told him we were happy where we were. Before he walked away he slapped the back of his hand on my chest and looked deep into my eyes, his face very serious. He stood on his toes to bring his face closer to mine. "Ten cuidado," he said in a clear and serious tone. *Be careful.* He turned and walked away.

We were in Chamula, a town at 7,200 feet above sea level in the mountains outside of San Cristobal de las Casas in the state of Chiapas. Chamula and other mountain towns in Chiapas are home to the direct descendants of the Maya, and to the *Ejército Zapatista de Liberación*

*Nacional* (EZLN), more commonly known as Zapatista rebels. Taking pictures of people, or within the church in Chamula is illegal and can get you on the wrong end of a group beating. It is the only town in Mexico with autonomous status, meaning that they make up their own laws, and Mexican police and military aren't allowed to enter the town. Needless to say, we didn't take any pictures.

Inside of the church, the explosions shook the walls, while the shrieking horns were muffled into a perfect horror film soundtrack. The scene inside the church was something from centuries past, almost supernatural. Thousands of candles filled the floor and every flat surface, the smoke of burning pine billowed up from a fire that lay smoldering on the floor near a shrine tended by two women, filling the place with a thick haze. The entire floor was covered in a thick layer of pine needles, giving us the feeling that we'd stepped back in time a thousand years. A man stood in the center of the church weeping inconsolably, speaking in Tzotzil, a Mayan dialect. He alternated his hand between his forehead and his chest, stricken with grief.

A family sat in the middle of the church floor wearing traditional tribal clothing, a hundred candles unlit in front of them. The pine needles tangled in the women's matted goat hide skirts, the children leaned against their mothers. A shaman sat with them wearing a white goat hide vest, its wool poking wildly in all directions. A chicken sat on the floor with them, a plastic bag restricting its wings. Four glass bottles of Coca Cola rested in front of the women. One by one the family lit the candles and for several minutes we watched them staring into the flames, speaking quietly. Suddenly the man picked up the chicken and snapped its neck; it flailed wildly, its head limply hanging from its body. The man held its legs still while the life faded from it, and then he placed its body on the floor near the candles. Its body produced an occasional twitch. One of the women picked up each Coke bottle in turn and waved it over the flames. The sacrifice of the chicken saddened and shocked us, but the feeling was mixed with a sense that we were catching a glimpse of something ancient. Here were the direct descendents of the Maya, still sacrificing animals and carrying out their rituals. Dominican missionaries forced them to accept Catholicism, but it was clear today that they accepted it with their hands behind their backs, fingers crossed.

Feeling shaky from what we saw in the church, the billowing smoke, the candles, and the Mayan faces ringed with emotion, we emerged into the throngs of people filling the vast central square. During the time that we spent in the church, things had intensified. The shrieking horns were being blown with greater vigor and the warriors moved more quickly around the circuit. New characters had joined the promenade, holding pots containing smoldering pine, which gave the zócalo the same smoky aura as the inside of the church. The shrieks, the smoke, the explosions, and the increase in tempo created a sense of impending calamity. The men were running now. We pushed ourselves back into the throngs so that we could see into the center of the commotion.

Suddenly from a side street, a long line of men wearing goat hide vests sprinted into the square pulling a long rope. Attached to the rope was an enormous angry bull. It kicked wildly and swung its head trying to impale its captors with its horns. As the bull passed by in front of us it lurched for the crowd. Everyone recoiled as it passed, while the brave and the drunk ran toward the bull and tried to ride it. Time and again the bull would toss the riders to the ground, and at one point it successfully gouged a rider with its horn.

As time went on, four more bulls were brought into the plaza, creating total havoc. Women and children curled up in the corners of open air food stalls as the bulls passed. Frequently the bulls jumped onto the sidewalks and tried to impale bystanders. Everyone remained serious and kept the emotion out of their faces. Two boys tried walking along the sidewalk in front of us toward a waiting bull, and one of the warriors ran in front of them, striking the ground at their feet with his wooden stick. They tried walking around and he advanced, jumped in the air, and brought his switch onto the ground at their feet again, creating a loud crack. He got up and stared into their eyes. There was no longer any confusion about where they were not to tread.

At the end of the day we shakily made our way back to the top of the hill on the edge of town to catch a *colectivo*. Seventeen of us piled into a 1970's Volkswagen van and then its teenage driver sped away, down the steep and twisting mountain road back to San Cristobal. We heard later that a couple of tourists had been chased down by a group of warriors with their wooden sticks for having taken a photograph. We didn't hear if they got away.

This is why we quit our jobs and left the comfort of home. To discover a world that we didn't know existed. To wander into Zapatista villages, to run away from angry bulls, to witness Mayan rituals, and to occasionally leap completely out of our comfort zone. Am I happy to be out of the mountains and writing this post safely from the comfort of a Caribbean beach? Well, yes.

# 16

*San Cristóbal de las Casas, Mexico — February, by Brad*

For a while I've been wondering what baby gifts we should get for our friends Jen and Eric, who are expecting twin girls soon. You could say I don't really "get" kids. When I speak to them I use long multisyllabic words, I assume that they want to talk about politics, or I force them to sit through my soapbox monologues about the intricacies of proper espresso preparation. It was thus with great joy that I discovered the two perfect gifts for Jen and Eric's future daughters while strolling around the artisan market in San Cristobal de las Casas.

The first thing I found was a great little handmade wool monkey, a mother hugging its baby. It seemed like a gift that would remind child #1, we'll call her Guadalupe, that her mother, like this monkey, is a caregiver. I don't know a damn thing about kids, but it seems like little Guadalupe will benefit from a constant reminder that her mother will give her a hug when she gets sad about petty injustices, or whatever it is that kids get sad about.

Later I was walking by a market stall when another gem caught my eye. For child #2, we'll call her Wanda, I couldn't pass up a handsome wool figurine of the masked leader of the Zapatista rebels, Subcomandante Marcos. He wears a black ski mask over his face and carries a camouflaged rucksack on his back to aid in his survival while camping in the mountains. His cute little wool hands tightly clasp a Kalashnikov machine gun. In times of despair, little Wanda can look at her Subcomandante Marcos doll and find solace in the idea that one day the evils of globalization will be put down and the mountain villages of Chiapas will once again thrive.

San Cristobal de las Casas was a beautiful town, and one of our favorites yet in Mexico. Its mountain location in a pine forest at roughly the same elevation as Flagstaff made us feel at home. Walking through the cobbled streets, through the brightly colored buildings and ample open air markets, we encountered a great number of women and children dressed in traditional Mayan clothing. Women wore long skirts made of black goat hide, still thick with unruly goat fur, and brightly colored cardigans. Every Mayan girl over the age of 15 or so had at least one baby in tow.

We found a campsite within walking distance of downtown, yet still tucked away in the trees at the base of the hills. By day we wandered the town streets or took short trips to the surrounding villages, while in the evenings we fell asleep to the sound of crickets. We spent one evening chatting with a couple from Switzerland who are on their way north from Argentina to the United States. So far we've met at least a dozen groups of Europeans doing this route, but pretty much nobody else seems to be heading south like us.

After a few days in San Cristobal, the ocean started calling to us. The surfboards were looking a little parched and the fishing poles still longed to be used for their intended purpose. And with that, we loaded up Nacho, secured our baby warming gifts, and headed east. Someplace warm. A place where the beer flows like wine. Where beautiful women instinctively flock like the salmon of Capistrano. I'm talking about a little place called Palenque.

# 17

*Misol-Ha, Mexico — February, by Brad*

At about 4:30 this morning, Sheena woke me up in a frantic scurry. With firefighter speed she exited the sheets, swung her legs over the edge of the upper bed, and dropped into Nacho's downstairs living quarters. She was sick in a bad way. As I lay there with my ears plugged, I thought to myself, *Poor little lady. And on her birthday of all days.*

Once per year it's up to me to turn an otherwise mundane day into a fantastic one. Instead of sitting at home in the snow, we go to the deer farm and risk getting Lyme disease while petting the mangy deer. Or we play hooky from work and drive up the hill to Snowbowl for a day of skiing. Today was no exception; I had stealthily sneaked to the cake shop in San Cristobal and bought a tres leches cake, and had successfully hidden it from Sheena. I had planned a day of wonder, as I do every year. "Just take some Pepto," I told her. "Everything will be fine."

Once Sheena had composed herself, we converted Nacho from living machine into driving machine and hit the road to the East. Palenque was 130 miles away, so I figured we could make it in a few hours tops. A few kilometers from Palenque we would stop at the Misol-Ha waterfall for Sheena's birthday celebration. It was to be so grand.

The road out of San Cristobal took us through incredible jagged mountains dotted with tiny Mayan villages, which, given the backdrop, looked like what I imagine one might see in the Nepalese Himalayas. The first half of the drive was through pine forests, while the second half was through jungle.

Occasionally we came across short men carrying enormous loads of firewood out of the forest on their backs using slings wrapped around their foreheads. Often men and women would be raking out coffee beans on tarps on the roadside to dry the beans in the sun.

In my driving time calculation I had failed to account for one thing: *topes*. The ubiquitous Mexican speed bumps were placed approximately every quarter mile on the 130 mile road from San Cristobal to Palenque. And in between the speed bumps the road would mysteriously be missing, fallen off the side of the cliff. Several times we came upon sections of road where literally half of the road had slid off the edge, leaving a jagged hole. Where the road hadn't fallen away, it was littered with sink holes in the pavement where it would soon fall off. The 130 mile trip took us six hours. But boy was it beautiful!

We arrived at Misol-Ha in the early afternoon and went down by the water for birthday cake. Sheena, being sick, was surprised about the tres leches, but wasn't exactly in the mood to stuff her face. After a spot of cake we went for a swim. The falls cascaded over the edge of an overhanging shelf and fell 100 feet into a large pool. A pathway led around the back of the falls to a subterranean river cave. Or, if you were totally hardcore extreme like Sheena and me, you would swim across the water to the cave. It's a feat that should only be attempted after copious amounts of Red Bull or tres leches cake, whichever is available.

While we swam in the pool at the base of the waterfall, tour buses made frequent stops at the falls. A line of tourists would file into the area around the pool, then go behind the falls and take a bunch of pictures. After a while we started to notice trends in the tourists' photos. It seemed that nobody could take a normal photo; rather, the person having their photo taken would spread their arms really wide and make a goofy smile (the most common), or else they would jump in the air (another favorite). Group photos often involved several strange poses, or sometimes everyone in the group would open their arms really wide as if trying to grasp the entire place in their embrace. We became intoxicated with this phenomenon, and eventually decided to take a few of our own, mimicking the poses we'd seen. It was all great fun, and at the expense of our vacationing countrymen.

At Palenque, a few kilometers away, we found a campsite within walking distance of the Mayan archeological site. The area was thick with jungle, and our campsite sat in a small clearing in the trees. As night fell, howler monkeys surrounded us and broke into their ritual noisemaking. As we sat listening to the monkeys, fireflies pulsated in the grass next to us. The monkeys were so loud that it was nearly impossible to fall asleep.

In the morning we strolled over to the archaeological site. From the depths of the thick jungle a whole ancient Mayan community had been uncovered, including temples, a palace, residential areas, and a canal. We spent the better part of a day exploring. This site, unlike many of the more widely visited sites in Mexico, still allows visitors to climb up the temple stairs, go inside the tombs, and explore at will.

And so the next day, in the way we do, we got back into Nacho and with firefighter speed we made way for the Yucatan peninsula. Our last stop in Mexico.

# 18

*Bacalar, Mexico — February, by Brad*

As we coasted at 80 miles per hour along well tended roads into the Yucatan peninsula, Mexico was essentially behind us. It was time to start our training. After two long months in the country we were almost to the Caribbean. Before entering Belize though, we had to practice laying around in hammocks, counting sand, and painstakingly ensuring that our tans were just the right touch of scorched paste. We decided that our first stop would be Tulum.

We found a campground on the beach and quickly got to work on our new training regimen. Sheena tested the hammock — sadly the first time we've pulled it out on this trip. Meanwhile I strutted around without a shirt, and later we both went snorkeling before retiring to the beach for a lounge. Our first day of Caribbean training was tough, but we survived.

Bright and early the next day we made it out to the Mayan ruins perched on a short cliff by the sea. They sure had a knack for choosing nice settings, but the ruins themselves were a far cry from the epic ruins at Palenque. All of the buildings were roped off, and the magnitude of the place was much smaller than our last stop. Still, we had a really nice time walking around.

With some laziness practice under our belts we headed South. We had to hurry up and act really lazy before leaving the Yucatan and putting our preparation to the test. The perfect place, it seemed, would be a small town that we'd seen on the way to Tulum. The town of Bacalar sat on the shores of a clear fresh water lagoon with a nice clean white sandy bottom, only a few miles from the Belizean border. We found a campsite right on the shore in a grassy lot. Later we would discover that our lot was in the territory of a queen ant who decided to lay thousands of babies inside of Nacho, but who on Earth could have seen that coming?

Over the ensuing couple of days we really did our best to get in some last minute relaxation training for Belize. We practiced the essentials: paddleboarding, swimming, regular dock diving, shrimp eating, hands-clasped-behind-the-back dock diving, strutting, muscle flexing, and flipping water with our hair.

We found Bacalar to be very enjoyable and laid back. It seemed most of the sun-seekers had skipped over it en route to the more popular Caribbean beaches farther east on the Yucatan. The visitors we met here were primarily Mexicans on vacation. We even ran into our first couple of Mennonite families; a group that has fairly extensive presence in Belize. We weren't really prepared to see people dressed like characters from Little House on the Prairie eating seafood at waterfront thatched huts. We continually caught ourselves staring at them, analyzing their every move. This was one thing that our extensive training program hadn't prepared us for.

# 19

*Somewhere in Southern Mexico — February, by Brad*

In America, our news outlets are all about sensationalism. If there isn't anything outrageously bad to report on, they'll revisit the terrible, heinous crimes from last month. This sensationalist attitude means that all you ever hear about Mexico is a continuous stream of negativity; terrible stories about kidnapping, dismemberment, and murders that occur due to the movement of drugs northward to satisfy America's own lust for illicit substances. Furthermore, everyone has heard about a friend of a friend with a corrupt cop story. Let's face it, Mexico gets a bad rap north of the border.

Before we left on our trip, people used to ask us how much money we were budgeting per day for bribes. Per day! After two months and 4,735 miles on the road in Mexico, we were never so much as pulled over by the police. We stopped at countless police and military checkpoints, but were met with nothing but smiles and friendly small talk. The police, by and large, aren't crooked. Foreigners who get pulled over and then offer bribes to "make it go away" are the real issue, as they create the impression that foreigners are stupid, and will part with their money at the drop of a hat.

As for the extreme danger due to the war on drugs, it never even crossed our minds outside of wondering, *what is the media talking about?* It never came up. Not in a conversation, not out of the corner of our eye, never. We felt silly safe every second of every day. Well, except for that strange day in Chamula with the bulls in the street and the animal sacrifices, but that was different. In short, America is missing out on experiencing a truly wonderful country to its immediate south due to little more than media fear mongering. If I sound dumbfounded, it's because I am. Should Europeans avoid travel to America because of gang violence in Los Angeles? Well, unless they're a member of a Los Angeles based gang, I'd say they have nothing to worry about. If the Mexican media reported on every single murder in the USA, they'd be scared to death too.

In Mexico, almost every day was an absolute treasure. The people we met were unfathomably kind, the weather was incredible, the food was life changing, and we feel that we've become better people for our experiences there. In the people we found a warmth and sincerity that we've never felt on such a universal scale. No longer do we dare pass someone on the street without greeting them with a smile and a "buenos dias." Whenever someone passes us on their way out the door of a restaurant, they invariably smile at us and say "provecho." *Enjoy.* Not just every once in a while, I'm talking about every time. Entire families will say this to us in turn as they pass. Even tough-looking teenagers. Mexico has taught us manners.

After two months in Mexico, we've decided that the country really deserves six. And to top it all off, it's cheaper to travel in Mexico than it is to stay home. Now I'm off to write a harshly worded letter to our friendly Arizona news network, and you can be sure I'll open with "buenos dias."

# Part 4

# Middle Americas

# 20

*Placencia, Belize — March, by Brad*

Before we got to Belize I didn't really know much about it. I knew that the official language was English and most tourists spent their time on the islands off the coast rather than inland in the jungle. I knew that Mennonites had a strong presence here. I knew that Floyd Landis was raised a Mennonite and ended up cheating to win the Tour de France. So the country had a strong presence of people linked to people who cheat to win the Tour de France. My knowledge was clearly a bit thin. I had heard that there were no fast food chain restaurants in Belize. Well at least that's redeeming. We were also told that we'd be robbed blind the minute we stepped over the border.

We beat the odds by crossing over the border and not getting robbed blind. Things were looking up. By the evening we had arrived in the country's capital, Belmopan. We stopped at a Chinese-run hotel and asked if we could pay to camp in their parking lot. They nearly robbed us blind, but then opted to let us camp there for free. Camping in a hotel parking lot in a country's capital might seem uncomfortable, until you realize that the population of Belize's capital is only 16,000. That's exactly 80 times the population of Farmersville, Pennsylvania, the town where Floyd Landis was raised as a Mennonite before growing up to be a big fat cheater.

While camping in the parking lot of that Chinese hotel in Belmopan, we made friends with Durman, the parking lot security guard. He told us that Prince Harry of England would be hosting a party in Belmopan the following evening, and everyone was invited. Our minds wandered to what could come of this. Belmopan's population was small, so the party would probably be small. We imagined ourselves laughing at really funny jokes with Mr. Prince, doing belly button shots, and making impersonations of Ace Ventura. Later, in a moment of weakness he would scribble his cell phone number on a napkin and invite us to stay in Buckingham Palace when we get to London.

We slept on it, but in the morning decided to forego Prince Harry's kind invitation and instead drive to Placencia to camp. We accepted the fact that we'd regret our decision in a couple of years when we find ourselves camping in a wet London back alley, creating little perimeter dams out of soggy saltine crackers to keep the hobo urine from soaking into our sleeping bags.

Accepting our fate, we drove on. A couple of hours outside of Belmopan we came across a sign advertising *Blue Hole*. That could mean anything, we thought. We pulled over and walked into the jungle to find a nice little swimming hole created by a sinkhole that had collapsed into an underground river. Just downstream from the swimming hole the river ducked under a mountain and disappeared into darkness. With a guide you can take an inner tube down the river into the dark subterranean cave, and presumably come out somewhere else. We didn't have a guide, nor an inner tube, so I just stood in the cave entrance and watched leaves disappear into the darkness as I dropped them into the current. It kind of felt like when I was a kid and used to send cow pie boats through the rapids in trout streams, except that if I slipped here I would be sucked under a mountain.

On our way to Placencia, a small town on the Caribbean coast, we passed through dozens of small villages. Standing in stark contrast to the scary robbers that we expected to see based on everyone's warnings, we saw the smiling, happy faces of Belizeans. Most don't own cars, so they walk or ride bikes. This gave us an opportunity to see hundreds of people on our drive across the country, and nearly everyone was smiling. Furthermore, we didn't pass a person on the roadside, be it a walker, cyclist, or someone sitting on the porch of their home, without them giving us a wave and a huge beaming smile.

Oh, but the fast food chain restaurant thing? Turns out it's not true. Subway opened a store in Belize City, but the government later required that they obtain their bread rolls from a local source. If Subway would exist in Belize, it would serve its sandwiches on Belizean rolls. They said "no way" and closed their doors. Later, McDonalds tried to open a branch in Belize City. They were given permission with one stipulation: they would have to source their beef from Belizean ranchers. They also said "no way" and pulled the plug. Later, Subway relented and reopened their doors. Now if you want to eat at a fast food chain in Belize, you'll have to find the only one in the country: a Subway serving its sandwiches on Belizean rolls. I don't know about you, but I find this story very refreshing.

What we thought we'd find in Belize based on hearsay: scary robbers. What stands out in or mind after actually having visited Belize: all smiles. To hell with naysayers. The Mennonites even looked nice and nonthreatening in their horse drawn buggies with their suspenders. So to hell with Floyd Landis too.

# 21

*Hopkins, Belize — March, by Brad*

If there's one thing we can say about Belize after having spent a little more than a week there, it's that the people are, as a whole, some of the happiest and friendliest we've come across in our travels thus far. When we arrived in the coastal town of Placencia on our second day, we asked a group of locals where we might find a camping spot.

"Yeah mon! You could prob'y camp in ya van at my gromma's house! Hey Priscilla, take these two ova to my gromma's house and ask if dey can camp ova der. When ya get ya van situated, come on back an' we can drink an' smoke togetha!"

When we were unable to navigate Nacho into the guy's grandmother's yard due to low tree branches we asked two other locals. One said we could camp in his front yard for free, although we kindly declined because it didn't offer much privacy, and another engaged us in an hour long conversation about Belizean national pride, although he didn't have a place for us to camp. In the end we opted to stay closer to the town of Seine Bight where we had seen an actual campground. All the while, everyone we passed on the roadside flashed a huge grin at us and waved.

We spent most of our time in Belize on the Caribbean coast between the towns of Placencia, Seine Bight, and Hopkins. We split our first few nights between the campground near Seine Bight and a spot at the Jungle Jeanie lodge in Hopkins.

Placencia is a small village at the tip of a long, skinny peninsula with equal parts indigenous Garifuna culture and foreign tourism. We had a good time hopping between restaurants and bars and hanging out with our campground brethren, but soon had our fill and headed off to Hopkins.

Hopkins seemed to better fit our style; to get there it required navigation of a rough dirt road, and the main street in town was mostly dirt. These obstacles have kept it slightly less discovered by tourism, and hence it seemed to retain its Garifuna culture a smidge more so than Placencia. Still, it had been outfitted with enough decent bars and eateries to keep us entertained for a few days.

One evening we had hoped to try some Indian food at what would have been our first Indian restaurant since leaving home. Unfortunately it was closed, so we opted to try one of the only places open that night: a foreign-owned place called Love on the Rocks. The idea is that you order an expensive fish dinner and then they bring it out to you uncooked along with a really hot ass rock. You then put your uncooked fish on the hot ass rock, where it proceeds to get stuck to the rock and burn the hell out of itself while you desperately try to get it unstuck with your fork. All the while the waitress stands there staring at you while you struggle. Finally, you eat your overcooked rubbery fish while the stuck fishy bits that remain on the rock turn into a smoldering black mess. Sheena thought it was awesome, as did several others we met in Hopkins, but I found it all very asinine. If I wanted to cook my own damn fish, I would have stayed home. And I certainly wouldn't have cooked it on a really hot ass rock.

The good part about the rock ordeal was that a Garifuna drumming group was playing. The Garifuna are an indigenous group in the area who are known for, among other things, their hand drumming. They're also known for a really tasty fish curry called hudut. Instead of incinerating the fish on a really hot ass rock, they make a curry out of coconut milk — which they make by hand — and pureed plantains, and then stew fish in it. It's served with cassava bread and mashed plantains, and it's absolutely transcendent. I know this because we tried it the following night at a local place called Innie's. But I digress.

Finally on our last day, after having waited out some rainy weather for a couple of days, we tagged along with a boat that was headed out for a day of snorkeling and fishing. We both knew that if I was going to catch a fish at all on this continent, I was going to need some professional help. Our group included Patrick the Belizean boat captain, and two other couples. We would go several miles out to the barrier reef — the second largest in the world — where there would be more to look at than in the murky water closer to shore.

As we made our way out of the Sittee River into the Caribbean, the weather wasn't looking promising. Storm clouds still filled the sky, and rain could be seen falling into the sea in the distance. Several miles offshore, as we approached the first barrier islands, it started to rain. Patrick steered the boat to one of the islands where we disembarked and took shelter under the thatched eve of a vacant hut. Once the rain passed we boarded the boat and headed into a shallow cove to net some sardines. If I was going to break my bad luck fishing streak, we were going to need some serious sardines.

Patrick's magic sardines worked wonders. Within half an hour we had reeled in several barracudas. Later we pulled in a couple of triggerfish, which are protected, so we released them, and a couple of red snappers. As a friend of ours was quick to point out, fishing from a boat is cheating. I would tend to agree, but we have to remember that I've discovered through nearly three months of field research that it's impossible to catch a fish from the shore. This indicates that I've been fighting a war in a place where my adversaries don't even live. Through the miracle of internal combustion I was able to bring my fight to the battlefield. We won't call it cheating, we'll call it strategizing.

Oh, and the snorkeling? The name "snorkeling" sounds ludicrous. Swimming around with fake webbed feet and an oversized drinking straw mouth extension is ludicrous. But once you get over the ludicrousness of the whole affair, it's really pretty awesome. We swam around, cheating evolution, for hours checking out coral and fish. We also stumbled across a couple of giant rays, which Sheena and I followed around at what we considered to be a safe distance.

On the boat we befriended a couple of professional hair designers from Connecticut who were preparing to retire to Belize.

Raymond, an energetic fellow originally from Hong Kong, and his wife Michelene invited us back to their hotel to barbecue our red snappers. However, before we could eat, Raymond insisted on giving both Sheena and me haircuts. He also taught me how to properly layer a woman's hair, so I no longer have an excuse not to cut Sheena's hair; we've been cutting each other's hair for years, but recently she's been asking for layering, which I've been able to dodge on the grounds of ignorance.

After haircuts and a delicious red snapper barbecue, Raymond and Michelene kindly offered us their room's extra bed for the night. In the morning they treated us to breakfast before heading back to the airport. I guess the locals aren't the only generous ones. We followed their lead and moseyed our way inland, to the west, toward the Guatemalan border.

# 22

*Hopkins, Belize — March, by Sheena*

Sheena here! While I originally intended to write regularly right from the start of our trip, time seriously does fly when you're having fun. Those who know me well might have guessed that the most likely thing I'd choose to write about would be food. I love cooking, baking, experimenting with new flavors, and finding healthy, wholesome ingredients.

Food preparation has become quite the challenge on the road, to say the least. How I miss the oven and a fridge large enough to pack five children inside. Not that I would ever do that. While we have a small refrigerator and most of the amenities for home cooking inside of Nacho, we still find ourselves eating out regularly. Fortunately we find a great deal of enjoyment in tasting the local foods while traveling. Brad and I are up for trying just about anything, anywhere; road side stands, local *comedores*, markets, they're all fair game. Given my slight stomach issues, some of you may be thinking I should be a little more selective and steer clear of mysterious street food and fare served from dubious grungy kitchens having questionable sanitation standards. Good news though, I've been training my weak tummy through street food therapy, building antibodies and strength for the next round of countries we are approaching.

With every new country, we've familiarized ourselves with a new set of flavors and sensations. I often forget how different the food truly is from home. Not so much the basic ingredients *per se*, but their arrangement into meal time staples. I've become well accustomed to the deliciousness of the mashed plantain; the dirt cheap bowls of fruit topped with yogurt, a choice of cereal toppings and honey; freshly squeezed lemonade; non-refrigerated, boxed UHT milk; eggs sold in plastic bags instead of cartons; water sold in bags instead of bottles; mangoes topped with chili powder; *tortillerias* on every street corner selling freshly made tortillas; and the ever present taco stand.

The same goes for the general way of life in Central America. It is no longer a surprise to see mangoes littering yards like garbage, or truck drivers taking midday siestas in hammocks strung underneath their big rig trailers. It's no longer strange to see livestock walking down a busy city street, two dozen people in the back of a pickup truck, red *tuk tuks* zipping through traffic, baskets being balanced on top of heads, and people taking baths in the river and drying their washed clothes on river rocks and barbed wire fences. It's rare not to see a hammock outside of every home. A few weeks ago we rented a room in a well off family's home, and interestingly, a hammock was strung up between two beams in their living room instead of a couch. So many sights have become normal, and we often forget how spectacular they are.

After traveling through Mexico, roadside food stalls have become not only normal, but an expected and relied upon means for obtaining meals. Our first food stop in Belize was at a road side stand worked by cousins – two chocolate skinned young girls, shy in demeanor, but unable to conceal their bright smiles. We sat down in the shade offered by a blue tarp strung up over a patch of dry earth, providing a small exile from the hot Belizean sun. We placed our orders with the smiling girls, and proceeded to stuff ourselves with rice and beans, barbecued chicken, and coleslaw. Every lunch from here on out was a similar concoction of fare: paper plate in hand and food doused in Marie Sharp's Hot Sauce and pickled hot peppers and onions. There were options of course; potato salad instead of coleslaw, pork instead of chicken, but every meal included a tall bottle of Marie Sharp's Hot Sauce. Marie Sharp has a monopoly on hot sauce in Belize, as every single back alley restaurant and mom and pop grocery store has bottles of it at the ready. I can only compare its popularity to a bottle of Heinz ketchup on the tables of American burger joints.

Breakfast in Belize has never failed to delight. After talking with Taiowa, a native of Belize that we met at our campground in Placencia, he insisted we must try the fry jacks for breakfast. They are made by deep frying a portion of raw dough, which become hollow and plump. They're perfect for stuffing with other morning staples like beans, eggs, meat, and fruit. They remind us of Indian fry bread made by the Native Americans in Arizona. And while I didn't see the Belizeans eating their fry jacks with honey or jam, I know this would be an undeniably perfect replacement to stuffing them with protein. Besides the fry jacks, there are also Johnny cakes, a fluffy local biscuit, sometimes made with coconut.

With every heaping mass of rice and beans consumed at breakfast, lunch, and dinner, there are equal portions of seafood devoured. No surprise here as the country's coast bumps up against turquoise waters laced with coral and schools of fish. A taste of lobster is a must here, but if you come during the non-harvesting season, like we did, then you'll have to go without, as they're illegal to catch out of season. And so it goes, no lobster for us, but we did get our fair share of red snapper, shrimp, and deep fried bunches of battered conch meat.

For something really authentic, we sampled a of few of the local Garifuna dishes. When shipwrecked and escaped slaves settled along the coast of the region, they mixed with the native Caribs to form a new ethnic group called Garifuna. The town of Hopkins was one of their primary settlements, and the place where we sampled the uniquely Garifuna culinary specialties of Hudut, Bundiga, and Cassava bread. Hudut is a coconut broth fish stew accompanied by mashed plantains and served with cassava bread, a hard flat biscuit made from the cassava root. Bundiga is made of clumps of grated banana, cooked in coconut milk, and served with red snapper. Both were completely unique, and both were absolutely delicious.

And best of all, my weak tummy left Belize in a state of happiness. Our strict regimen of local foods seems to be working, and I can't wait to see what will be served up next.

# 23

*Tikal, Guatemala — March, by Brad*

Up until a couple of years ago, I spent my days as a medical products design engineer. The best days were spent in the lab testing design iterations and new materials. Most days, however, were spent parked in front of a computer designing the products, writing test plans, communicating with vendors, writing reports, or analyzing test results. On the odd day when the computer system would go down in a storm, operations would come to a screeching halt. When we arrived at the Guatemalan border that old feeling returned. The computer system had crashed and we would have to wait indefinitely.

For the next couple of hours we sat with a fellow stranded traveler, a Mennonite farmer. His family farmed rice in Belize, but export taxes imposed by Belize, combined with America's subsidies for imported Asian rice, had made it impossible for him to make a living farming rice in Belize. He was thus relocating his family to Guatemala where labor and export taxes were cheaper, which would allow them to continue farming. As rough as we may think we have it sometimes, at least we don't have to relocate our families to a third world country just to stay above water.

We finally made our way through customs as the sun went down, and then found a camp spot in the yard of a hotel a few yards from the border. By morning we were on our way to Tikal.

The following morning, we pointed Nacho down a road that remained largely unpaved, so we put the van in first gear and sat back for the hour-long haul. This exercise has become far too common these days; slowly creeping along for hours on end in first gear. Soon enough we arrived at the gates for Tikal, one of the most elaborate and extensive Mayan ruins in existence.

Since we had arrived at the peak of the afternoon heat, we figured we'd set up camp in the grassy camping area and rest until evening. When the afternoon heat passed, we headed out for a hike, having decided that we'd hit the ruins first thing in the morning before it got hot. It wouldn't be so. As we passed the guard shack we were stopped and asked for our tickets to see the ruins.

"We're just going for a hike in the jungle. We'll use our tickets to see the ruins in the morning."

"Oh no, you have to use the tickets today. They're only good for one day."

"But we will use them for only one day. We'll use them for tomorrow."

"I can sell you more tickets for tomorrow, but you will have to pay full price. These tickets will be no good."

After having been put in a bad mood by the "foreigner" price, which was over six times the "local" price, things were only getting worse. "So you'd like for us to pay the full foreigner price again, meaning that we will have paid the price of twelve local person tickets, just to see the ruins one time? Why can't you can just reissue us some tickets for tomorrow?"

The guards conferred, and then one of them approached me as if he had a good idea. "Tell you what. You can just pay him the price for two more full price tickets, and you'll be able to enter the park at 4:00 AM and spend all day looking at the ruins."

We had no choice but to spend the last two and a half hours of the day looking at the ruins. We didn't have much time, so we hurried through as much as we could before the sun went down and the park closed. The area contained a vast collection of pyramids and buildings, which used to support a community of over 100,000 inhabitants.

The following day we woke up early so we could do our hike in the jungle. We had heard that there were some hiking trails but weren't sure where to find them. As we walked along a path leading toward the ruins we saw a small trail ducking under some vines that disappeared into the jungle. It looked like a hiking trail, so we took it.

After a few minutes we came across a long concrete building in a clearing. As we scoped it out we saw two men come out of the jungle carrying machetes. They seemed to be guides for the park. One of them called out to us.

"Are you looking for the ruins? You should be careful, it's very dangerous in the jungle."

"What do you mean? Are there dangerous animals?"

"Not really, but it's very easy to get lost."

We thanked him for the advice and found another trail that disappeared into the dense vines and walked on. Heeding the guard's warning, we devised a nearly fool proof method of not getting lost in the jungle: every time we came to a junction, we made a wooden arrow showing us how to get back the way we came. As long as there weren't any malicious people or monkeys behind us, we ought to be in good shape.

Our trek took us down several trails before dropping us onto a rough dirt road. We followed the road for a while until we saw a place where two faint tire tracks could be made out heading off into the jungle in a different direction. We took these, but they petered out after about a half an hour of walking. It looked like two or three Jeeps had ever made it to where we were.

Finally, as we began to consider turning back, the outline of blocks in the undergrowth caught our eye. In some places it looked like someone had shoveled away a few inches of topsoil to uncover the outlines of some buried structures. We walked into the undergrowth, away from the tire tracks, and found more blocks forming the outlines of rooms; in all we found ten or twelve rooms. It appeared to be a residential area where there must have been many homes. We had stumbled into an unexcavated Mayan ruin.

On the way back we thought about how many ruins must be hidden in the jungle around Tikal. For a site with so many enormous temples and gathering places, there must have been extensive residential areas sprawling out beyond the excavated center. As we discussed this, Sheena froze in the path. Her eyes grew into cue balls, her lungs filled, and her breathing stopped. Her mouth formed into the ecstatic smile of a crazy person. I looked ahead in the path and saw the object of her elation: a miniature deer. It was like a normal deer, but it was the size of a whippet. When it saw Sheena's crazy eyes it turned and walked into the jungle on its pencil-thin legs.

For the next few minutes the conversation shifted to Sheena's new favorite animal.

"You know, I've always wanted to see a miniature deer," she said, matter-of-factly.

"I didn't even know they existed. How long could you have possibly wanted to see one?"

"Oh, many years," she said.

In the end, despite the negative impressions on our first day, our jungle excursion gave us an opportunity that most Tikal visitors don't get to experience. It was like going to Disneyland and finding a ride that nobody else had ever seen before. Except there weren't any pedophiles dressed up as cartoon animals lurking about. And best of all, Sheena got to fulfill her many years long dream of spotting a mini deer.

Things won't always go our way. But just because things aren't going our way, it doesn't mean that they won't turn out to be better in the end.

# 24

*Fray Bartolomé de las Casas, Guatemala — March, by Brad*

On our map, the road to Sebol looked like a highway. In reality it was a potholed, muddy dirt track that threaded itself like a needle through dramatic mountain spires jutting up through dense rainforest. We put Nacho in first gear and slowly clambered through the mud and rocks. Once in Sebol, we planned to head south to the town of Semuc Champey where we would bask in clear pools and explore a network of caves.

After two hours of slow dirt road crawling, we arrived at pavement. We put Nacho in third gear and sailed through the torrential rain into the tiny pueblo of Fray Bartolomé. Moments later, a metal-on-metal whooshing sound erupted from Nacho's left rear wheel. As we came to a stop in a mud puddle the wheel let out a groan. Our hearts sank; for the second time in a month the driver's side rear wheel bearing had failed.

We were hosed. I had used up all of my spare bearings in Mexico, so we would have to rely on locals to find new bearings for us. I looked across the street: the sign in front of a simple cinderblock building read *Hotel Fontana H*. Two buildings away there was a *mechanico* filled with broken down chicken buses and beat up trucks. It could have been worse; we could have broken down in a Mayan shantytown, or worse, in the middle of nowhere. Mari, the caretaker of the hotel, would later tell us that *Dios* had sent us to break down in front of her hotel. I made a mental note to write a harshly worded letter to this *Dios* of whom she spoke.

We started the engine and slowly crept across the street to the mechanic. He took the hub apart and verified again that indeed the rear wheel bearing was destroyed.

"Can you get parts?" I asked.

"I'm not sure, but I'll try. It could be three, four days." he said. This was not a good sign. Four days in Latin American time could be six weeks! He let us plug the van into the electrical outlet in the shop since we wouldn't get any solar energy there, and then we gathered our things and sulked over to the hotel where we fell heavily onto our dingy mattresses. My mood sunk to an all time low for the trip. Sheena entered the beginning stages of a near nervous breakdown. The stained shower curtain separating the toilet from our room hung limply in the dank air, oblivious to our mood.

We collected our wits and headed out to a run down *comedor* next to the mechanic called Restaurante Manatí for a late lunch. I ordered the standard Central American lunch staple of grilled chicken with rice and beans, while Sheena ordered a bowl of soup. We tried to find the bright side. Everything was going to be fine. We would get Nacho fixed…some day. We would be done with mechanical issues…until next month. Our hotel was cheap, so we were saving money. Nothing really seemed to elevate our mood.

We asked for the bill.

"Señor, how much do we owe?"

"It is 320 Quetzales." He said.

"320 Quetzales!?" I asked, startled. That's $42. The typical daily wage for a Guatemalan worker is between five and nine dollars. Our hotel was eleven dollars per night, and a typical lunch in a restaurant will set you back a measly two dollars. "That's a lot of money for lunch!"

"The chicken is 50 and the soup is 200. Your drinks were 70, so it's 320 total."

We hadn't inquired about the unlisted prices before ordering, and quickly realized that he was robbing us. There was nothing we could do once we exhausted our bewildered inquiries. We had to pay him. In writing this well after the fact, I wish I could report that this was an isolated incident, but it was not. In Guatemala, and in no other country we've been to thus far, merchants repeatedly tried to take advantage of us. After having more experience with dishonest Guatemalan vendors I would have certainly handled this situation differently if I were able to do it again.

We returned to our hotel exhausted, infuriated, and overwhelmed. Overland travel has its highs and its lows. This was a very low, low.

The next morning I went to the mechanic for news on our bearings. He had put in a request with his suppliers in Guatemala City and was waiting to hear back. When I arrived I saw that Nacho had been unplugged from the electrical outlet. I went to ask why when I noticed that the outlet where it had been plugged in was blackened and melted. I looked at our extension cord and saw that it too was melted, and had welded itself to Nacho's electrical hookup.

"Last night there was an electrical storm." It was the mechanic, approaching from behind a building. "The security guard called me and I came over. There was smoke coming out of the wall so I unplugged your cord."

I quickly went inside of Nacho and checked the electrical panel. The 110V breaker hadn't tripped for some inexplicable reason, meaning that the wiring inside of the van had probably been destroyed as well. I found the multimeter and checked. Sure enough, there was continuity between the positive, negative, and ground leads. Like us, our wiring was hosed. By some stroke of luck Nacho hadn't gone up in flames. I made a note-to-self to try to find a surge protector if we ever became free from this hell.

I found a screwdriver and removed the hookup from the outside of the van, allowing me to peer behind the cabinets. I could see a melted mess of wires leading behind the water tanks. I could also see that the scorching hot wires had melted through one of our drinking water lines; the resulting water leak had probably kept the van from burning down.

I decided not to go back and report this news to Sheena for fear that I'd trip her over the edge into a raging nervous breakdown. Instead I took a tuk-tuk to the gas station and bought a new extension cord and some 110V wiring. I spent the rest of the day dissecting Nacho's interior, rewiring the 110VAC electrical system, and patching our severed water line. By the end of the day it was back to normal. I returned to the hotel with all of our food so that we wouldn't have to run the refrigerator. There was still no sign of wheel bearings anywhere in the country.

As the days passed we made friends with the family that ran the hotel. It started with high fives and knuckle bumps with Debora and Jordi, the children, when we would pass them in the reception area. Soon we were having conversations with Rodolfo and Mari, the parents, while the kids watched cartoons. After a while congregating in the reception area became our daily ritual.

Mari was happy to show Sheena how to make tortillas in the hotel's makeshift outdoor kitchen, and told us why they had come to Fray. In her home town she tried to sell tortillas on the street, but was unable to sell the 30 tortillas per day required to make ends meet. The people there were too poor to buy them. She was equally outraged to find out that Restaurante Manití had charged us ten times her daily wage for lunch.

On our third night we decided to make the family a nice dinner. We walked down to the *Dispensa Familiar* and bought supplies for shrimp risotto and one of Sheena's killer salads. In Guatemala we'd been having a hard time finding ample vegetables to eat, or really much of anything besides the typical meat and beans staples, so we really splurged. For the shrimp risotto we bought broccoli, peas and Argentine wine. For the salad toppings: walnuts, strawberries, avocado, apples, broccoli, tomatoes, cheese, raisins, and almonds. On the side we would have some of the fresh tortillas that Sheena and Mari made.

While we cooked the children stood on boxes so they could watch. They periodically snatched strawberries and broccoli, stuffing them into their mouths. It was clear that they too were craving some fresh fruits and vegetables. While the risotto simmered they showed us their favorite dances. First, Jordi and Debora twisted around the room in a rudimentary version of the tango. Next, as Jordi put it, "I'm dancing with my legs!" This basically entailed holding his upper body straight while stepping around with spaghetti legs. Debora loved it as much as we did, and went wild in a tirade of squeals and laughter.

Dinner delivered much needed nourishment and reminded us of how fortunate we are to have good food available to us so ubiquitously back home. Mari and Rodolfo had never tried walnuts or broccoli before. They each had seconds and thirds, and then asked to keep some of the leftovers. The next day Rodolfo asked if we could make the salad again. For the next few days every time we heard them on the phone they spent considerable time recounting the meal. "The gringos...shrimp in the rice...Argentine wine...salad with nuts..."

The following day I returned to the mechanic to see about the progress. "They have found some bearings. They will arrive tomorrow at the gas station on a bus from Guatemala City." It seemed too good to be true. That night we celebrated over a dinner of fried chicken with rice and beans that Rodolfo and Mari cooked for us.

On the final day I walked in the shop just as the mechanic was reassembling Nacho's hub. I had ordered an extra set of bearings so that we would have a spare on hand, but there was bad news. When the new bearings arrived at the gas station, the gas station attendant had taken the initiative to help us out by pressing the bearings into the hub using his hammer. When the mechanic picked them up he found that the use of a hammer had completely destroyed the bearings. He had to remove them and use the spare set instead. In the end we were really lucky to have ordered two sets; if we hadn't we would have been stuck in Fray Bartolomé for even longer.

As the mechanic put the finishing touches on the hub, I took some time to do an oil change and a tire rotation. The mechanic asked a young boy who had been watching us to help me rotate my tires. It turned out that he actually worked there.

"How old are you," I asked.

"Thirteen," he replied.

"Do you go to school too, or do you just work?"

He looked at me as he jacked up the front of the car, his eyes giving away a hint of melancholy. "I just work."

That night we reflected on the privileges afforded to us simply by being born in the United States. We had enjoyed carefree childhoods. The worst part of each summer was the act of back to school shopping, marking the momentary end to fort building, sleepovers, and back yard baseball games. We had grown up taking family vacations to the beach and to amusement parks. Neither Rodolfo nor Mari had ever been out of the small region in Guatemala where they were born. I had gone on a school trip to Peru when I was twelve.

The next morning we said goodbye to our new friends. Mari told us that the kids would probably cry for a long time once we left. Rodolfo jokingly offered to give us one of them as a gift. At that, Mari asked us to wait and went into her room. She came back with a ceramic angel with a broken wing.

"I wanted to give you this gift so that you will never forget us."

Driving away from the *Hotel Fontana H.* filled us with relief to finally be free. But then again, we've been free all along. Sometimes we just take it for granted.

# 25

*Highway 7W, Guatemala — March, by Brad*

When we left on this trip, I knew next to nothing about Guatemala. I take that back. When we left on this trip I knew *absolutely nothing* about Guatemala. It should thus come as no surprise that we found ourselves in this predicament.

You may recall that our original plan was to drive from Tikal to Semuc Champey in one day. We ended up camping out in the schoolyard of a Mayan village in the middle of nowhere after the main highway on our map turned out to be a really rough, really long dirt road. We spent the evening surrounded by dozens of Mayan children staring at us while we sat in Nacho, staring back.

The next day, you will recall, we barely managed to get off of the terrible dirt road before our wheel bearing failed, leaving us stuck in a ramshackle town for five days. A demoralizing affair, you will recall.

By the time Nacho was ready to go, we had talked ourselves out of going to Semuc Champey, as we were told that the road to get there included 3–4 hours of hellish, rocky, Nacho-killing steep dirt roads. It sounded like a surefire way to destroy more wheel bearings, so we opted to scoot on a mere 155 miles to the mountain town of Nebaj. Only three and a half hours away, Google Maps said.

What we didn't expect was to drive from Fray Bartolomé to Coban, a distance of 80 miles on paved roads, in first and second gear. But mostly first gear. The road was never flat; it oscillated between straight up and straight down. While climbing, Nacho insisted on being in first gear. While descending, Nacho's brakes insisted on being in first gear too. After our early morning departure, we arrived in Coban, the halfway point, in time for a late lunch. We would have been faster, of course, had we not taken the time to stop for breakfast next to a river, and to give a firewood-carrying old man a ride. We're supposed to be enjoying ourselves, right? And doing charitable things for the elderly?

At Coban, the capital of the department of Alta Verapaz, we were sure our luck would change. We were turning onto a new highway, the CA14, followed shortly by Highway 7W. They were big thick red lines on our map, ensuring fast-moving smooth travels. Minutes later we realized that we were wrong again, as the road snaked into a dramatic mountainous ravine. We reminded ourselves how little we knew about Guatemala. Mountains? All of it?

When we hit the 7W it didn't take long to turn to dirt. We had traveled 95 miles by this point and had not managed to move beyond 2nd gear. When the road turned to dirt we slowly crawled over a few off-camber deep ruts studded by sharp rocks before we stopped and looked at each other.

"Are you kidding me? Is there some other way we can go?" I asked.

It didn't look promising. The next place of interest for us after Nebaj was Lago de Atitlan, which would put us nearly out of the country after a really long detour. We couldn't keep skipping sites because of the roads. We reluctantly drove on.

After a couple of hours of slow, first gear crawling, we came to a split in the road. Straight ahead the path was full of tall weeds and it seemed to head straight for a cliff. To the left the road pitched straight down at what seemed to be a 35 degree slope, at least. If we drove down, there was no way we'd get back up. The downhill road clung to the side of a steep rock outcropping before plunging off the end and around a corner at an even steeper pitch. A man had parked his bicycle and was urinating in the middle of the weed-patch road. We felt uneasy. I tapped the gas and sent Nacho sliding down the loose, dusty incline straight down the side of the mountain.

By the time we reached the second or third corner, maybe three hundred yards down the road, I pulled onto the embankment to let the brakes cool down. If I didn't keep it at a walking pace, then our tires would slip under braking. As we sat on the roadside the urinating bicycle man slowly rode past us, his rear wheel locked, skidding. Sheena got out and walked the next corner. Safety first.

We alternated between driving and letting the brakes cool for what seemed like an eternity. The road kept switching back, diving lower and lower down the side of the mountain. Suddenly, as we came around another vein of rock jutting out of the mountain, our jaws dropped. The entire face of the mountain in front of us had peeled off and slid down into the valley below. All that was left was an enormous scar where a mountain used to be. The road wound its way right through the middle of the landslide, weaving through rocks the size of buildings, clinging precariously to the side of the rubble-strewn slide path. Where the road had split before the steep downhill, we had turned onto a makeshift road since the old way had apparently been wiped off the side of the mountain.

We slowly crept along through the rubble, crossing a stream that continued to erode away the mountainside. As soon as we made it across the landslide, the road pitched straight up. We would have to climb all the way back up to where we started, but on the other side of the slide.

Due to the steepness of the road, there were times that we would bog down in first gear and it didn't seem like we'd make it. Nacho is big boned and doesn't like hefting his 5,800 pound body up really steep stuff. In these cases, just as it seemed we'd stall, I would push in the clutch, rev the engine, and release. It's a great way to destroy a clutch, but given the alternative, it seemed right. It was that or face the wrath of a raging wife. *What do you mean we're STUCK? And in DANGER?!* In the end, we made it to the top, albeit just barely.

A couple of hours later, as we continued to slog through landslide after landslide (although much smaller than the first), Sheena read the following in our Lonely Planet:

*Renowned for its incredible views, highway 7W was until recently the most direct route from Huehuetenango to Coban. But in late 2008, disaster struck when a mountain collapsed atop the road, leaving its east end in shambles.*

*There's been no official attempt at rebuilding, but locals have carved out a hastily constructed detour that's generally considered unsafe. Buses from Uspantan to Coban regularly plow through the debris anyway, despite the dangers. By all accounts, it's a hair-raising journey and things worsen when it rains and drivers refuse to risk the gap, making passengers hike through the mud for 2km to continue the journey.*

*The saner alternative is backtracking via Guatemala City, a loss of about 4 hours, but an infinite gain in peace of mind.*

Well crap.

After a couple more hours we finally reached pavement again. For the first time, after eight hours of driving, I put Nacho in third gear. A few seconds later we came across another landslide covering the pavement, so we put it back in first and felt our way through it. First, second, third, landslide, repeat.

As we approached the high mountain town of Nebaj, night had closed in on us. We wound our way up into the mountains in first gear, 15 miles per hour, ever higher into the night sky. As we traversed one switchback after another, we looked out the window at the twinkling lights overhead. In the deep black of the night we couldn't tell if we were looking at stars, or at the lights from homes clinging to the mountainsides above us.

By nine o'clock we pulled into the small Mayan town of Nebaj; headquarters of the rebel army during the country's recent civil war, chosen for its natural defenses against enemy attack. The trip of 155 miles took us 11 hours. An average speed of 14mph. Screw you, Google Maps.

In Nebaj we admired the traditional dress of the local Mayans, shopped in the local market, and hiked through a mountain pass to the even smaller and more remote town of Acul. In the mountains we took pity on the hordes of children emerging from the dense forest with loads of firewood on their backs. We awoke each morning to the smell of pine burning in wood stoves and admired the blue skies and vast mountainscapes.

On the morning of our third day we pointed Nacho skyward, climbing the mountain rim surrounding the town. Once at the rim we pointed downward, into the switchbacks. From Nebaj to Lago de Atitlan we continued our slow progress across Guatemala, in first and second gear, at somewhere around 15 miles per hour.

# 26

*Antigua, Guatemala — March, by Brad*

"Who's that old creeper hanging out with all of those high school girls?" Those who passed the open window of the chocolate making school in Antigua were all certainly wondering the same thing. Sure, Sheena and the girls' chaperone were both my age, but they blended into the sea of adolescent femininity like snakes in grass, leaving me the odd man out. The 28 year old creeper.

The class was riveting, and our high school classmates were a vivacious bunch. They hailed from Georgia (the state), and were in Guatemala for some kind of weeklong church trip to a Mayan village. With the help of our instructor, Pablo, we roasted cocoa beans and turned them into all sorts of goodness. After having shelled, and pulverized the beans in a mortar, we made Mayan hot chocolate. As I sipped on my tiny ramekin of hot cocoa I spied something that nearly caused the spicy concoction to squirt out of my nose: one of the high school girls tilted her head in such a way that she looked almost exactly like our friend Shawn. It was uncanny! *Who's that old creeper staring at that high school girl? Creeeepyyyyyy!*

We arrived in Antigua, in the southwestern corner of Guatemala, after having crawled across the country over the course of two weeks at a mere 15 miles per hour, give or take, due to heinous roads. At long last, we had reached the final major outpost before the Salvadorian border. While Antigua was a well cared for colonial town, we had unexpectedly found the country to be, by and large, economically ravaged. I suppose it's only natural given their turbulent recent history.

In 1954, the CIA sponsored a military coup to overthrow the government of Guatemala. It's well documented, not conspiracy theory. The goal was to create an authoritarian government in place of Guatemala's functioning democracy for the sole purpose of protecting US corporate interests (primarily a banana company that supplied fruit to the USA). Between 1954 and 1990, about 300,000 civilians were murdered and the country's economic development remained at a standstill. And that's what I mean by *turbulent recent history*.

When we arrived in Antigua we made our way to the office of the tourist police, the *Asistur*, where we had heard we could camp for free. Lo and behold, just outside of downtown we found a walled compound filled with abandoned cars, bombed out buildings, and a small office containing the tourist police. It had a nice view to the southwest of a live volcano, only a couple of miles away, which erupted every day. We drove in and found a place between the Australian couple we'd met in Tikal, and the French family we'd camped next to in Lago de Atitlan.

Running into the same group of overlanders has become a regular and welcome occurrence. At any one time there are a number of groups making the trip down the Pan-American Highway on similar schedules. The result is that every week or so we come across someone we know. There's Thomas, the Swedish guy we met Palenque, Mexico, who takes public transit, and whose good looks have made him irresistible to even the most macho of male Guatemalan hotel employees. There's the French family driving in an RV and homeschooling their two children along the way. The Australians Chris and Wendy, as well as the Americans James and Lauren, are both driving Toyota 4Runners and making us jealous with the speed at which they can drive over *topes*. Toughest of all are Barbara and Achim, the German couple, riding their bikes from America to Argentina. They're on flat pedals with hiking shoes, always seem to be in a good mood, and are keeping pace with us in our van.

As we settled into our place at *Asistur*, chewing the fat with the French and the Aussies, who should come strolling into our camp but

Barbara and Achim. Wendy and Chris, having planned to leave that day, decided to stick around for another day just for the hell of it. We had catching up to do. We would spend the next four days hanging out with Barbara and Achim. Friends, just like back home, except that we're all homeless and unemployed.

It just so happened that we had arrived in Antigua just in time for the pre–Semana Santa religious processions. In this display, families stake their claim on a patch of the procession route; a daylong circuit winding through the streets of Antigua. The families spend immense amounts of time creating beautiful "carpets" In the street. The carpets are actually artistic scenes made of colored sawdust, flowers, vegetables, and other objects, and are created by the devotees on the day of the parade. They're an obsessive compulsive person's dream: sawdust grains ordered in such a way, and on such a grand scale, that it blows the very minds of any and every observer.

As the procession passes through the streets, the carpets are destroyed by the trampling of men and women wearing pointed caps, brandishing instruments, and carrying heavy wooden floats adorned with fake Jesus puppets spewing pump-driven fake blood. One million people packed into Antigua's streets like sardines to watch the carnage. It was like a religious Disneyland.

Sitting at the German microbrewery in Antigua with our Bavarian friends, we reflected on Guatemala. It was tough. I do realize that we plan to drive our van through China, India, and the Middle East, and that those will undoubtedly be tougher. But we're just getting started, and Guatemala was tough for us. We're still in the shake down period, figuring out what works and what doesn't, but this country was a test. We ordered new car parts and had them sent to Costa Rica. We compiled lists of lessons learned. We hit many lows and not very many highs. But we made it through. And after all of that, we took our pent up frustration out on a bunch of cocoa beans, yielding a mediocre ramekin of sugary chocolate milk, and the everlasting impression burned upon the minds of those who passed by us, of the Antigua Creeper and his cohort of Georgian high school girls.

# 27

*Antigua, Guatemala — March, by Sheena*

Walking through the crowded weekend market in Nebaj, Guatemala, I continuously glanced over my shoulder, searching for my honey. These markets aren't made for tall people. The law of survival of the fittest has alienated any shopper of non-Mayan descent. Watching Brad attempt to maneuver through the crowd was painful, as his height of 6'3" made it necessary for him to walk with a bend at the waist and in a low crouch. Even then, his head skimmed the tarps strung above the stalls and dirt walkways. A steady stream of women shuffled around him, plunging him into a human whirlpool that he couldn't escape. Every other shopper walked effortlessly, head held high, baskets atop, and holding live chickens under their arms.

The Nebaj market was mesmerizing, not only for its people but for its food selection. Large plastic rice bags sat plump on the ground and on the tables, sides rolled down to reveal the dried goods inside. Grains, dried chilies, spices, flour, beans, unroasted coffee, and cacao beans. Every stand had a different selection of fruits and vegetables piled high; heirloom tomatoes, juicy beets, yucca, carrots.

I hand selected my tomatoes and piled them into a bowl, and then gave the bowl to the Mayan woman sitting on the ground next to s scale. She methodically placed the bowl on one end of a balance scale. Holding the scale up high from the middle, the small-framed lady eyed it with concentration, throwing a few more tomatoes in until level with the one kilogram weight (a bag of rice) on the other end. On the way out, we passed a group of women working a tortilla stand. I watched as they broke off balls of dough, smashed them between their palms, pinched the edges to perfection and threw them on the skillet. They looked a little different than a standard corn tortilla.

"*Hola, qué es esto?*"

One of the women looked at me strangely, unable to understand why I couldn't identify what she was making and said "*Tortillas dulces de platano.*"

Ah, sweet tortillas made of plantain. That was a new one. We bought a dozen and off we went. Brad breathed a sigh of relief as he stretched out his back.

Much of the Guatemalan food came as no surprise, with corn *masa* continuing to be the staple, served with meat, rice and beans. We did, however, run across some delightfully new dishes.

In Antigua, we often visited the local market for lunch. While there were plenty of sidewalk restaurants and cafes targeting the tourist crowds, we found the local market to be more our style. As we walked down a row of food stands, people leapt out from every corner, blocking the walkway for as long as we would permit them, all the while shouting out the meals of the day. One young lady spoke so rapidly that I quickly became hypnotized, my eyes locked on her bulging neck vein, ready to rupture from the physical endurance of nonstop announcing. Her sales pitch didn't lure us in so much as the visible popularity of the restaurant. Two long benches stretched parallel to each other were packed with local families and workers. As a man in Mexico once told us, if you don't know which food stands are the best, just look for the one with the most locals and go there; you are guaranteed good food and affordability. Here we had the *pollo en pipian*, chicken in a tomato-pumpkin seed sauce, a local Antiguan dish for $1.50.

In the same market on a different afternoon we tried *chiles rellenos*. These were much different than the spicy Mexican *chiles rellenos* we've come to know and love, which are usually stuffed only with cheese. Guatemalan *chiles rellenos* were on the lighter side, having no cheese but rather stuffed full of finely minced meat, carrots, green beans, and spices. They were then covered in egg batter, fried, and topped with tomato sauce.

During the craziness of *Semana Santa*, we came across a church with hundreds of people pouring through the arched entrance. Inside we found a sheltered area containing dozens of food vendors. I presumed, based upon the organized groups of purple robed men, that it was one of the staging areas for the religious processions. This is where I discovered *platanos con mole*, or plantains served with a sweet and spicy cacao sauce. Heaven!

The last gastronomical wonders of Guatemala were the *licuados*, a frothy blend of fruit, ice, and water or milk. While they may sound just like smoothies, they decidedly are not. *Licuados* are lighter and thinner in consistency, having only enough ice to make them cold and slightly thick. When blended they produce a frothy top with flavorful liquid at the bottom. The perfect way to cool off after emerging from a hot, crowded weekend market in Guatemala.

# 28

*Nicaragua — April, by Brad*

Keeping a level head: I consider it a strength of mine, with a few notable exceptions. There was the time I flipped out on our neighbors in college for staging a boxing match against our front door in the middle of the night. By the time I realized what was going on, I was standing in the chilly air in the middle of the fight in my underwear, screaming like a banshee. And there was the time I unleashed my verbal wrath on Tom Danielson, now a top ten Tour de France finisher, after he acted like a sally girl crybaby during one of our mountain bike races. But in general, I'm an even-tempered guy. And it was with this even temper that I envisioned myself dealing with police on this trip. *Just be cool*, I tell myself when I practice in front of the mirror.

For nearly three months; through Mexico, Belize, Guatemala, and El Salvador — some seven thousand miles in total — we had not been pulled over by the police. As we bumped along the potholed highway in southern Honduras, our luck finally changed. The police had set up cones in the roadways and were waving people over to the shoulder, seemingly at random. Somehow we'd made it to within a few miles of the Nicaraguan border without being stopped, and then sure enough: the point, followed by the wave.

"Dammit! Just be cool, okay?" I said, pulling Nacho onto the dirt shoulder. Sheena nodded, wide-eyed.

"Okay, I'll be cool!" I wasn't talking to her, but I kept this detail to myself. We were expecting the full body cavity search, or worse.

*No bribes. No bribes. Just be cool. It's just a full body cavity search. Be cool…*

The officer slowly strode over to our window, chest puffed out. He looked over my head before snapping his face downward, peering at me over his aviator sunglasses. Classic.

"Where you coming from? Where you going?" He seemed like a man without emotions. The worst kind of man.

"From El Salvador to Nicaragua," I said in the coolest way I knew how. He looked up the road, then down the road, and then over my shoulder at the interior of Nacho before looking at me again. His movements were slow, as if he were conceiving an evil plan.

"So," he said, "have you tried the white melons?"

"Uh, what?"

"The white melons. Have you tried them?" He lifted up his left hand, in which he was carrying a large white melon. "They're the richest melons in Honduras." He peered over his aviators, expectantly.

"Um, no sir," I said, still being totally cool. *What the hell?*

He reached his hand through my window and handed me the melon. "Try it. These white melons are so rich." Then he stepped backwards, held up two fingers in front of his face, and flicked them to the side. Move along.

Showed him. Oh, and he was right. The melon was rich. Maybe even the richest in all of Honduras.

A couple of days passed without much in the way of police activity, although Nicaragua turned out to have the same type of police stops: cones in the road, officers pulling people over at their leisure. One day we made the decision to scoot from the north end of the country to the south end so that we could find a secluded beach spot to wait out the weekend craziness of Semana Santa. We were asking for trouble.

At the intersection of two main thoroughfares somewhere in the Nicaraguan countryside, a police officer waited. I was nervous. I looked both ways and then pulled out, making a perfectly executed left turn, if I do say so myself. Seeing a livestock truck fast approaching from behind, I signaled and changed lanes. Textbook. At this, the police officer shook his head in pity and waved me over. I had apparently done something very wrong.

"You made an illegal turn" he said, slightly invading my personal space bubble as he stood next to my window. He was messing with me. I felt my heart rate increase. I had a flashback of Tom Danielson and I wanted to punch him in the face. This was unsportsmanlike.

I pointed out my window at the road I'd just come from. "I just turned from over there, into the left lane. Then I signaled and changed lanes. That's not an illegal turn."

He shook his head wildly, looking down, his eyes closed. Clearly I knew nothing about driving. "You made an ILLEGAL turn! Big ticket. BIG ticket!" he said, flailing his imaginary pen against an imaginary paper in his hand like he was going to write me a ticket.

"Not a big ticket," I said, "No ticket. I know the laws sir, and I know how to drive. I didn't break the law, so I don't get a ticket." I was struggling to keep my composure.

He pointed his finger at the sky. "Only God is perfect" he said, shaking his head at me like I was some kind of heathen.

"I'm not claiming to be perfect, but I am claiming to know the law." I said.

He stood at my window in silence staring at me. I stared back at him. Maybe he was waiting for the *How can we make this go away* schpiel, but obviously he was not privy to my personal promise not to pay bribes. After a minute he took a small step back.

"Can we go?" I asked. He said nothing. I eased my foot onto the gas, watching for a reaction. There wasn't one, so I pulled away.

We made our way down the road in silence. "I think he wanted a bribe," I said. "Yeah, I think you're right," Sheena responded. I told her what he had said about God and she giggled. He was really trying.

Our freedom only lasted about an hour before we were summoned to the roadside again. This time we'd done nothing out of the ordinary, so we weren't too concerned. We were already acting really cool at the time, so we just kept doing it as Nacho came to a stop.

"Coming from? Going to?" The officer asked.

"From Playa Poneloya to Playa Majagual" I said.

"All right. May I see your license, registration, and insurance?" At this my heart skipped a beat. Car insurance isn't required in most countries, and we usually buy it at the border where it is required. If you had car insurance down here you'd spend years trying to collect on it in the event of an accident, so we don't bother unless mandated. We didn't have it for Nicaragua, as we didn't think it was required (hindsight note: it is).

I got out my license and registration and handed it to him. "Here you go." I hadn't formulated a plan yet, and hoped he'd forget about the insurance.

"Insurance. Can I see your insurance? You do maintain insurance, right?" He said. I needed more time to think.

"Que significa 'seguro'?" I asked, pretending not to know what the word for "insurance" meant. My mind raced. I recalled that in Belize, the fine for driving without insurance was $3,000.

"If you get into an accident, insurance pays for the damage. Do you have insurance?"

"Ohhhhh! Of course!" I said. I slowly unlocked the security box under my seat where we keep our important paperwork. I figured I'd rifle through some papers and then pretend I couldn't find it. At least it would give me time to think.

As I leafed through the folder, I saw it: my full coverage insurance, expiring in 2014. I had completely forgotten about it! The only trouble: it wasn't real. I'd felt foolish and a little dirty while creating it in Photoshop several months before our trip. The idea had come from the Bumfuzzle blog during their around the world sailing trip. From their website:

*We, like at least half the cruisers out here, consider ourselves to be self-insured. However, a promise that we'll pay for any damage that we do doesn't seem to cut it here. Fortunately we foresaw that this was going to be a problem and we created our very own self-insurance company. We pay a deductible of $0 per month to ourselves in exchange for coverage equal to the amount of our bank balance. We even issued ourselves some insurance paperwork that looks pretty official and passed some very close scrutinizing by the Greek authorities.*

*Should I use it?* I wondered. Before my more sensible side had a chance to pipe up, I was handing our fake insurance to the officer. Confidently, of course, and in a totally cool way. He seemed confused and stared at the paper for a long time. My heart pumped and I felt like the veins in my neck would explode. *You're going to jail, punk!* I thought to myself. *This is serious. Don't drop the soap!*

Sheena's eyes were burning a hole in the side of my head, I could feel it. Before either of us lost consciousness though, the officer handed my paperwork back.

"Have a nice day," he said, and we were off. I had a little explaining to do, as Sheena was not privy to my criminal preparations prior to this. "You're welcome." was my only defense. She pretended that I was a complete moron, but I could see a smile through her condescending frown.

The final shakedown, the big test, came with our next and final traffic stop, not thirty minutes later. It was getting old, and I was getting cocky. The officer pointed to us, then pointed to the side of the road.

"License, registration, insurance please."

"Here you go," I said, handing him our mix of legitimate and illegitimate paperwork. He matched my license up to the registration and looked satisfied. He took one look at our insurance and held it up for me to see. He paused. I nearly crapped my pants, but then caught myself.

"This isn't valid in Nicaragua."

I knew he was right, but I had to keep the ball rolling. My mind flashed back to the USAA insurance I used to have back home.

"Actually this insurance *is* good in Nicaragua. It's the official insurance company of the US Military. It's good everywhere in the world. You know, if you're in the military you never know where you'll end up." It was a Hail Mary. I had dragged the US Military into my lie. If there is a hell, I would certainly end up there.

He called another officer over. "Hey, does this insurance work here? This guy says it does."

"Nope, it's no good." The other officer said. Just then, a car came racing through the checkpoint and the second officer ran to stop it. Our officer seemed unsure what to do, and tried to get the attention of his colleague. After a few attempts he gave up. He handed me the papers and looked at me.

"Am I free to go?" I asked.

He shrugged his shoulders, so I drove away.

"Gracias!" Sheena squealed from the passenger seat. Way to play it cool, Sheena. Way to play it cool.

# 29

*Playa Coco, Costa Rica — April, by Brad*

Several years ago my dad opened a Mexican restaurant. The main goal for any enterprise is to make money, and so it might seem strange that there was one item on our menu on which we consciously lost money. Every time someone ordered guacamole, we lost $1.00. Why? Because our guacamole was like crack and it drove business through the doors, but it would have been too expensive if we actually charged people what it cost to make it. We bought fresh ingredients from the farmer's market in Flagstaff and made it by hand. It was with this proud guacamole heritage that Sheena and I prepared for the impromptu Guac-Off at Sole and Diego's house in Playa Coco, Costa Rica.

As with most of the positive aspects of our life these days, we fell into this situation by way of not having a plan. We had arrived on the Nicoya Peninsula that morning, and decided to head to Playa Tamarindo. It wasn't because of anything specific we'd heard about Tamarindo, it was merely the only place on the peninsula we'd ever heard of.

As we approached Tamarindo, we passed a break in the trees where we could see a beach. People basked in the sun on the white sand and surfers were lined up in the water. It had all of the ingredients of a good day, so we rolled Nacho to the roadside and pulled out the surfboards.

It might be of interest to know that neither Sheena nor I really knows how to surf. We've been attempting, with varying degrees of success, to catch waves ever since we put down tracks in Baja California.

Nevertheless, I sat out there on the longboard while Sheena paddled around on the stand up paddleboard (SUP), and we took turns getting pulverized by waves. In between watery punishments, we noticed a guy and a girl successfully surfing on their SUPs. After we'd had enough, Sheena decided to ask them for advice.

It turned out that the SUPing couple were Diego and Sole, owners of a paddleboard tour company in Playa Coco, about forty five minutes up the peninsula. With them were a couple of American friends who had recently moved to town.

"We're having a guac-off tonight," they said. "You guys should come. You can sleep in our guest room."

And with that we abandoned the idea of Tamarindo and headed back the way we'd come. There are rules to this game, and rule number six says if you get invited to a guacamole making party, you drop whatever you're doing and go. Especially when you have guacamole heritage in the family. The thought of a real bed was also appealing.

And so it was that forty five minutes later we were stepping through the doors of Sole and Diego's extra nice, super comfortable condo in Playa Coco. It was the first time in three months that we'd set foot inside of a modern home; uniform walls, granite countertops, plush couches, decorations, curtains, and nice beds, not to mention a nice patio overlooking the town.

We weren't there long before we were whisked out the door by the Americans Heather and Jeff, and their Costa Rican friend Sandy. There was to be a guac-off, so we had to loosen up. We drove Diego's truck through the mountains and down a 4×4 track to a hidden beach in a cove. Diego had told us that a red tide had come a few days before, meaning that a bacteria bloom had occurred, but that it should have been gone by now.

I brought along my speargun and snorkeling gear, as I was told that this cove had crystal clear water, and was basically an underwater seafood buffet. In the Pacific Ocean of all places, where my research has shown a distinct lack of fish. Jackpot. As I entered the water, however, something didn't seem right. Funky smell. The water was rather opaque. "It'll get better," I thought. I spent a few minutes fumbling with my flippers and snorkel, then loaded my speargun and put my face into the water. I'm color-retarded, so it took me this long to realize that the water was dark red. I swam away from the shore, thinking that perhaps deeper water would mean more currents and clarity.

After a few minutes I had a boogie man moment. I decided to see how bad the visibility really was, so I placed my hand in front of my face. I couldn't see it. Being that I was born and raised in a forest, and had spent considerable time in deserts (all far from the ocean), this instantly sent my mind into all kinds of worst case scenarios. Red tide! Still here! Can't see anything! Could be rocks! Could be sharks! I'm a sitting duck! I've wet my pants! Am I drowning? I might be drowning!

I put my little blue flippers in high gear and quickly brought myself ashore. Once I was safely out of shark territory I slowed down and adopted more of a David Hasselhof saunter towards the others. *Did you see me almost bag that roosterfish?*

Once back at Sole and Diego's house, it was game time. There were three guacamole entrants; Sandy (using her husband's secret recipe), Heather and Jeff, and Sheena and me. Diego and Sole made homemade garlic aioli, salsa, grilled chicken, carne asada, and taco fixings. While we made guacamole, Sole kept the margaritas flowing. She may have been trying to throw us off our game, but Sheena and I took our margaritas in stride and perfectly executed our guac.

In the end, each of us put our own spin on the traditional preparation. Heather and Jeff infused theirs with finely chopped bacon and ample bacon grease. Sandy added a dash of sugar, extra lime, and some cream cheese. Sheena and I blackened some garlic cloves, turned them into a paste in a mortar, and then stirred them into the guacamole. The stage was set. Judge Diego positioned himself in front of the bowls.

We looked on eagerly as he cycled through the bowls. Chip…dip…taste…(shifty eyes)…chew…(eyebrows tilt)…nod of the head...swallow. So much was riding on the verdict. *If we lose*, I thought, *I will never be able to look my dad in the eyes again. Black sheep.*

Finally he finished his rounds and we waited in anticipation. He grabbed a bowl and held it up. "This one is the winner!"

It was our bowl! It had been a while since we'd won at anything, so this was thrilling. Oh, the sweet taste of victory! I strutted around with my chest puffed out while Sheena squealed with excitement.

In the end we had a really nice dinner with our new friends. We rested in a clean and comfortable bed, ate great food, and laughed our brains out, thanks entirely to the kindness of strangers.

We didn't follow a recipe for our guac, but if you want to make it on your own, here's approximately what we did:

## Nacho's Guac-Off Championship Winning Guacamole

Cut up the following and put in a bowl:

- One large tomato
- One small white onion
- A handful of fresh cilantro
- Five avocadoes (cut them in half and spoon the insides into the bowl, save the pits for later)
- A teaspoon of salt, and one of pepper
- The juice from one lime

Now do this:

- Throw five or six garlic cloves in a skillet with a splash of oil and fry them until the skin turns black
- Mash up the garlic in a mortar or in a bowl with a spoon. Now add it to the guac bowl.
- Stir up all of the ingredients with a fork, mashing the avocadoes as you mix. Once everything is a nice chunky

consistency, stop mixing. Don't get it too creamy, you want it chunky.

- Throw the avocado pits back into the bowl and stir them in.

Taste with a spoon, add some salt, taste, add salt, etc. until it blows your mind.

# 30

*Nicoya Peninsula, Costa Rica — April, by Sheena*

Every year, the ritual goes, for our birthday, the birthday boy or girl requests whatever cake their heart desires. The other must then make the requested cake from scratch. No pre-mixes or jars of frosting are permitted. No problem. I love making cakes for Brad. There are numerous reasons why, but who am I kidding, the main reason is because I have a strong addiction to eating cake batter. No, raw eggs don't deter me. I will take my chances with salmonella any day. A deep contention exists in our relationship around this one idea.

It all stems from differences in the way Brad and I were raised. When I was a young girl, after helping my mom make the batter for cookies or banana bread, she always made sure to leave an excessive amount of batter in the bowl, just for me. I was never all that interested in the finished goods. Sometimes we'd even save more and stick it in the fridge. On the contrary, Brad's mom always scraped out every last smudge, and only then was the bowl handed over to the three brothers, who proceeded to lick it clean like baby kittens. Brad insists this is how it should be, forcing the scavenger to cherish every savory drop instead of gluttonously indulging in spoonful after spoonful of sugary batter. Which tradition will live on when we have kids in the future? Well, let's just say that Brad is the barbeque guy in our relationship and I, the goddess of the oven. Just try and stop me from bringing that kind of joy to our future offspring.

For my birthday one year I requested from Brad a Mexican *tres leches* cake. What I got was a 8"x12" rectangular mass of sponge that, instead of absorbing the "three milks," floated and bobbed about in a pool of liquid. We tried to save it, and in the end pierced so many forks holes in the top that it ended up looking like a piece of yellowish foam caught in a shoot-out. We drained the liquid and ate what remained, and I vowed to one day take the reins and make it myself. This day did come, and what should have been a cake that leaked a creamy concoction from every pore, once again floated instead of absorbed. It was starting to seem as though homemade *tres leches* was unattainable by *gringos*.

This year the idea of baking cakes was scrapped. No oven, no cake. Instead, back in February, Brad bought me a *tres leches* cake at a bakery in San Cristóbal de las Casas. It was a proper *tres leches* cake, but while trying to hide it from me over the course of a winding mountain road, our shoe bin fell on top of the flimsy cardboard box that contained it, smashing it. The universe didn't want me to have *tres leches* on my birthday.

A few days before Brad's birthday, we were wandering the grocery aisles in Playa Coco, Costa Rica. It was like no other store we had seen in four months of driving in Latin America. The selection was outrageous and we left with a massive quantity of food, including all of the ingredients to make tiramisu for the birthday boy.

From the store, we headed South down the Nicoya peninsula to the neighboring beaches of Playa Avellanas and Playa Negra. After snaking through a field of mangroves and emerging at the intersection of the ocean and a river mouth, Brad hopped on the surf board. Soon the waves proved too much, and as a present to himself he fell off the front of a wave and landed on a sandbar on top of his surfboard fin before being picked up and pummeled by the wave. When he finally pulled himself to shore, it became clear that he'd taken a surfboard fin to the shoulder, producing a long shallow cut across the front of his chest. It sucks getting older, but that's what birthday cakes are for.

# 31

*Atenas, Costa Rica — April, by Brad*

By 10:00 on Friday morning, I had given Sheena up for missing. I had never lost my wife in a foreign land before, so I wasn't quite sure what to do. Do I call the hospital? Issue an Amber alert? Do I press the S.O.S. button on our GPS Tracker? The last option was a sure fail, as the tracker stopped working three weeks into our trip and hasn't started working again, even after receiving a new unit from the company. How the hell did this even happen anyway?

We had arrived in Atenas, Costa Rica a week earlier, and were given the keys to our friends' vacation home. The house sits high on a mountainside outside of town, up an impossibly steep dirt road, in the middle of a small coffee plantation. We had arrived after four months of solid overland travel and were frankly ready for a recharge. A vacation from the vacation, if you will. For the first several days of our stay we lazily slept in, lounged about in our pajamas, went for swims in the pool, prepared extravagant barbecued meals, and ate breakfast high on our second story breakfast nook overlooking the San Jose valley and its surrounding volcanoes. In short, we acted in the same way that rich actors must behave during long periods of no work. I came to see myself as a young Clint Eastwood. I started wearing my sunglasses indoors at night, just like rich and famous people do.

By the time the first week of our stay came to an end we were ready to change out of our pajamas and host our first guests, our fellow Pan-American traveling friends James and Lauren.

James and Lauren just happened to be passing through Atenas, and would be picking up Lauren's mom and sister from the San Jose

133

airport the following morning. A worry-prone mother, fearful for her vagabonding daughter's wellbeing had joined the picture, so the stage was set for some catastrophe to happen. The only thing missing was a catalyst; some terrible idea that would set Murphy's Law in motion.

"Let's go for a hike!," Sheena exclaimed to Lauren.

"Oooh yeah, we can go early so I can be back in time to pick up my mom from the airport!," Lauren said.

The shit had been thrown. All we could do was sit back and helplessly wait for it to hit the fan.

Lauren's mom would be in at 11:15 AM, so they decided to leave on their hike at 7:00. Two independent sets of neighbors had vouched that the loop would take an hour and a half, and that there was no possibility of getting lost.

"There's no way they could have gotten lost!" Darlyce said in self defense, after the girls had become hopelessly lost.

Initially James and I were comfortable with the idea of a morning lady hike. This would give us a chance to sit around and do manly stuff without female distraction. Crimp wires with greasy wire crimpers, organize heavy things, open bags of tortilla chips without any notable struggle, sit backwards in chairs. Bro time.

The first inkling that something might have gone terribly wrong came when the ladies failed to materialize by 8:16. Sheena and Lauren are both fitness aficionadas. They do things like running and P90X workout videos. But they don't do the workout videos in air conditioned living rooms like those sissy ladies back home, they do them in the jungle after they spent the night sleeping in their car. They're tougher than nails and they don't do hour-and-a-half hikes in an hour and a half. They do them in an hour and fifteen minutes. By 8:16 they were assumed to be missing in action.

James and I took silent note of this fact, but continued opening bags of chips and organizing heavy things as though nothing were amiss. Only namby pambies sit around worrying about where their ladies are.

9:30 came and went, and it was clear that something had gone terribly wrong. Could have been anything; kidnapping, hit and run, drive by shooting, starvation.

"Come on ladies," James said nonchalantly as he loaded their things into their 4Runner. The clock was ticking, and their predetermined airport departure time was only 30 minutes away. I tried to busy myself by rearranging liquor bottles and eating really spicy salsa without wincing. Every once in a while I would walk outside and stand on the property wall overlooking the road. Not because I was worried or anything, but because standing atop a high rock wall made manliness exude from my every pore. This was Bro Time, after all.

"If they don't show up by 10:00, we're going for a drive," James said. This was good. We would spring into action and swoop in to save our ladies from whatever ailed them. We would drive this hour and a half loop and see why the heck they'd been gone for over three hours.

In the 4Runner we silently drove the circuit in reverse, climbing steep mountain roads in four wheel drive, keeping a keen eye out for distressed women sulking about.

"So…what should I tell Lauren's mom if I we don't find them and I have to go to the airport by myself?," James asked.

"Just tell her…uh…" I can usually B.S. my way through just about anything, but this time I came up empty handed. We continued bouncing along in tense silence. By 10:30 we'd seen no sign of our fitness queens, so James dropped me back at the house and high tailed it to the airport. He would have to tell Lauren's mom that her daughter was a missing person. Like that *Locked Up Abroad* show on TV, only worse because we didn't even know if they were locked up at all. Only one thing was certain: they were abroad.

After thinking about what I should do – Amber Alert, S.O.S. button, et cetera – I decided to drop by the neighbor's house. Darlyce could surely shed some light on the seemingly hopeless situation.

"There's no way they could have gotten lost!" She said. She hadn't shed the light on the situation that I had imagined she might have. We went inside and her husband Alex made some calls to see if anyone knew where they might have ended up. In the end, we hatched a plan whereby I would scour the mountains with the gardener as a passenger in his gardening truck. In time, I was told, we might find them. Somehow.

By now I was coming to terms with the real possibility of my untimely death by strangulation that would ensue upon my telling Sheena's father that his daughter, too, was a missing person.

As Diego the gardener and I walked to his truck, we noticed a small red car in front of our house. We watched as Sheena and Lauren emerged from the back seat. No blindfolds, just the grimace of shame that can only be the result of a near international missing persons fiasco. The little red car swung out of the driveway and into the road. It was a taxi. Our fitness queens came home in a taxi.

"Oopsies!" Sheena said, totally downplaying the seriousness of the situation. "We got SO lost!"

"Yeah, SO lost!," Lauren added. "We took a wrong turn, but we were talking so we didn't realize it for a VERY long time."

"Yeah, and then we turned around and started going back, but then we didn't know where we were, and then we took another wrong turn," Sheena said. "After a while we knew we'd be late, so we started running downhill as fast as we could. And it was SOOO steep! But after like 10 minutes we realized that we were running the wrong way."

"Yeah, we started running through a bunch of leaves, and we didn't remember any leaves, so we knew we were VERY lost," Lauren said. Things were worse than I had imagined.

"Finally we decided to ask for help, so we looked for a house with a car. We thought maybe they would bring us home. But when we told them we needed a ride home, we couldn't remember where we lived. We didn't even know the name of the town!" Sheena seemed to think that this was all very funny.

"So a taxi came and got us and we told him we lived in 'San something', so he started driving us around. Finally Sheena started to recognize stuff and she was like, 'oh, oh, I REMEMBER this!' And that's how we got back here!"

James called me from a payphone as the plane was touching down and I was able to report the good news. When Lauren's mom and sister met him, they asked where Lauren was. "She's not here, but she's okay" was his response. The perfect words to keep a mother from worrying. Disaster averted.

# 32

*Dominical, Costa Rica — May, by Brad*

Lying on my back under Nacho on the side of the road, my hair becoming matted in oily mud, it occurred to me: this is probably the first time in five months that an office desk didn't seem like a bad place to be. The events over the last sixty five miles leading up to this point were almost unbelievable. Like listening for hours on end tf the bone-chilling sound of children's laughter, this too was a test of endurance.

In Costa Rica, our planned two week stop in Atenas had turned into a month. We had dropped Nacho at a shop for a week of TLC, but after a week they hadn't yet started to work. After two weeks, the engine and transmission were on the ground, but no real progress had been made. Meanwhile, Sheena and I were going stir crazy. The list of jobs I gave to the mechanic at the beginning was a half page long, including the replacement of several oil seals, new brake rotors, a clutch inspection and slave cylinder rebuild, and a full-fledged investigation into why our rear wheel bearings kept failing. At this rate, we would be back on the road in a year. Maybe two.

Week three in the shop saw me spending every day there, doing much of the work myself. There was no other way we'd get back up and running otherwise. By the middle of week four, Nacho was ready to roll with new engine oil seals, transmission seals, an inspected clutch, new valve cover and water pump seals, new brake rotors and front wheel bearings, and all new fuel lines in the engine compartment. I also managed to install an industrial fuel filter before the fuel pump to combat silt-laden gas later in our trip. Notably absent from our list of complete projects was the full-fledged investigation into our rear wheel bearings – the main reason we stopped in the first place. After a month, however, we were unable to hang around any longer. The rainy season had come, and we had long overstayed our welcome at our layover house.

At long last, a full month after we arrived in Atenas, we hit the road. Our friends had invited us to go trout fishing in the mountains outside of Cartago, and as we climbed the steep road into the mountains, we saw the first bad omen: our oil pressure light started to flicker. Without an oil pressure gauge, there wasn't much I could do, so we kept driving. Before long, we arrived at the dirt road that led to the trout pond. Waiting for us at the turnoff were our friends James and Lauren, who, after having seen the road, assumed (correctly) that we'd need a tow up the steepest section.

A hundred yards down the dirt road, all hell broke loose in Nacho's front end; in an instant it sounded like our van was being attacked by Langoliers. You know, from that Stephen King movie.

I got out in the pouring rain and mud, and jacked Nacho up. It was immediately obvious that something had gone horribly wrong; the front wheels were *totally effed up*, as we engineers say. I took the wheels off and found that both hubs were about to come apart, and both wheels were hanging onto their spindles by a few threads. Further investigation showed that our mechanic had failed to adequately peen both front hub locknuts, and they had almost completely backed off. I disbelievingly unscrewed them the rest of the way with my fingers.

I reassembled the hubs and torqued the locknuts to the factory spec, and then peened them in place. After putting everything back together we again got underway. Some of the noise had subsided, but it still sounded like a dominatrix was whipping Nacho with a chain as we drove. It was bad. We were only a few hundred meters from our camp, and decided to press on and figure it out later when it wasn't dark and raining.

In the morning, I found that one of our front brake caliper bolts had fallen out, and the other one had backed out 90% of the way. This would have been due to improper torque being applied by the mechanics when they reassembled the brakes after they swapped brake rotors. Our caliper had been smashing around as we drove on the dirt road, making all kinds of racket. We walked back on the road and miraculously found the missing bolt, and then I remounted the caliper and set the torque on all of the brake caliper bolts. With a torque wrench. The way Mother Nature intended it.

At the trout farm we met up with several of our overlanding friends; James, Lauren, Jessica, Kobus, and Jared. We spent two days stream fishing (with limited luck), pond fishing (with ease, as the pond was stocked with trout), Dutch oven cooking, and seeking refuge from the newly arrived rainy season. The pond was so well stocked, in fact, that it seemed like a great idea to try spearfishing for some trout. You see, after so much time away from academia and other forms of intellectual stimulation, my mind is becoming soft like baby fat.

On the second morning, I wrestled myself into my wetsuit and donned my flippers and mask. I slipped into the black, icy cold pond carrying my speargun, and put my head under the water. It was worse than the red tide in Playa Coco. In a small pond containing hundreds of slimy, writhing water-breathing beasts, I couldn't see a thing. Do trout have teeth? So terrifying. I held the speargun up in front of me, but couldn't see as far as the tip. It should have been obvious to me that if you can't see the spear tip, you won't see anything in front of the spear tip either. The odds were stacked against me, but the frigid water was constricting the blood flow to my baby fat mind. I hunted on.

After 15 minutes I had failed to spear anything and was teetering on the edge of hypothermia. Our new friend Juan even came down and chummed the water all around me with dog food in an attempt to give me a clear shot. Even with hundreds of trout bodies slapping up against me in a feeding frenzy, it wasn't to be. My repeated blind shots failed to kill anything except for my dreams. The trout had won.

Back on the road, we pointed toward Pavones in the far South of Costa Rica. If all went well, by the following morning we'd be surfing the world's second longest left hand break. The mechanical gods had a different idea, and a few miles after leaving, while traveling up a long climb in the pouring rain, our front brakes overheated. We pulled over as smoke billowed out from our front wheels.

After pulling the wheels off, it became clear that our front brake pistons were frozen. This meant that when I applied the brakes, the pads would squeeze the brake rotor, but wouldn't retract, leaving our brakes on at all times. I removed the brake pads and cycled the pistons in and out, trying to loosen them up. I noticed that the rubber piston seals were shredded, allowing water and grit to fly right into the calipers.

Back on the road, we made it no farther than a few more miles before we smelled the unmistakable odor of burning asbestos. My half-assed brake fix had failed to solve our sticky piston problem. We pulled to the roadside, this time on a descent leading into an enormous valley in the middle of nowhere, and settled in. I decided to rebuild our calipers there on the roadside, and make a crude repair to the dust seals with some RTV silicone. We were ready to spend at least one night on the side of the road.

While removing the first caliper my wrench slipped and I ripped a chunk of flesh from my thumb on the fender well. Not a great start. As I pulled the first caliper from the van, a man walked up to us. His engine had blown a few kilometers down the road, and he was trying to find some food for his waiting family. He told us that if we were able to coast down to where he was stopped, his son, a mechanic from San Jose, would be arriving at 8:30 that evening to give him a tow. He called him and verified that he would be able to help us out.

At 11:30 PM, the man's son and another mechanic showed up and started working on Nacho. Rather than rebuild the calipers, they opted to cycle them in and out as I had done earlier, only this time they sprayed WD40 into the pistons. Not quite as good, but it was enough to get all four pistons moving enough to safely drive a short distance. We spent the night by the roadside, and in the morning we headed out. I would just have to find a couple of caliper rebuild kits soon. My new rotors had already warped due to the stuck pistons, and I would need to get everything back to normal before any more damage was done.

We carried on through San Isidro, and started the long descent to the coast. I put Nacho in first gear and slowly crept along so as not to have to rely much on our brakes. We arrived at the coast late in the day and turned South on the coastal road. A mile down the road, I heard a light tapping from the rear wheel. I swerved a couple of times to assess where it was coming from, when all of a sudden we lost all engine power and a rapid beating sound erupted from our rear end. It sounded like we'd run over one of those improvised explosive devices, but I quickly ruled that out. Seemed unlikely.

As I got out, my mind first went to transmission failure. I really hoped it was a failed CV joint instead. In the sweltering heat and humidity I lowered myself into the dirt and crawled under Nacho's underbelly. I grabbed the axle and it spun freely in my hand. Somehow the passenger side outer CV joint had come completely unbolted from the stub axle. All six bolts, the ones I've been battling for the last two years to keep tight, the ones I replaced right before the trip and slathered with "permanent" Loctite, had all come out.

Since the CV joint was exposed to the elements, I had no choice but to unbolt the entire axle and rebuild it. I used the sand ladders on our front bumper as a workbench, took the joint apart, cleaned everything until it shined, rebuilt it and packed it with grease. What I didn't count on was the downpour that started just before I was ready to crawl back under Nacho to bolt everything back in place.

As I lay there on my back, my hair becoming matted and my shirt becoming soaked in oily mud, I couldn't help but laugh to myself. This whole ordeal had started with preventative maintenance. Then, in a span of 65 miles we had a tire puncture, an oil pressure light, had to be towed up two hills, our hubs came loose, our brake caliper bolts fell out, our brake pistons seized up, and our axle fell off. Now I was lying on my back in a mud puddle with mosquitoes buzzing around my face while I slowly hit each of the 12 passenger side axle bolts with brake cleaner, wire brush, Loctite, and a torque wrench.

I will henceforth be doing all of my own auto mechanics, and that's final. There's a reason I spent two tedious years learning how to work on Nacho correctly. And while many days make our hearts want to explode with overwhelming joy, days like this remind us that it's not all rainbows and unicorns out here. But we've come this far, so what the hell. Might as well see what tomorrow brings.

# 33

*Colón, Panama — June, by Brad*

Standing in the cramped bathroom of the Subway sandwich shop, I counted the money: $2,100. I uncrinkled the oil-stained cookie bag that I'd snagged from someone's tray as I had walked toward the bathroom, and slid the one inch thick stack of twenty dollar bills inside. I folded the oily bag around the stack of money, slid it into my pocket and then stared at my tired, unshaven face in the dirty mirror. I hadn't done anything this shady since I lent that beleaguered Nigerian Prince my whole life's savings. But we needed to get across the Darien Gap – the 80 mile long swath of impenetrable, guerilla-ridden jungle separating Panama from Colombia – and it had come to this. The Subway cookie bag was our ticket to freedom.

The only way to cross the Gap with a car is to place the vehicle in a shipping container and retrieve it on the other side. We were teased with the promise of a new ferry service that would connect the two sides, but on the day that we went to the ferry office in Panama City to reserve our spot, they told us that it had been delayed by another month. The next morning we began the dehumanizing process of getting Nacho on a ship.

In the morning our shipping agent emailed us, describing how to find the nondescript building in a Panama City ghetto where our car was to be inspected. The first step to safely crossing the world's most deadly stretch of jungle was to drive into an equally deadly ghetto and have a guy look at our engine. The directions weren't confidence inspiring:

> *"Go toward Sante Fe hospital and continue as if looking for*
> *Albrook...Stay in the left lane when you turn to Santa Fe...and when you*

*see the bridge don't take it...on the left where there are buildings – ugly buildings hahaha...there in the open ground – where there is construction for roads...this is vehicle control...there will be various automobiles. Climb the ladder to the metal door, announce yourself and open your hood to cool. Important...announce yourself because these are special cowboys..."*

Detecting our navigational ineptitude, the agent's daughter ultimately met us on the banks of the Panama Canal and led us into the heart of the ghetto herself. As it turned out our actual agent lived somewhere in Argentina and was using her daughter as a proxy assistant. After a hair-raising drive through Panama City traffic and an hour sitting in the dirt parking lot surrounded by slums, we were informed that no inspectors had come to work that day.

"Tomorrow they will work," our agent promised. We would have to venture into the belly of the beast one more time.

The next morning we sat around the ghetto parking lot wiping the egg from our faces after the inspectors failed to materialize again.

"They are in a seminar," our agent told us, "they will be back at noon."

"Great, so we'll just wait until noon and they can inspect our engines when they get here," I said.

"Not possible. They only inspect engines between 10 and 11. Noon is not between 10 and 11." We had to remember that this was Latin America, where things don't always happen in a logical fashion. Inspecting our engines at noon would cut into lunch, and if lunch were pushed back, it would cut into the two hour afternoon naptime. That would inevitably cause issues with the period of late afternoon lazing around. Don't rock the boat. Monday was only 3 days away.

Before we left the ghetto, I decided to give away a pair of Sheena's old running shoes. I saw a crazy man in a wheelchair without any shoes in front of one of the slum buildings, so I called to him to see if he wanted them.

"Man, I'll take the shoes, but I can't wear 'em," he said.

I didn't want them to be sold, or else traded for crack, so I decided to give him 50 cents instead. I couldn't just leave him hanging, so I ducked through the chain link fence and handed him two quarters. He dropped them into his lap and then snapped his head back quickly, staring straight into my soul with his crazy Jack Black eyes. He started making shapes with his mouth, flexing every muscle in his stringy face. I thought he might be having a heart attack. Suddenly he started scratching at his chest and somehow managed to wrestle his shirt off. He reminded me of a swamp rat. He still hadn't muttered a word since taking my quarters. Before I had time to retreat, he started waving his arms around slowly while shifting his eyes from side to side. His arms snapped into a karate chop to one side, then the other. Several tai chi moves culminated in a series of fast karate chops at an invisible enemy.

His eyes again locked on mine and it looked like he was in deep thought. Although his hands were still stiff and weapon-like, he had forgotten about the karate. Slowly his head tilted back, he closed his eyes, and opened his mouth wide like a wounded spider monkey. He winced hard as he mouthed silent screams into the air while clubbing at his bare chest. His head straightened and he looked at me again.

"Muy impresionante," I said. What the hell else was I supposed to say? I took a few timid steps backwards and then hurriedly ducked back through the chain link fence to the relative safety of our ghetto parking lot.

The process of getting Nacho onto a ship became a series of long waits punctuated by hurried, stressful visits to various customs offices, government buildings, and port officials. During the periods of waiting, we did our best to fill our time exploring Panama City. Our guide to the city was Ciro, whose exceptionally pleasant mother operated a guest house called *Jamraka*, our homestay on the edge of the city. With Ciro we explored the inner workings of Casco Viejo, the colonial portion of the city. We dined at street carts serving up plates of rice and barbecued pork, explored the district's bars, and spent one evening on a rooftop terrace overlooking the city with a film crew celebrating its completion of a Panamanian beer commercial.

Over the weekend, after two unsuccessful attempts at finding the inspectors at work, we opted to tempt fate by taking Nacho on a road trip to the abandoned fort at San Lorenzo, and to the small Caribbean town of Portobelo. Bearing in mind that Nacho had just suffered a long string of breakdowns, we threw caution to the wind and loaded the van with our road tripping crew; Ciro, our new friends Margaret and Madison, Sheena and me; and hit the road.

After driving across the width of the isthmus from Panama City to Colón, we turned westward and followed a string of dilapidated roads through an abandoned military base and into the dense jungle. We crossed the Panama Canal below the enormous gates of the Gatún Lock while four foot long fish jumped like dolphins in the turbulent water, once again proving that the Caribbean is well endowed with fish compared to its scant Pacific counterpart. Winding through the jungle on the approach to San Lorenzo we followed an anteater before it ducked into the undergrowth. We ended the perfect day by eating seafood while overlooking the bay at Portobelo.

While our time in Panama City was spent waiting for inspectors to do their jobs, in Colon it was our shipping agent who no longer felt like working. "Be at the Super 99 at 8:30 sharp so Boris can meet you and take you to the port." Our instructions were clear, so we awoke bright and early for the hour drive.

When we arrived at the Super 99 in Colon's seedy center, right on time, Boris was nowhere in sight. After 30 minutes we called him.

"I will be there at 11:00," he said. At this I reminded him that he was supposed to meet us at 8:30, and that we preferred not to sit in the parking lot for two and a half hours. "Yes, but the port doesn't open until 11:00," he said.

"Boris, we still have to go to customs before we can go to the port," I reminded him. "Okay, okay, I will come at 10:00." This Boris was not making a good impression on me, nor the rest of my shipping partners; Mark, the Canadian who I was to share a container with; Bart, the Dutch legume salesman; and Alejandro, the Mexican lady's man who was making the trip to Argentina in a clapped out minivan, and was paying for his trip by selling postcards along the way. "In Nicaragua nobody would buy my postcards, so I make a fire show in the street," Alejandro had told us.

By 10:15 there was no sign of Boris. I called him and got his voicemail. For the next several hours I continued to call him, but he never answered. Finally, at 1:00, he picked up his phone. "Oh hi, are you at the port or at customs?" he asked. "Boris!" I yelled, "We're still in the damn parking lot, REMEMBER!? We've been here for five hours!" At this he acted surprised and promised to have one of his guys pick us up. Ten minutes later a man showed up on a motorcycle to lead us to the customs office.

The unwritten laws of inefficiency in Latin America would dictate that our simple tasks at the customs office would not go smoothly. First, it was discovered that Alejandro had accidentally overstayed his visa. Next, Mark was accused of forging the stamp on his car importation permit. Each was demanded to pay $250. Of course they refused, and an hour long debate ensued. Arms flew into the air, sad faces abounded, pleas were made, several calls were made, and ultimately Alejandro's bribe was reduced to $10. They also agreed that, in fact, Mark hadn't forged his import stamp. At 4:30 we emerged from the customs office, ready to drive our cars into their containers.

"It's 4:30, you're too late. You must load the containers tomorrow," our moto guide told us. At this we became furious. Our shipping agent, through laziness, had forced us to miss our time for loading the containers, and we would have to grab a hotel in Colón. An angry phone call to Boris ensued, but he played innocent. Mark, Bart and I split a hotel while Alejandro raced the minivan back to Panama City to party the night away.

The next day unfolded in much the same way as the first; we waited for an hour for our motorcycle escort to show up, after which time he escorted us a few hundred yards before waving us on without him. At the port we waited for another hour for another motorcycle man to show up, and then once he showed up we waited longer while he talked to people. Finally in the afternoon we loaded our containers and locked them up for the short trip to Cartagena.

After waiting for an hour while yet another moto man brought us a handwritten receipt for our container fees, we took a taxi back to the seedy parking lot in Colón's center, being followed by our moto guide. After going to the ATM it was time to pay our dues. We walked into the Subway restaurant and bought some drinks. I snagged an oily cookie bag off of someone's tray and walked into the bathroom.

When I emerged I looked at Luis, our motorcycle guide, and gave him a nod. He followed me out the front door and we stood on the curb, looking out into the parking lot.

"Do you have the money?" he asked.

"Yes, it's in my pocket."

"Do not let anyone see it. They will rob me if they know I carry money." Truth be told, this was one of the nastiest cities I'd ever been in. I didn't blame the guy for his caution.

"Did you count it?" he asked.

"Yes, I counted it. Do you want to count it?" It was feeling more and more like a dirty drug deal.

"No, I won't count it. I trust you." We stared at the parking lot. Timidly, I pulled the oily bag from my pocket and slyly handed it to Luis. He didn't look at me. He slowly strode to his bike, pulled his helmet on, gave me a quick nod, and sped away down the dilapidated street, weaving through traffic.

The taxi ride from the Subway to the bus station was like a trip into the ravaged center of Mogadishu or Kabul. Choose your favorite bombed out third world capital. Cracked buildings were held together by plaster, clothing hung from every window, trash piles littered every open space, and people hobbled around like injured hobos.

"This is the RED zone, man! You don't WALK here! You get yo self ROBBED…or SHOT!" Our elderly taxi driver was from Panama, but had spent his life in Texas and his accent was proof of it.

He continued to murmur his warnings as we weaved past the bombed out building carcasses. "ROBBED!...or SHOT!...the RED zone..."

All of a sudden there was a gap in the bombed out buildings and there stood the Colón bus station. Our taxi driver steered over to a group of police officers and cracked his window.

"These guys need to get on the BUS! They're FOREIGNERS!" At this we got out of the taxi and were shrouded by the police officers. One of them signaled for us to cross the street, and he flanked us on one side as we crossed, rapidly moving his head around in all directions to keep watch. As we got to the other side of the two lane street, he ushered us onto a waiting bus and slammed the door behind us. He had literally escorted us 15 feet. We sunk into the seats for the long haul back to Panama City.

# Part 5

# The Deep South

Drive Nacho Drive

# 34

*Cartagena, Colombia — June, by Sheena*

I have rivers of sweat running down my legs and beads of perspiration dancing on my skin. Having grown up in 115 degree weather, I know what hot feels like, but it sure didn't prime me for the kind of heat rising off of this cement. I may as well have taken a shower with my clothes on. Despite the heat, every morning I attempt to run along the water front promenade. And without fail, by 7:30 my run turns into an unsteady trot and then into a sad, overheated limp.

After spending the morning recovering from near heat stroke, Brad and I pop our heads out of the hotel in search of lunch. One day, as we walk around a corner in the Getsemani neighborhood where we're staying, we're drawn into a packed eatery buzzing with a multitude of oscillating fans. Not a single table is vacant so we squeeze into a small table occupied by a lone female. A chalk board outside lists the options for the day. As with most Colombian midday meals, this one comprises two courses, starting with a bowl of soup. As my internal temperature continues to rise, I watch the locals happily eat their steaming bowls of *sancocho*, a thick stew of bone-in meat, herbs, yucca, plantain, yam, and corn. It seems that national eating customs don't change just because you are in 112 degree Cartagena. When in Rome, do as the Romans do; I eat the first course. Love at first sip.

Next up is *seco*, literally the 'dry' portion of the meal – rice, beans, *patacones* (mashed, fried plantain), a small salad, and meat. After dozens of standard rice and bean lunch platters, I quickly realize this one is special. The rice is stained brown in a caramelized mound, molasses in flavor and laced with plump raisins. I vow to search high and low until I figure out what I've put in my mouth, and I eventually find it. Secret ingredient for *arroz con pasas*: Coca Cola! This one side dish alone will bring us back to *La Tertulia* three more times, wanting more.

While we pig out, Nacho claustrophobically waits on a ship inside of a cargo container, awaiting transport from Colón, Panama to Cartagena, Colombia. Any day now he'll brave the high seas and slip past the infamous Darien Gap. Until then, we wait. Luckily, Cartagena is a gem of a city – a 16th century Spanish port on the Caribbean Coast.

Wandering the historic district within the 11 kilometers of city walls is an attraction in itself; beautifully cobblestoned streets, bougainvilleas draping from balconies, and plazas lined with food vendors. The walls of the city, once used to protect the city against pirates are now a place of congregation. Friends assemble on top of the walls while business takes place down below. Shaded by the sturdy wall, a barber purposefully cuts hair while a lady sits slumped back in a plastic lawn chair nonchalantly giving pedicures, her client's toes tanning in the morning sun.

In the morning a P.E. teacher blows her whistle while students take turns running up and down one of the many ramps of the wall. In the evenings along the wall in front of our hotel, local baseball teams gather to play games in the cool of the evening. On Sunday the crowds gather in the morning, blocking the street with lawn chairs, for a day-long baseball tournament. Home plate and third base are painted on the sidewalk on our side of the street, while first and second base are on the opposite sidewalk. The pitcher's mound is painted in the middle of the street, and the city wall acts as the edge of the stadium. Intense yelling battles erupt as opposing fans shout accusations at one another. The desire for more space forces the locals to pull their lawn chairs off the sidewalk and into the street, and many more accumulate atop the city wall. Cartagena is very much a living city.

Things invariably slow down midday as the sun relentlessly beats down, forcing everyone inside, to a shady spot, or to the juice stands. Large aquariums on wheels filled with icy cold fruit juice are easy to find on the street, manned by a person with a ladle and a stack of plastic cups. Every flavor under the sun can be had — watermelon, mango, strawberry, *tomate de arbol* — but *limonada* seems to be the people's choice. Other men push carts down the street filled with carafes of coffee. Small Dixie cups are offered, filled with either *tinto* (black coffee) or *café con leche* (coffee with milk) as a quick pick-me-up. In addition to all of the drink options, there are plenty of vendors selling sticks of meat or fried treats. One popular greasy item is the *arepa con huevo*: a thick corn tortilla cut down the middle, whole raw egg cracked inside and then fried.

Sweets are sold in jars along the famous arcaded walkway known as *El Portal de los Dulces*. In the adjoining *Plaza de los Coches*, which was formerly a slave market, you can watch traditional Carib dancing. As Shakira, a native Colombian, would say: these hips don't lie. These people can dance. And as we have come to find out, these people can eat too. Colombia is looking pretty good from here.

# 35

*Colombian mountains — June, by Brad*

Before we started our trip we were warned about Colombia. Namely, we were cautioned about the possibility of getting kidnapped by the FARC. We tried to ignore the stories, but when my beloved *This American Life* podcast ran a story about a Colombian radio station that exists for the sole purpose of communicating with the country's kidnapping victims, our ears perked a little bit. However, after speaking to people who had spent considerable time overlanding in Colombia, we were put at ease. "Just stay on main roads and tourist areas and you'll be fine. The rebels operate in the remote jungles and mountains now." Easy! We just hadn't realized how easy it would be to wander off the main roads. Soon enough, we found ourselves several days' drive from civilization in the middle of the Colombian mountains, in what has historically been a FARC *red zone*.

Nacho had arrived on the ship at the port in Cartagena, and with it started my second round of hoop jumping to get our wheels out of the port. A ride on an airliner, several taxi rides, various port and customs offices, and too many hours were spent sitting around waiting for things to happen. I was denied entry to the port without proper footwear, so ended up spending a full day walking around the port wearing Sheena's shoes.

To describe the convoluted, inefficient mess that we endured to get Nacho out of there would stir up far too many painful memories for me. I'll just wave my arm and say that many things happened, and in the end Nacho emerged from the port being driven by a guy named Mark. When it was all over, we happily putted away from the overheated city, looking for adventure. Our research revealed that there was a mountainous national park on the Eastern end of the country called *Parque Nacional Natural El Cocuy*, so we pointed Nacho's big blunt nose Eastward and sat back for the long, slow haul.

The first two days of driving went off without a hitch, but by the end of day three it was about time for Nacho to break down. After all, we hadn't broken down in a few hundred miles. Lo and behold, as we topped a mountain on the edge of Chicamocha canyon, our oil light started to flicker. Usually it only flickers when it gets wet, because the water causes the decomposing sensor wire to short against the engine. This time it wasn't raining, and I pulled over to discover steam pouring out from under the van. We hastily removed our belongings from the back of the van – shoe bin, Dutch ovens, my clothing – and opened the engine compartment. Sure enough, the plastic nipple on the rear coolant bleeder valve had somehow broken off, causing our coolant to empty itself all over the engine. The wet coolant had caused the sensor wire to short against the engine, alerting me to the impending disaster through the oil pressure warning light. I knew there was a good reason not to fix that wire! I whipped out the Dremel tool, created a new nipple, reconnected the coolant hose, refilled the coolant, and slapped on an additional pipe clamp for good measure. Disaster averted, and we were on our way.

By the end of the day we made it to San Gil, where we set up camp for the evening. Since leaving Cartagena we had been looking for a paper map to augment our GPS, but had found that the only places in Colombia that sell paper maps are the toll booths. And so far, every toll booth gave me the same answer when I asked for a map: "no hay." In the morning, a quick search around town revealed no paper maps, so we reluctantly drove off the grid, mapless, towards the tiny mountain town of Mogotes.

The paved road to Mogotes switchbacked straight up the side of a mountain, and then descended the other side into a river valley. We drove for an hour or so along the river as it wound its way between enormous mountains, until we reached the town. A short distance beyond the town the road turned to dirt, marking the beginning of a multi-day dirt road drive through the mountains. I had flashbacks to that fateful day in Guatemala when I graduated from boy to man over the course of twelve hours on the death highway. This was poised to make that drive look like mere child's play. We dropped into first gear and started creeping, slowly, toward El Cocuy.

The road between Mogotes and San Joaquin started so sweetly, like Martha Stewart, but after winding through the foothills the gradient pitched upward and the road revealed her darker side. We soon found ourselves plodding straight up the side of the mountain toward our first dirt road mountain pass. While the horizontal distance between Mogotes and San Joaquin is only a few miles, we found ourselves feeling uneasy at how long it was taking to climb the enormous mountain separating the two towns. The road narrowed and to our left the river valley spread out thousands of feet below us.

Near to the top of the pass, we encountered our first challenge. The road steepened abruptly before crossing in front of a waterfall. The road had been washed out, and subsequently repaired with concrete. The water, rather than flowing over the repaired road section, had found its way under the concrete, and had since washed all of the soil out from underneath it. The concrete remained, several feet of unsupported four inch thick roadway suspended in mid-air, while the river had left a gaping chasm that funneled into a ravine.

We gunned the engine, Nacho let out a battle cry akin to that of a handicapped newborn pony, and we came to an uninspired halt in the middle of the abrupt uphill section before the waterfall. A classic display of Nacho's frailty. I attempted to back up to have another run at it, but in doing so got us stuck in the ditch, wedged against the canyon wall. Just then, as if to add insult to injury, the sky opened up in a magnificent downpour, further weakening our four inch thick concrete bridge and my confidence in getting to San Joaquin in one piece. After a while the rain stopped, we negotiated our way out of the ditch, and a few repeated attempts at the climb saw us safely on our way.

After reaching the top of the pass we rested for a moment before putting Nacho in first gear and lurching downward, toward countless switchbacks and dozens of landslides strewn across the road as it wound along the razorback spines of the mountain. Each time we crept through the path of a landslide I allowed my gaze to wander over the edge to see what kind of carnage it had caused farther down the mountain. On one occasion we spied a truck at the bottom edge of the slide, at least a thousand feet below. Sheena and I shuddered. Nacho shuddered.

We slowed down long enough in San Joaquin to verify that we were traveling in the direction of Onzaga, the next tiny mountain hamlet, and then carried onward, skirting the river at the bottom of the canyon. Our GPS had suggested that midway between San Joaquin and Onzaga there would be a road passing directly over the top of a mountain to our left, which would lead us to the town of Soatá. The road didn't exist on any map we'd seen, but if it existed it would put us within a half day's drive of our destination, and would save us a full day of driving. As we approached the point where our GPS showed the road, we found a small bridge over the river to a dilapidated building. I parked Nacho in the middle of the road and got out to investigate.

As I rounded the side of the building, I was met by several men sitting outside on benches, beers in hand. Their eyes were all glazed over, and several of them had *wookie eye* – their eyes pointing off in different directions like the cookie monster. The drunken glaze in combination with the wookie eye sent mild waves of fear down my spine. When they saw me they all stood up and surrounded me. Someone whispered something about what I was selling and another kept counting to ten in English, his wookie eyes staring off into the trees behind me. After a while I ascertained that in fact the road did not go over the mountain, and that we'd have to get the hell out of there as soon as possible and drive to Onzaga after all.

A man and a boy seemed insistent that they were coming with us, but I pretended not to understand them. Another man who had been shaking my hand continuously wouldn't loosen his grip on me. He

159

stared at me, his wookie eyes burning holes in the sky to either side of my head. I managed to squeeze my hand free, wave goodbye to the group, and quickly retreat to Nacho where Sheena sat wondering what was taking so long. Our would-be passengers looked totally betrayed, their eyes gazing randomly all over the place.

Our slow crawl through the mountains continued, and by nightfall we reached Onzaga. The town was quiet and only a few souls stirred in the street as we pulled up to the first hotel we saw. When we walked inside we found the owner and her friend, a truck driver, sitting around a plastic table. We checked into a room – nothing more than a concrete cube with two rock hard beds – and came back to the common area to talk. Using our GPS, we showed the truck driver our planned onward route, and although captivated by the touch screen, he was quick to inform us that our route was clearly dreamed up by a mere amateur, and that he had a secret route that was way better.

"You see this part? No good! Totally mountains. No good! You drive to Covarachia, good! Your plan, no good!"

He spoke with a confidence that said *I know what I'm talking about and you'd be a fool not to listen. A FOOL!* He scribbled some rudimentary directions on the back of a napkin so that we could find his secret road, but we were still leery. I checked Google Maps, Google Earth, and our GPS, but the road didn't exist on any of them. Not only that, but we couldn't even see a road on any of the satellite images that we found. What to do? The man was pretty assertive, so in the morning we left at the crack of dawn toward the truck driver's secret road.

Many days later while chatting with a local man, we told him of the convoluted route that we'd taken to get to El Cocuy.

"Yes, we definitely took a hard route to get there. We passed through San Joaquin, Onzaga, Covarachia…"

"WAIT!" he said. "You went to Onzaga?!"

"Uh, yeah. It was pretty quiet. We felt like aliens there," I said.

"Didn't you know that Onzaga used to be completely controlled by the FARC? All of these little towns are home to the FARC. Until very recently it was called *The Red Zone*."

Looking back on the advice given to us about where to travel in Colombia, we realized that we'd done exactly the opposite of what we were told. We somehow found ourselves leaving a former FARC outpost on a tiny mountain dirt road so small that it didn't even exist on any map or satellite image.

We left Onzaga at the crack of dawn, following the truck driver's hand drawn map. We had scoured all of the online maps and satellite photography we could find, but had failed to locate the road between Onzaga and Covarachia that he had sworn was the fastest route to reach El Cocuy. We were lost before we even made it out of the village. After stopping several times for directions, we crossed the river and made our way along the base of a mountain, heading North.

The truck driver had told us that we would reach some dilapidated houses, and then make the first right. Shortly after the houses we came to a fork in the road, the left road having been taken out by a landslide; we were happy to turn right. After a mile the tire tracks became less defined and eventually succumbed to a covering of grass, while the edge of the road had largely flaked off into the river. We came across a man with a machete and a severe case of wookie eye, and we asked him for directions. It turned out that when the truck driver had said "turn right," he actually meant "turn left." It was our first inclination that he'd never actually driven his secret road before.

After retracing our tracks to the fork in the road, we stared disbelievingly at the path ahead. A landslide had wiped out the road, but it looked like a tractor had driven across it and cleared the way. It was going to be a long day. We reluctantly followed the tracks through the slide, after which the road turned upward and began snaking up the side of the mountain.

Before long, the road became narrow and rocky. The several days leading up to this had been on roads that could accommodate two vehicles side by side. The truck driver's secret road was a single lane, and based on its condition it clearly hadn't been used very often. We gradually crept up one steep incline after another, interspersed with water crossings, landslides, ruts, and rock gardens.

After one water crossing, the road pitched steeply upward over a series of rocks and ruts. It seemed we wouldn't make the climb unless we carried some momentum into the rocks, and if we were unable to make it, we'd have to backtrack several hours and find a different route. We had to make it.

We stopped to inspect the water crossing, and then backed up and took a run for it. We made it through the water, and then bounced into the uphill rocky section. After a couple of hard bumps our front wheels both came completely off the ground, throwing Nacho into a totally gnarly wheelie. We came down, and the recoil from the shocks caused us to bounce into the air again. It was totally gnarly, again. When we stopped bouncing we had lost much of our speed, and barely made it past the rocks and onto a less severe incline. And we wonder why poor Nacho keeps breaking down.

After three hours and as many mountain summits on the truck driver's secret road, Sheena became nervous and started reading an e-book. This is her way of hiding from the reality of the nerve-wracking roads we encounter. Shortly thereafter, we approached a vertical rock crevasse in the side of the mountain, having sheer rock cliffs rising vertically to either side. The road seemed to dive straight into the crack, but I couldn't discern an exit. We crept closer, but I remained puzzled. As we reached the crevasse, I was shocked to see the road make a tight switchback inside of the crack, and then cut back abruptly against the opposing rock wall.

As we rounded the chicane, I could see that the cliff-hugging road had a rock wall on one side, and a sheer drop on the other. The road was the width of one vehicle, was strewn with rocks, and was bloody steep. I gunned it and Nacho raced forward like an injured turtle. As we bounced over the rocks I looked over the edge – only a couple of feet to my left out the open window. The height was dizzying and I felt nauseous. I stole a glance at Sheena, but she was oblivious to the situation, engulfed in her coming of age princess novel. Or whatever it is that women read on their e-readers.

By lunch time we emerged at the intersection of a slightly larger dirt road, only a few miles from Covarachia. We had cheated death and the mechanical gods once more. We parked Nacho in the road and ate some cereal out of plastic cups while we gazed into the valley below. Perched on the side of the road was a statue of a saint, where passersby could stop and make an offering for their safe passage. I poured out the remnants of my cereal milk at its base and got back in the van.

Finally after half a day of driving, we emerged at the tiny mountain town of Covarachia, not having seen a single other vehicle since daybreak. From Covarachia the terrain became more desert-like, the road being lined by a mix of agave and prickly pear cactus, tall green grass and bamboo. We switchbacked down the side of the mountain to the town of Tipacoque, where we intersected a larger road running along the side of Chicamocha canyon.

After reaching the town of Soatá, having sworn never to take directions from another truck driver, I entered a small *tienda* where I was given directions by a mute man aided by his toddler grandson. We filled our gas tank and then headed eastward, through canyons, winding roads, and mountains, inching ever closer to our destination.

As the sun sunk low in the sky, after four solid days of brutal, twisting, slow, yet stunningly beautiful driving, we arrived in the pueblo of El Cocuy – the gateway to Colombia's Sierra Nevada range and final outpost before our destination: *Parque Nacional Natural El Cocuy*. We found the *Hotel Villa Real*, and inside, our friends James and Lauren who had arrived a day earlier from a different direction.

Before leaving Onzaga, we had told James and Lauren to watch our GPS tracker map embedded in our website, as we would be updating our location every 10 minutes throughout the day. This would allow them to keep tabs on us and know when to expect us. If the tracker sent repeated updates from the bottom of a ravine, they were to alert the proper rescue authorities.

"So…you chose an *interesting* route from Onzaga," James said as he welcomed us into their hotel room. He had watched as we had driven away from all of the possible routes on the map, and instead drove over an entire mountain range through an unmapped no-man's land.

"Damn truck driver never drove that road in his life. Last time I take driving advice from someone whose name isn't Garmin."

We grabbed a room — an unremarkable plywood cube with a rock hard bed — and refueled in the downstairs restaurant. In the morning we would make the final oxygen-starved push into the heart of the mountains.

When the sun came up, we loaded our trusty steeds, stocked up on empanadas for the car and non-perishables for the days of hiking that lay ahead. We checked in with the park ranger and pointed upward and to the East. Destination: *Nacho Basecamp*, elevation 13,000 feet.

After close to 30 hours of driving through mountains over the course of the previous four days, the hour and a half drive from El Cocuy to our first camp seemed to fly by. We threaded through the mountains, winding past Swiss-looking backdrops of green mountain pastures and high peaks.

Finally, only a few dozen meters from the top of the final pass, Nacho stalled out. The 12,800 foot elevation, in combination with a tricky rock climb and Nacho's hamster wheel engine proved too much. James towed us up the last incline to the summit like a high altitude porter and his unfit mountain climbing client. At the pass, we stopped to take it all in.

A short distance from the road, we came across the foundation of the old park ranger's cabin. Although details of the story are hard to come by, I had gathered that El Cocuy was used as a base by FARC rebels and other paramilitaries due to its remoteness and natural defenses. They had occupied the area since the 1970's, forcing the boys in the surrounding villages to join them, and executing those who wouldn't comply. In 1999, FARC rebels forced their way into the ranger's cabin, killed him, and set his house on fire. After some time, President Uribe's government sent in 20,000 troops to secure the region. A short but bloody battle ensued, and in 2003 the park was finally cleared of rebels and considered safe to visit. It hasn't yet been "discovered" by adventure tourism – likely due to the difficulty in getting here.

After catching our breath we put away the tow strap and coasted the last half mile to our camp site. We had driven as far as it is possible to drive into the Sierra Nevada. After pulling up to the edge of the ravine above a glacial stream we popped our tent, extended the awning, thanked Nacho for his hard work, and cracked open celebratory brews all around. We'd finally made it.

Over the ensuing days we would hike to *Paso de Cusirí* and *Cueva del Hombre*, we would sleep in the cave and awake to a morning of snow, halting our plans to hike to the glacier. We would awake each morning and have to pinch ourselves at our good fortune at having chosen to trade the nine to five routine for this life, and we would leave El Cocuy following James and Lauren through the rough roads of the Colombian Andes. But nothing could prepare us for what would come next.

# 36

*Susacón, Colombia — June, by Brad*

As soon as I knew what it was to want, I desired nothing more than to be the commander of an intergalactic space shuttle. Later on I decided that I would make a better commercial fishing boat captain. For a short time in 5th grade, my best friend Nick and I decided that we wanted to be nefarious gang members. We even went so far as to form our own gang called *The Bloody Devils*; we designed a logo that we intended to get tattooed on our arms (a dagger with dripping blood), and declared the southwestern corner of the Heritage Middle School playground as our turf. My mom, ever the supporter, bought me a red bandana so there would be no confusion as to the level of my badassedness.

During recess we would defend our turf by staging shirtless wrestling matches against our rival gang members, who weren't even nefarious enough to have a gang name, a logo, or a turf on which to stage their own turf wars. However, after a few weeks of prepubescent territorial squabbling, our aspirations shifted to the NBA and our turf fell into the hands of Eric Seeley and his nameless, logoless cronies.

These last few weeks I've been wishing to be Barbara Walters, or some other tough talking interviewer. I wake up in the middle of the night waiting with anticipation for the Colombian mechanic to answer my question: *why did you do it?* I tried to get away from these mechanics, but they wouldn't let me go. *Why didn't you just leave me alone? Answer the question! WHY DID YOU DO IT?!*

We had left El Cocuy feeling that we had just experienced the greatest highlight of our trip thus far. What we hadn't realized, however, was that we were driving in a ticking time bomb.

We had followed James and Lauren out of the village of El Cocuy, intending to reach Villa de Leyva by evening. When we reached the town of Guacamayas I thought I smelled a coolant leak, so when James stopped his truck to take a picture, I ran out and smelled his engine. As I leaned over to stick my head in the wheel well of their 4Runner, my eyes were drawn to the stream of oil gushing out of Nacho's belly. I flashed back to my days as a gang member, and remembered that liquid gushing out of the belly could only mean one thing.

Nacho's nizzle had been shizzled.

*Oh no – shizzled!* My brain went into analytical mode to try to figure out what was happening, but my body took over and bolted like a newly dead chicken – a flurry of uncoordinated arms and legs. While I flailed around my brain tried to make sense of my train of thought: *Nacho bleeding! Dark oil between engine and transmission. No oil trail – must have started when I stopped. When I stopped I turned the engine off. Must restart engine!*

Sure enough, restarting the engine caused the oil to slow down, and revving it to 3,000 RPM caused it to stop leaking. I wasn't about to be stuck in the middle of the remote Colombian mountains – nine hours from a big city – with a major mechanical issue. I would just have to keep the engine speed above 3,000 RPM until we could get to our next stop, where I could set up shop for a while to fix whatever was wrong.

Forty five minutes passed and everything seemed to be going okay. On occasion I would stop and run out to see if the leak had worsened, but it seemed to be holding at a steady drip. As we began descending into Chicamocha canyon, the transmission made a funny sound. Actually, there was nothing funny about it. The transmission made a sound scary enough to make a grown man wet his pants, but only just a little bit. I admitted defeat and pulled under a shade tree next to a grove of prickly pear cactus. A small stream of transmission fluid coated the dry grass while I sat staring out of the windshield. Sheena knew better than to ask what I was going to do. No, by now she knows that these moments of silence are my time to come to terms with the fact that I have no idea what to do.

By now it was clear that the transmission, and not the engine, was bleeding out. A small feat of German engineering called the "oil slinger" was keeping the oil from pouring out of what was probably a failed transmission oil seal – but it only worked above 3,000 RPM. What had caused the seal to fail was anyone's guess. I decided to use our reserve of gear oil to refill the transmission and try to get to Villa de Leyva. We had long since, and perhaps foolishly, waved James and Lauren on, promising to meet up with them at the campground.

After the transmission refill – a procedure that takes close to an hour on the Vanagon – we finished the descent into the canyon, crossed the river, and then started the switchback ascent up the other side. By the time we reached the village at the top of the climb I was feeling more confident that we could make it. We were done with the toughest part and had reached a more frequently trafficked road.

It was in between the towns of Soatá and Susacón, while I sat there with a smug look on my face thinking I was so damn smart, that Nacho lost all power, came to a stop, voided his bowels right there in the middle of the dirt road, and started rolling backwards. My smug look evaporated and I stared out of the windshield. Sheena knew better than to ask what I was going to do. I cycled through all of the gears, but forward motion was not to be. Nacho had failed an epic fail.

After cursing our luck, we put our friendly hitchhiker faces on and tricked a nice Colombian man into helping us out. We roped up to his truck and settled in for the short three mile haul to Susacón. The alternative was our winchless self-recovery system, which somehow felt far under qualified for the job. Instead we just sat there, Sheena restraining from asking me the obvious question.

If there's one thing I've learned about Latin American car mechanics since starting this trip, it's that 99% of them don't have the faintest clue how to work on cars. They take things apart really fast until they feel like they've sufficiently destroyed whatever it is they were working on, and then they start putting things back together incorrectly, while leaving some things out and then tightening the bolts as much as their fingers or pliers will allow. I recently made a decree not to let anyone who isn't me touch our innocent little Nacho ever again. A transmission failure, while a much bigger job than anything else that's gone wrong, would be no different. I figured I would get the transmission out so I could see what was wrong, and to do so I would just need to borrow a jack. I asked the man to tow us near to the town's mechanic shop so I could ask about borrowing a jack. He happily obliged, and we soon found ourselves parked on the street in front of a grungy dirt-floored hole full of rusty junk. We left Nacho parked on the street and set off to find a place to stay for the night.

In the morning I walked to the mechanic's shop to ask if I could rent his jack to remove our transmission. One might try to defend the mechanic for his idiocy by suggesting that something was lost in translation, but no. The discussion went *exactly* as follows, except in Spanish. I know, because I've dreamt it over and over in my Barbara Walters dream:

"Hi, our transmission has failed and I'll be needing to do some work on it. I prefer to work on my own car, but I don't have a jack. Would it be possible for me to borrow your jack later so that I can work on my transmission? I'd be willing to pay you."

"Yes, no problem. I have a jack that you can use. Just come and find me when you need it; I'll be in my house."

With that out of the way, I went off to the internet café to seek advice on the interwebs and from my brother, who is a master technician for BMW. After almost two hours, due to a slow internet connection, I was back on my feet headed toward Nacho. Nothing could have prepared me for the sight I saw.

There, right in the middle of the street, the mechanic and the hotel owner from across the road were sprawled out under Nacho. All around them were mounds of nuts, bolts, washers, spacers, and unidentifiable doo dads. For some inexplicable reason the mechanic had taken apart my driver's side rear hub, and my drum brake was hanging from my now bent hydraulic brake line. To remove the hub housing from the swingarm, he removed all of the bolts using vice grips. These bolts are tightened to over 100ft-lbs; needless to say he destroyed all of the bolts.

He wanted to remove my shift linkage from the transmission, but rather than removing the single nut that connects it, he first attempted to take apart the universal joint at the opposite end of the van. Unable to do so, he left the joint partially destroyed and instead disconnected the splined shift linkage interface – which you're NOT supposed to touch! EVER!

Having successfully obliterated my shift linkage, he set to work on getting the actual transmission out. He started by undoing all of my CV bolts with a pair of vice grips, destroying all twelve bolts in the process.

After incorrectly disconnecting the transmission from the frame, he let the whole engine and transmission assembly fall some unknown distance to his jack, which caused the air filter box to rip clean off of the engine compartment wall. He knew so little about what he was doing that, by the time I found him, he had already started trying to pull the drive flanges out of the side of the transmission while it was hanging there.

"STOP! What the hell are you DOING!?"

It was all I could think to say. For several seconds I reprimanded him, but since the transmission was lying on his chest he didn't make much of an effort to move.

"I need to replace the clutch."

"No, you need to get the hell out from under there!"

In a flurry of vice grips and oily hands the two of them, ignoring me, separated the transmission from the engine, unbolted the clutch pressure plate, and removed the clutch.

"Give me the new clutch," he said, holding out his grease-covered grubby little hands. He actually expected that I would give him my brand new clutch disc from my spare parts box so he could destroy it by covering it in grease and gear oil. Furthermore, I actually think he planned to install it and put it all back together so I could drive along on my merry way. Clearly this guy was a deranged maniac. I tried to think what I would have done if I were a gang member, but somehow taking off my shirt and wrestling him seemed wildly appropriate.

At long last, the deranged maniac got out from under Nacho, whereupon I continued to yell profanities and disbelieving questions at him. "What were you thinking? What didn't you understand about my simple instructions? Did you know I used to be a nefarious gang member!?"

After the moron finished hastily slapping our hub back together, I grabbed our transmission and put it in the back of the van. I crawled under Nacho and placed all of the nuts and bolts in a plastic box and set them inside for later, and then used several ratchet straps to hold the axles and the engine up, which he had left hanging without any support. Once Nacho was sufficiently buttoned up, I went back to our temporary home – a farm with a guesthouse called *Hospedaje La Violeta* – and told our host, Luis, about what had happened.

As evening fell, Luis and I snuck over to Nacho by cover of dusk and hitched a tow strap to the front bumper. Without being detected by the deranged mechanic, despite operating under his bedroom window, we slipped away to the relative safety of Luis' gated farm. When we reached the farm, several of the young men who helped out on the farm joined in pushing Nacho through the wooden gate leading to our small cabin on the edge of a eucalyptus grove. With Nacho out of harm's way, Sheena and I slipped into our cabin where, for night after night, I would dream that I was Barbara Walters chasing the elusive truth within the deranged mind of the mechanic of Susacón.

# 37

*Susacón, Colombia — June, by Brad*

In my fourth year of engineering school I decided to do an independent study project. This meant I would choose a problem, and then engineer a solution to it while reporting my progress to my academic advisor. Initially I felt inclined to improve the aerodynamics of a rotating bicycle wheel—a problem that keeps us all awake at night, I'm sure. At the last minute, my advisor mentioned that an off-grid ranch near Flagstaff wanted to switch their power supply from a diesel generator to a hybrid of solar and wind power. They just needed a sucker to design the system for them. Wait a minute, *I* was a sucker, I thought. This would be perfect for me! I chose the ranch project and walked out of my advisor's office with a stack of books.

I will wave my arm and say that many things happened, and at the end of the semester I had over-engineered the process in a big way. In an effort to optimize *everything*, I had written a full library of computer code to do everything from product performance simulation, to weather prediction and statistical analysis. My advisor told me I should commercialize what I had done.

I will again wave my arm and say that many things happened and my social life suffered. A few years and several programming languages later, I had started a business and commercialized my software. A short while later my company was acquired, I quit my day job, and overnight I went from being a designer of medical products to being a renewable energy software development manager.

So what's the point, and why am I not talking about our trip? Because I want to demonstrate that sometimes things happen in our lives that seem trivial, but they can alter our path in unexpected ways. This is what happened the day Nacho's transmission went belly up three miles from a small Colombian mountain village.

By our original plan we should have been sitting around a campfire with our friends in Villa de Leyva, laughing at things so funny that expensive cognac would be shooting from our noses while watching a beautiful sunset and looking so chic in our turtleneck sweaters. Instead we rescued Nacho from the grasp of a demented maniac, retreated to the safety of a gated farm, and spent the first night teetering on the ragged edge of a nervous breakdown. In Guatemala we were stranded for a week and it was devastating. We had heard about a couple of fellow Volkswagen travelers who had suffered a transmission failure in Honduras, and it had taken nearly 70 days to get back on the road. By all estimations we were in for a hellish time.

For starters, there are a few things to know about Colombia, Vanagons, and why breaking down in the latter while visiting the former is a bad thing. The first thing to know is that there are more unicorns in Colombia than Vanagons. In a place where Vanagon sightings make tabloid news, finding parts for our transmission would be virtually impossible. Next, the Colombian government recently passed a law prohibiting the importation of used car parts. New parts can be imported, but they are taxed as high as 50% of their retail value. Yes, even if you're leaving the country with said parts in a matter of days. The last thing to know is that new Vanagon transmissions don't exist. They haven't been produced in many, many moons, and so the only way forward is to buy rebuilt ones. When I say *rebuilt*, you should hear *used*.

After a couple of evenings we had identified three options for getting ourselves out of this mess.

## Option #1: Bring our failed transmission to an inept local mechanic to be rebuilt, locally, and ineptly

When we got back to the farm and got settled in, I took a closer look at our transmission to see what had happened. The reason we stopped moving forward was immediately apparent. The input shaft, which connects the engine to the transmission, connects to the transmission's gears by a grooved metal sleeve, held in place by a circlip and a threaded rod. Somehow, the circlip had come off, the threaded rod backed out, and the sleeve slipped out of the way. With nothing holding the input shaft in line, it had gone all willy nilly. This willy nillyness caused the input shaft to melt the main transmission oil seal and destroy the oil slinger. At this point, Nacho's mojo leaked out and he voided his bowels.

After removing the bell housing from the transmission, I noticed that the ring and pinion gears were missing a couple of teeth, and the ones that remained intact were so pitted and cracked that it made a meth addict seem like a Colgate poster girl. To go the local rebuild route, they would have to import a new ring and pinion, input shaft, oil slinger, seal, and whatever else might have been wrong inside of the gear cluster. By my estimation, this would take a month and would cost at least as much as a new transmission stateside. Given the ineptness of the local mechanics, they would probably make all new parts out of beer cans and solder, and our transmission would fail again within a few hundred miles.

## Option #2: Buy a rebuilt transmission in the USA, ship it to Colombia on a cargo plane

You will recall that ordering a rebuilt transmission and having it sent to Colombia is illegal. No problem, those are the rules, and rules are made to be bent. We would just buy the transmission from a rebuilder who could be coerced into lying on our receipt to say it was new. What are the chances a customs agent would be able to tell the difference? We found that Aeromexico had cargo planes going from LAX to Bogota, and could carry our transmission for the low cost of $330 plus import taxes. We would just have to figure out how to get it to LAX, and bingo bango.

Almost bingo bango. Turns out you can't just go into the cargo port and pay your import taxes. That would be too easy. Instead you have to hire a professional customs broker to do the process for you. After calling around, I found that customs brokers only deal with freight forwarding companies, and not individuals such as myself. I considered incorporating my own Colombian customs brokerage for the occasion, but it seemed like a wildly inefficient idea.

## Option #3: Buy a rebuilt transmission from the USA and put it on a drug lord's motor boat

I'm being a little hyperbolic here, but the third option is a little on the shady side. We were told about a freight forwarder in Miami that could export used car parts to Colombia. I don't know how, and I didn't ask. All I would have to do is buy a rebuilt transmission and have it trucked to this company in Miami. They would then put it on a ship, which would take it to Colombia's North coast. At this point it would somehow go through customs, and be placed on another truck that would take it to Bogota, where I would pick it up and bring it to Susacón on a bus. By my estimation this would take about a month, and would cost somewhere around $1,000 in shipping all said and done.

For a week Sheena and I weighed our options, I made phone calls to Bogota and the USA, spoke to customs brokers, posed questions on internet forums, begrudgingly spoke to Latin American car mechanics, and generally tried to figure out what the heck to do. The more I found out, the less I liked our options. I just wanted it to be easy, but that was option #4, and so far we hadn't identified that option. As the days passed, we became more and more comfortable at the farm.

Our accommodations were in a private cabin on the outskirts of the village, at the edge of a eucalyptus grove. Out our front door, beyond the eucalyptus trees were several varieties of fruit trees, heavy with fresh fruit ripe for the picking. Sheena spent much of her free time picking figs and figuring out different ways of making dessert out of them. Our patio overlooked a meadow of tall green grass with weeping willow trees, grazing dairy cows, and little frolicking baby cows. On our second day a baby cow was born a stone's throw from out patio. For our little cabin we paid $25 per night.

Each day, our hosts Hernando and Constanza would show up at our door bearing housewarming gifts. Some days they would have a pitcher of fresh squeezed juice from one of their fruit trees, or a platter of fresh fruit. One day Hernando dropped off a bag of fresh coffee that he had just roasted using beans from a neighboring farm. Constanza dropped off a bowl of freshly ground beef from one of their cows so that we could make barbequed hamburgers on the wood fired grill. They brought over a bowl of dessert figs that Constanza made, lighting a fig fire inside of Sheena that would prove impossible to extinguish.

Once we discovered the bounty available from the surrounding farms, we began to subsist entirely on things that came from within the village. We bought peaches from the farm up the hill, raw coffee beans from the farm down the canyon, which I would roast in a pan, fresh honey from another farmer, and fruits and vegetables from the Monday market. After discovering that Hernando and Constanza had fresh beef from their cows, we kept ourselves in good supply of filet mignon for the grill. For around $30 per week we stayed stocked up on fresh local food and ate like kings. Well, a king and a queen.

Our evenings were spent barbequing, watching fireflies in our meadow, and curling up to watch movies. We awoke each morning to sunlight filling our cabin through the curtains, followed by a tired stumble through the meadow to fill up our morning milk pitcher directly from the cow's udder. Somehow, the importance of choosing an option for how to fix our transmission seemed a distant second to living the good life.

Each morning Sheena and I donned our running shoes and stole away into the hills surrounding Susacón. We ran out the back of the farm, up the cobbled track that leads past the pigs, under the giant willows, and past the monument to the revolutionaries who marched this way on their way to the Battle of Boyacá. We ran up a steep hill until we met the dirt road that wound its way through the forested hillsides toward Chicamocha canyon. We ran under cover of eucalyptus and willow trees, passed by raspberry bushes, agave, and prickly pear cactus. Each day we saw the same old woman with her bowler cap and woolen shawl, who asked us how we were dong, told us how wonderful the day was, and asked how we were liking Susacón. After cresting the hill, we descended into a meadow where the track wound past two large weeping willows before disappearing around a bend; a Monet painting in real life.

One morning, Hernando offered to bring us hiking in the mountains above Chicamocha canyon. To get there we drove the road where we took our morning runs, but this time continued until we reached the edge of the canyon. There, his aunt lived in a picturesque house with a commanding view of the Susacón valley. After coffee and a couple of shots of a local liqueur, we continued on our way along the rim of Chicamocha. When we reached a landslide blocking the road, we left the car and hiked to a peak overlooking the canyon.

After telling us about the area and pointing out the places where his family had historically operated farms in the surrounding hills, Hernando left us and headed back to town in his car. Sheena and I would laze about for a while, have a picnic on the edge of the canyon, and then hike back to town. As we sat, we talked about how much we'd fallen in love with Colombia. Being stranded in Susacón was really a blessing and we didn't much care to leave.

On the hike down, Sheena and I begrudgingly brought up the topic of what to do about our transmission. Cycling through our options made my head hurt. Nothing was going to be easy, and nothing would be cheap. I thought about driving around the world with a transmission rebuilt by a deranged maniac and it made my stomach turn.

"Why don't we just go home and pick up a transmission ourselves?" Sheena asked. The idea had come up before, but it was likely the most expensive option and it didn't make any logistical sense. We reiterated this and put the idea away. We hiked on in silence. I turned the idea over in my mind as we walked through the eucalyptus and weeping willows, the raspberries and the stone fences. I thought about how much this place seemed like Northern California or Oregon.

It was true, going home would be expensive and there would be easier ways of getting a new transmission. But why not go home? It would cost more money, sure, but it would be refreshing. We could catch up with friends and family, reacquaint ourselves with American pizza, Mexican food, mountain biking and microbrewed beer. Colombia would be an easy country to come back to. In the end, which path would make us the happiest?

"So, what do you think about going home?" I said, to which Sheena's eyes almost popped out of her head. "Let's do it!" And just like that, we had created our own Option #4 and had selected it. Three days later we would be hopping on a plane from Bogota bound for Phoenix, retracing seven months of driving in a single day. It's funny how one thing can lead to another.

# 38

*Arizona, United States — July, by Brad*

Standing on a granite boulder in the middle of the creek, my neon green fly line whipped back and forth in ten-and-two motions overhead. In one final throw, I set the fly upstream of a large boulder and let the current carry it past what was sure to be an underwater lair filled with hungry fish. Moments later my line was taut, having coaxed a large native brown trout out from under the boulder. After a short battle, it jerked hard and broke my line. Sheena and Lauren had given us one mandate before we stepped out the door: bring back enough trout to eat for dinner. After two hours of fishing in Sedona's Oak Creek Canyon, we had managed to catch and release a couple dozen six inchers, and the one dinner-sized one had gotten away.

Later, while standing downstream of the bridge to Garland's Cabins, a vacationing Mexican family walked past me and stopped to watch. I put a halt to my unfruitful fishing and excitedly recounted to them how we had left Mexico five months ago, and that I had spent every night since then crying myself to sleep thinking about the Mexican food we'd left behind.

I told them how on my recent flight home I had stopped over in Hermosillo, Mexico, with only one thing on my mind. I described how after the plane had landed, I had bolted away from the airport on foot, how the heat had enveloped me as I left the terminal, and how the air smelled like nostalgia. I was alone; for reasons not worth mentioning Sheena was on a different flight. Despite the absence of my navigator, I knew where to find my fix. I ducked into the first neighborhood I came across looking for a dealer who could feed my addiction. I wandered only a short time before finding what had been haunting my dreams, like a crack addict finding his next fix. As I approached the open air taco stand the husband, wife, and son were just setting up for the day. It was eight o'clock in the morning, the crock pots of beef and pork let off a hint of chili-scented steam. I dropped my backpack and melted into a familiar red plastic chair. A fly buzzed around the table, and the wife started slapping dough between her hands to form the fresh tortillas that would be the foundation for the many tacos on which I would gorge myself. The endorphins coursing through my veins put me into a stationary runner's high. True happiness, I told the family as they sat on the bridge straddling Oak Creek, is a Mexican taco stand.

We returned empty handed to Mike and Lauren's cabin on the banks of Oak Creek. Fortunately, Lauren was an avid reader of our blog, and knew that this would happen. She and Sheena had gone to the store while we were out, and nodded an unsurprised nod as Mike and I came through the door with nothing but our fishing rods. Without grocery stores we would have starved to death long ago.

With gas in our borrowed little car and freedom in our little hearts, we had set off from Phoenix to the Great White North: our adopted hometown of Flagstaff. After a quick and, given all of the excellent establishments we could have chosen, utterly unexplainable stop at Carl's Junior, we knocked on the door of our good friends Brigit and Bret. We had crashed at their downtown home for the week prior to our departure, and when we arrived our room was just as we had left it; the same books were stacked on the desk, and the Flight of the Concords poster hung inanimately on the wall next to the bed. Bret, a magician when it comes to baking, hastily got to work making a fresh batch of his famous chocolate chip cookies.

In an uncanny display of perfect timing, we had arrived in Flagstaff just in time for the annual *Clips of Faith* festival; an outdoor gathering to celebrate brews and short films put on by New Belgium Brewing Company. Accompanied by our friends Nathan and Claire we made our way over to the park, bought a handful of wooden tokens, and passed the evening sipping remarkable beer, catching up with friends, and being entertained by this year's selection of short films.

The day after Clips of Faith we decided to continue the merrymaking on our own. Being that the New Belgium crew was already in town, we threw together a beer tasting at Nathan's house and invited some people from New Belgium Brewing Company. Nathan supplied a few bottles from a recent business trip to the East coast, while Grant, a New Belgium sales rep, supplied several experimental brews from the brewery and an especially rare and expensive bottle of 2002 Stone Vertical Epic, of which he had found an entire case buried in his garage. Matt, a brewer from New Belgium, spent the evening ensuring that our palates were well calibrated to the treats he expertly brewed up back in Fort Collins.

We spent our time in Flagstaff catching up with good friends and eating good food. We paid the exorbitant price of $18 for a hamburger and a drink at Diablo Burger, had the world's best breakfast burritos at Tacos Los Altos, induced food coma over a plate of Fratelliquiles at Martanne's, and gave ourselves wasabi head rushes at Karma Sushi.

The climax of our "Reacquainting with Long Forgotten Foods of Home" tour was a visit to our favorite restaurant, the Himalayan Grill. Arriving for dinner was like coming home from war; Ramesh welcomed us with a huge smile, Jit came out of the kitchen to chat and hear about our trip, and Karan and Jyotsna told us all about their newborn son. Ramesh brought me a beer from a local brewery, and Karan made Sheena a melon flavored cocktail, which he delivered with a big smile. "I always wanted to be a bartender in New York when I was growing up. This is a drink I made up." The food, as usual, was awesome.

As we headed for the door, Ramesh corralled us into the bar and sat us down. "We must drink a toast!" Several shots of tequila and rum later, we were fully toasted and ready to walk home. As I clambered out of the bar to pay for our meal, Ramesh waved his hand. "We're glad to see you, it's on the house!" He then reached behind the register and produced a bag containing two dinners to go; Sheena's favorite: *saag paneer*. "Now you don't have to cook tomorrow," he said, as he whisked us out the door. Some people just exude awesomeness.

After the first couple of weeks at home it was clear that the fourth option was the right one. I was enjoying a much needed respite from Vanagon maintenance and transmission problems, and a steady diet comprising mostly Mexican food had put a temporary end to me crying myself to sleep. While it is no exaggeration that true happiness is a Mexican taco stand, there is no denying the fact that no number of taco stands can rival the happiness that time spent with friends and family can deliver. Now, if only traveling halfway across a hemisphere could heal a man's inability to catch a fish worthy of eating.

# 39

*Cave Creek, Arizona — July, by Sheena*

When we began our quest last January, a loaf of banana bread, a few slices of quiche, and a bag of my aunt's cream cheese cutout cookies were safely stashed in one of Nacho's cabinets. When I ate the last slice of quiche somewhere along a deserted highway in Baja California, I had a strange sensation of helplessness as I realized I was devouring the last tangible piece of home.

Fortunately the mind is a vault, and the sensations, emotions, and experiences tied to this place we call home are easily recalled. Within a split second, I'm home. When I close my eyes, I am back at my doorstep on Skyline drive. In the foreground, Black Mountain rises high in the crisp blue sky. The smell of desert rain is irresistibly and deliciously potent, and from every direction, the long reaching shadows of saguaros paint the volcanic rock. Rabbits and families of quail scurry through the cholla cactus and aloe vera patches. And inside, saltillo tiles lead to the kitchen and the aroma of banana bread from the oven chokes the air.

And then there's my other home, two hours north, rising high above the desert. Here, the pine forest stretches for as far as the eye can see and the San Francisco Peaks create a backdrop to our home. When I step outside of our dollhouse in the valley, I stand and stare. I've come out the front door to the sight of massive herd of elk bugling on the hillside. I run alongside the river, flowers in bloom, briefly stopping at the pond to catch my breath and to watch the mother duck and her trail of babies, bottoms up, scanning through the depths of the water for food.

This July I'm not dreaming anymore. Our impromptu trip home lands us back in Brad's home town of Prescott just in time for the 4th of July festivities. Brad's family and mine gather en masse, grilling up hot dogs, burgers, and corn on the cob. In true Southwest fashion, mounds of guacamole, spicy salsa, tortilla chips, and salt rimmed margaritas line the flagstone countertop.

Farther down the desolate back roads in Prescott, more relatives spoil us with their delightful food.

July is also the perfect time to visit the Red Rocks of Sedona and the overflowing blackberry bushes that line Oak Creek. After a wonderful day of mountain biking, Brad and our good friend Mike insist that they can catch us some trout for dinner. In return for their hard labor, Mike's girlfriend Lauren and I will make them a blackberry pie and fudge. While they fish, we put on our pants and long sleeved shirts, ready to put in a good fight with the massive web of thorny blackberry bushes. We lay down planks of wood through the bushes, gaining us access through the mess until we leave in victory, bowls full of lusciously ripe blackberries in hand. It's no big surprise that Brad and Mike return home empty handed from their fishing trip, but we gorge ourselves on blackberry pie nonetheless.

Back in the desert, my list of nostalgic things to eat is satisfied in its entirety, and Brad's is too. He requests that we make it to Barro's Pizza, where history took place here for the two of us. It seemed like a decade ago, and in reality it was. During high school he'd come in and watch me work while dipping fat slices of pepperoni pizza into ranch dressing.

My mom toils away in the kitchen, cooking up batches of banana bread, quiche, and French toast. Most certainly, if I were to make a cookbook of family recipes, these would easily be the top three. I wonder what foods make home "home" for other people, so I asked Brad. Chilaquiles from Martanne's, curries from the Himalayan grill, our homemade burgers on the grill, and our daily cappuccinos from our home espresso bar.

Our trip back home is fulfilling in so many ways. The food only adds to the enjoyment we receive by our unexpected visit with friends and family. We never know where life will take us, but there will always be a special place in our minds for memories of home.

# 40

*Bogotá, Colombia — July, by Brad*

Although we were having all kinds of fun, it had come down to game time. We were home for a reason, and we couldn't avoid it any longer. We needed to pick up a transmission, put it in a suitcase, check it onto an airplane, and somehow get it through Customs in Colombia without being caught. Since being home, we had also managed to acquire an eighth grade girl's weight in other car parts, fishing equipment, clothing, and more car parts. We knew it would require a great deal of savvy and luck to pull it off, so we trained for it in the only way we knew how: we played horseshoes to hone our precision, and we rode our bikes to build our endurance. We saw a large billboard on the side of the road in Prescott that proclaimed in bold letters "Guns are why America is still free." This billboard seemed to associate guns with freedom, which we were going to need, so we got some guns and shot some little clay disks. We were willing to try anything for the promise of freedom.

Our first step was to swing by the shop and pick up our transmission. I was pleased to see how shiny and clean it looked; this would play a key role in my ability to lie my way through Customs in the event that I was caught trying to smuggle a used transmission into Colombia, which of course, is illegal.

Next, we had to pack it up. We needed to make it as small as possible so as to fly under the radar of the Colombian Customs agents, and we needed it to be light. The maximum weight allowed for a checked bag, regardless of how many crisp Benjamins you flash in front of the ticket agent's face, is one hundred pounds. I decided to remove the bell housing to make it sleek like supermodel, and then build a slim wooden box in its place to protect the input shaft. With any luck the box would survive a fall from the airplane's cargo door. Just to be sure, I wrapped the thing in a whole bunch of bubble wrap. We didn't want to sneak through Customs only to discover that we had a trashed transmission again, so we used wood and plastic. Nature *and* science.

My original idea had been to try to bring the transmission in my carry-on bag. Everyone said I was crazy, but it made good sense to me. First of all, it would save us $350 in overweight baggage fees. I mean seriously, who has ever had to weigh their carry-on? All I would have to do is put the transmission in a backpack, and then pretend that the backpack weighed less than twenty pounds so that no official types would think anything was fishy. Then, I would have to ensure that I could lift the transmission over my head and place it in the overhead compartment, while not leading on that it weighed more than twenty pounds. And lastly, I would have to hope that the overhead compartment didn't come crashing down, killing someone's child. That would make all of my sneaky heavy lifting effort null and void. In the end I decided against it, but only for the children.

Finally the day had come. Sheena went on her merry way to United Airlines carrying two checked bags. In those bags were many illicit objects, including a transmission bell housing, a new starter, some new LED interior puck lights, new spark plug wires, a clutch master and slave cylinder, a new flyfishing rod, a spare alternator regulator, some new brake lines, and a few other odds and ends. Her bags were, in short, Customs lightning rods.

In my bags, things were looking no better. I went off to the Aeromexico counter carrying a transmission, two salvaged rear hub housings made of rusty cast iron, a slightly modified and very rusty catalytic converter, two stub axles, a fancy air filter, a timing light that looked just like a gun, and some corrosive fluids. All very illegal. My bag containing the transmission ended up weighing 94.5 pounds. Just under the legal limit. When the nice Aeromexico ticket agent weighed my bag, she looked rather shocked. She told me, pity in her eyes, that I owed her

$350. I nicely asked her in her native tongue if she would give me another twenty pounds for free, and she instantly obliged, knocking $100 off of my fee. Things were going great so far! Good thing we shot those guns!

The trip to Colombia went off uneventfully. My stopover in Hermosillo was too short to dart out to the taco stand like last time, but I did manage to gorge myself on tacos on my second stopover in Mexico City. Poor Sheena ate at an American chain restaurant in Houston, and nothing more.

When I stepped off the plane in Bogota, Sheena was waiting for me at baggage claim. She already had her bags full of illegal contraband, and waited patiently while I recovered mine. I found a note on my bag saying that US Customs had seized something from inside the bag. I unzipped it in a panic, and quickly found that they had only stolen my brake fluid and the cleaning agent for my new washable air filter. I zipped it back up, swallowed hard, and Sheena and I coolly walked toward the exit.

"Don't worry, Sheena," I said, "I shot a gun before we left. We *will* have freedom."

Everything was going great and soon enough we could see the exit doors; the rays of light streamed through the plate glass like bullets from a freedom gun. As we approached the Customs agents, a mere fifty feet from the exit doors, I whispered for Sheena to look straight ahead and be cool. I casually checked my watch, sighed, and pretended to see someone I knew outside. This gave me a reason not to make eye contact with the agents. And then, all at once, we were accosted. An agent stepped in front of us and pointed to the x-ray machine. His gaze said it all: "I know you're smugglers, you sons of bitches!"

We pretended it was no big deal, and walked to the x-ray machine with our 244.5 pounds of illegal imports. Sheena put her bags on the conveyor first, and I helped her stand them on their sides in just such a way so that the bell housing would be less obvious, and the starter would look less like a bomb. I hefted my transmission onto the belt next, followed by my hubs, axles, catalytic converter, and gun-like timing light. I stared at the agent behind the computer, trying to avert her gaze from the screen using extra sensory perception.

*Look away…look away…look away…look—*

"We have something here! We have something here!" She looked around, hand in the air, calling for backup. Sheena and I looked at each other; we had seen *Broke Down Castle*, and knew that these situations usually ended up with the smugglers spending the rest of their lives in an all-women's Thai jail. The agent spun the screen around so I could see it. Sheena's bags were still in view, but she was pointing at mine.

"What is this!?" She seemed angry, pointing directly at the transmission. I tried to think of something quickly that would make her believe that indeed this was not a car part. Anything but a car part. If she knew it was a car part, it would be all over. Our illusion of freedom would disintegrate like the crumbling walls of an all-women's Thai jail.

"Uh…it's a car part." *Doh!* "It's…um…it's a transmission for a car." *Doh! Doh!*

She moved the conveyor, burping Sheena's illegal contraband out the end. "These are car parts TOO!," she said, pointing at my next bag containing a whole gaggle of car parts. As the woman continued to call for backup, I gave Sheena the nod. She quickly snatched her bags and speed walked out the door and into the street. It had only been a few seconds, but I could no longer remember what freedom tasted like. Whoever made that gun billboard was a liar and a moron.

A woman named Alicia, someone I would come to know all too well over the course of my Customs incarceration, led me across the linoleum floor to the DIAN office. "Everyone fears the DIAN," Constanza would later tell us. "They are the IRS of Colombia. Everybody must pay the DIAN."

I sat in an uncomfortable chair against the wall while I watched a young man being humiliated by a DIAN agent as he pulled illegal electric motors from his suitcase. "They are for my father's business," he said. *Your father can't save you. You're in DIAN now, son!* I waited my turn, what seemed like hours. I would have to get used to waiting, as I was now a common criminal in the Colombian DIAN justice system. Just another scumbag smuggler, trying to outsmart The Man.

"Car part smuggler? DIAN will deal with you now."

# 41

*Bogotá, Colombia — July, by Brad*

"What are these car parts?" I had been sitting at the DIAN office for hours as Alicia tirelessly entered information about my illegally smuggled goods into her computer. One should expect nothing less from a Colombian version of the IRS. Sheena still sat outside on a concrete island in between two lanes of traffic, studiously reading her e-book.

"In the one bag I have a transmission. The other suitcase has wheel bearings, nothing more." I was lying, but only because I didn't think it mattered. It probably made no difference to Alicia, on whom the difference between a hub, a stub axle, a catalytic converter and a wheel bearing would be lost anyway.

"And what is the value?" I just wanted to get out of there, so I made something up. "The transmission is about $700, and the wheel bearings are $85." It was my second mistake, because at the time I didn't know that I would have to back it up with official proof. I was digging myself a deep hole. After a few hours of paperwork and computer entries, all I had to do was go to the Cargo Port and pay my import taxes.

"Just tell them that the parts are *elementos de arte oficio*," a random stranger told me as I left the building. "Otherwise you'll have to pay high taxes." I told him I didn't understand. "You're only allowed to enter the country with personal items. If you're a tennis player and you enter with a tennis racket, this is an *elemento de arte oficio*. It's something that you use to perform your hobby. It's a personal item. Just tell them you're a mechanic and these things are for you to perform your hobby. They're like your tennis racket."

At the cargo port, I was told to find an agent, give them my Customs papers, and pay the associated taxes. According to Alicia, I should be suckling the sweet milk of Freedom's teat by day's end. I promptly found a customs agent, handed him my papers, and told him I was there to settle my debt. "It should be quick," I said, "these are *elementos de arte oficio*." He mustered a contrite giggle. "Sorry, I don't think so," he said. So much for that idea. And not only was he sorry about my lame attempt to sidestep the laws of The Man, but furthermore I was not even allowed to handle payment of my own import taxes. I would have to employ the services of a customs broker, or find someone who lived in Colombia with a commercial license to act as a customs broker. Importing my contraband-ridden suitcases basically involved the same process as importing our van.

Day one came to an end and our transmission was still on lockdown in the DIAN office at the airport. I regretted not pepper spraying the Customs Agent and making a run for the door when I had the chance. That evening I put out the word on our Facebook page that we needed help, and a few hours later we were in luck. The coworker of a friend of one of our Facebook followers would meet us the following morning and accompany us to the Cargo Port to pay our simple fee. DIAN had gone too far this time – we had gone to three degrees of separation for help.

Omar met us in front of our house at nine o'clock in the morning where we hailed a really expensive cab. Upon arriving at the Cargo Port, we were told that we must use a special software program to fill out more paperwork before we could pay the import tax. They had a computer with the software that we could use, but no user manual. The efforts of Omar, a professional importer, and me, a professional software designer, were useless against the confusing and non-user-friendly DIAN software. Recognizing our conundrum, we opted to visit a customs broker in Bogotá to see if they could help. Another expensive taxi ride ensued, and we soon found ourselves sitting in the broker's office. The prognosis? In three days we could have our illegal contraband, and it would cost us $180 on top of the import fees. We declined the nice agent's offer and took another expensive taxi ride back to the Cargo Port, where we withered away the rest of the day. On our way out of the building to hail another expensive taxi, we found a mysterious fortune teller type named Miss Ofelia who could meet us in an internet café the next day and fill out our paperwork for a fee of $90.

The next morning Omar took another day off of work and met us at the internet café. I was armed with fake Photoshop receipts for my transmission and "wheel bearings," reflecting the exact values I had reported to Customs. Miss Ofelia clicked away on the computer for a couple of hours, eventually producing separate sets of paperwork for each illegal item I was importing. All I had to do was bring them to the Customs Agent to pay my taxes.

Of course, it couldn't be so easy. When I presented the papers to the Customs Agent I was told I could only pay my taxes at the bank, and that I should bring my receipt back to him get another official receipt with a stamp on it. Only then could I bring that receipt to DIAN where more paperwork could be done.

I went to the bank and paid my import taxes – another $200 – but I couldn't get a receipt because the computer system was down. After a few hours the system returned, I got my receipt, and we headed to the DIAN office at the airport. Now it was time for Alicia to actually inspect my bags to be sure everything was as I said it was.

Together we inspected the transmission. She looked at it cluelessly as I described what it did and ensured her that it was brand new and not used. Next it was time to inspect my pack of lies – suitcase number two. When I opened it, Alicia looked so disgusted I thought she would lurch all over my stuff. She looked at the pile of rusty parts and the timing light that looked like a gun. "Those parts are all used. It's illegal to import used car parts. And is that a gun?" I tried to explain how the hubs and stub axles were somehow actually wheel bearings. I placed a stub axle into one of the hubs and spun it, "See? It spins, so it's a wheel bearing." I next tried to explain that the catalytic converter didn't really count, and that I'd forgotten about the timing gun. After a few minutes of my backpedaling she finally took pity on me.

"I didn't see anything," she said. "Just wrap up those parts so I can't see them. I never saw anything." Next, she grabbed the catalytic converter and handed it to me. "Put this in your bag. It was never in the suitcase at all. I never saw it. Also, take this gun, throw away the packaging, and put it in your bag."

Somehow rules were being bent in our favor. We had out-patienced the Colombian IRS! I walked out of the quarantine room with a backpack full of undocumented contraband, watched Alicia type some more information into the computer, and then I was handed a piece of official-looking paper.

"You're free to go," she said. All at once the taste of freedom came rushing back and I remembered what liberation felt like. I grabbed my suitcases and wheeled them out the back door into the overcast, chilly air of Bogotá, handing my official papers to the police guard at the door. All said, including airline baggage fees, import taxes, paperwork fees, and three days of taxi rides, it had cost us $721 to get our transmission and other assorted parts from the USA to Colombia.

After a daylong car trip from Bogotá to Susacón with Hernando and Constanza, it was time to get back to work. We reacquainted ourselves with our little cabin and took a day to relax. We stocked up on firewood and filet mignon for the grill – we weren't here to rough it, after all – and prepared ourselves for the work ahead.

As a warm up for installing the transmission, I decided to start off by replacing our rear hub housings, stub axles, and wheel bearings. We'd had two wheel bearing failures in close succession in Mexico and Guatemala, and I wanted to be sure that those were behind us. I installed the salvaged hub housings and stub axles from my smuggled inventory, and replaced the wheel bearings for good measure.

The next step was to remove our air conditioner. I never bothered to hook up the wires to get it working properly, but after much thought decided to remove it altogether. We've found that whenever we get into a new climate, it takes about a week to get used to it. After that, the weather doesn't bother us and we stay relatively comfortable. But air conditioning, while quite comfortable, insulates us from the environment. As long as there is air conditioning to come back to, we never adapt to the weather and are always in a state of discomfort. Besides its extra weight and the downside of halting climate adaptation, it also served to be in the way of me accessing the left side of the engine. Once I got it all out on the ground I felt a lot better, and in the process Nacho lost about fifty pounds.

Over the ensuing days I fixed all manner of things that had been troubling us mechanically; I rebuilt our CV joints and safety wired the bolts, replaced the starter, rebuilt the front brake calipers, replaced all of the brake hardware, springs, and front brake hoses, installed a manual battery separator switch, and serviced the rear brakes.

To my dismay, but not disbelief, I found that the deranged mechanic of Susacón had sabotaged my driver's side rear brake while he was in the process of sabotaging my transmission. When I removed the rear brake drum on that side, I found that he hadn't bothered to tighten the bolts that hold the brake system to the hub housing. And while he was at it, he stole both of my brake shoe return springs. Hernando volunteered to go over to his shop to get them back, but the maniac denied everything. Instead, I was forced to manufacture new return springs using things we found on or near the farm. I knew that watching MacGyver would pay off some day.

Finally I had procrastinated enough and it was time to install our new transmission. Since trying to borrow a jack from the local mechanic had backfired, I decided to try it without a proper jack. I rigged up a series of ratchet straps instead, which would allow me to hoist the transmission into place. I replaced the pilot bearing, clutch, and pressure plate, and then hoisted the transmission. The ratchet straps turned out to be less than ideal for the job, so I had to position myself under the tranny and basically hump it into place using my pelvis. It was the most grotesque thing I ever did to a tranny.

In the last few weeks before the transmission failure, the starter had occasionally ignored my pleas to start. I took the initiative to replace it as well before it left us stranded. With everything in place I turned the key and pumped life into Nacho for the first time in six weeks. Everything went great until I depressed the clutch and tried to shift. From Nacho's belly the sound of crunching metal emanated. Something was totally whack with the transmission. After much debate and many phone calls I decided to remove the transmission again to see if all was well within the bell housing. This time I located a proper jack to help me along.

After removing the transmission I found that everything was as it should be in the bell housing, although I noticed that the bracket that stabilizes the clutch slave cylinder was, and always had been missing. At this realization I sprung into action and employed my blacksmithing skills to create a new bracket out of a piece of steel I found in the barn. I also noticed that the reason for the metal grinding was an incorrectly installed clutch throw out arm. I fixed the arm and got everything ready to reinstall.

With the jack, the installation went much more smoothly the second time. I jacked that puppy into place, reattached the CV joints and safety wired them in place, and then bolted all of the other associated doo-dads in place. I re-bled the clutch one more time for good measure and fired Nacho up. This time when I changed gears I heard nothing but Nacho's deep purr.

Later on I did a full tune up; new fuel filter, spark plugs and wires, new air filter, distributor rotor, and a new idle stabilizer. I finished it all off by adjusting the timing to add a few extra hamster wheels to Nacho's total power, and then took it for a test drive. Cruising the streets of Susacón filled me with a sense of liberation akin to that of Timothy Robbins after he'd crept through the sewers and stumbled into the forest in *Shawshank Redemption*. On my way back to the farm I passed the deranged mechanic of Susacón walking on the sidewalk. Our eyes connected for a split second and it felt like I was staring into the devil's soul. When I got home, Sheena and I celebrated with a barbeque and some Club Colombia beer.

The following morning we loaded Nacho and said goodbye to Luis and Constanza. In a display of true Colombian hospitality, they told us we could stay in their home in Bogotá for as long as we wanted as a liberation gift. We locked up the cabin, pointed Nacho's big, dumb, blunt nose out of the farm gate, and slowly pulled out onto the winding mountain road toward Bogotá. Susacón, it's been lovely. Maybe one day we'll meet again.

# 42

*Susacón, Colombia — July, by Sheena*

Dozens of figs had swelled to a purple mass, soft to the touch, and desperately hung on to their stems for dear life. Literally, it was a race with the birds. The ripest fruits were already pecked to death, left hanging to taunt us with what we had failed to discover in time. Birds had wings, but we had sticks. Hernando had warned me to be careful when picking the figs from up high because they leaked a sticky white sap when broken free. I stood on my tip toes, arm fully extended, beating the figs free from their stems. I wanted those fruits, badly.

I had at least a week to burn while waiting for Brad to maneuver Nacho's new transmission back in place, plus a laundry list of other projects to increase Nacho's mojo. I started the day as I started every day, by running through the eucalyptus trees and alongside the fields of grazing cows and corn fields. At my turning around point, I stared out at the countryside in utter disbelief of its beauty. I continued, stopping to greet the many families of baby cows and the truck driver who passed me every day on his way to drop off his workers to tend to the sheep.

I found myself reflecting on the impressions that most Americans have about this country: that it is defined by cocaine and violence. There is no denying that both of these things exist, but there's no sign of them here, and it's hard to even imagine that they exist in this peaceful and beautiful place. They certainly don't represent Colombia as a whole.

When I returned home each day, Brad would already be working on the vehicle and would stop briefly when I yelled breakfast was ready. For the remainder of the day, the Olympics played in the background while I painted, basked in the sun, watched the cows, cooked, wandered through the yard, or kept Brad company. The extra special days were those when Constanza and Hernando took the time to show me how to cook up some local dishes.

Before we left Susacón the first time around, I attempted to cook dessert figs. I failed miserably and realized I needed some expert advice. Cos accepted the role and tutored me on how to cook figs in sugar water, infused with cloves and cinnamon. While the figs simmered, I learned how to make a custard dessert called *Postre De Natas*.

A few days later, Hernando showed me how to make *sarapas*, a corn-based pancake. This variation was a close relative to the *arepa*, also a corn-based pancake offered on every street corner and home in Colombia. After we made a stack of a dozen or so, Hernando made hot chocolate, also a staple in the Colombian diet. Next to the spatulas and spoons in the Colombian kitchen, there is a special stirring stick made solely for mixing and frothing hot chocolate. There is heaven on this earth, and its name is Colombia.

# 43

*Quito, Ecuador — August, by Brad*

Crossing into Ecuador from Colombia marked the first time in three months that we had driven across an international border under our own power. The previous night we'd driven twelve hours, our long push culminating at a Texaco station high in the mountains where we set up camp. Shortly after our arrival all four of our tires were promptly marked by a band of rogue dogs, as happens every time we stop.

Having driven the last four hours at night, I hadn't seen a rock in the road and hit it at around 45 miles per hour. The rock flung up and hit the propane hose that feeds our stove, creating a gash that caused most of our propane to leak out. I noticed the smell as we settled down for bed, and closed the valve so as to retain what little propane was left, and to avoid waking up dead. One more thing to fix.

The following morning, after a short visit to a church built over a gorge where a crazy person claimed to have seen the Virgin Mary, we crossed into Ecuador to find the Pan-American a beautifully manicured four lane highway. We continued South to the town of Otavalo, and after a couple of uninspiring days there we were ready to say goodbye to the Northern Hemisphere.

By early afternoon we had arrived at the equator. We found a restaurant near the equatorial line, where we were welcomed by a bunch of cardboard cutouts of Dave Zimmern, the host of some American strange foods show. He had apparently stopped here and eaten a guinea pig, as evidenced by the myriad photographs, quotes, and faded cardboard cutouts of him holding said guinea pig. We spied several guinea pigs impaled on sticks over a fire, so we inquired. In a country where lunch rarely costs more than $2, we regretfully turned down the $20 price tag and instead ate what the locals were eating. The proprietor seemed extremely dismayed that we were unwilling to purchase one of her exorbitantly priced rodents. We paid the $2 for our lunch and made our way to the equator.

The equator, for all its fame and reputation, was about as interesting as a line painted on the ground. We checked it with our GPS and found it to be several feet from the real equator. It wasn't merely disappointing in the way that your children don't like The Rolling Stones as much as you do. No, it was really disappointing. Like the kind of disappointment you feel when your children quit their perfectly adequate jobs to go live in a van. This fact didn't stop us from doing silly poses and, most impressively, planking the illegitimate equator.

A few small issues had popped up with Nacho since leaving Susacón, so we decided to spend a couple of days taking care of them in Quito; one of our inner tie rod ends had developed some slop, we now had a bad propane line, and we found – to my utter dismay and disbelief – that our new transmission had come with a leaky drive flange oil seal. As we drove, the bottom of our engine and transmission were being covered by a continuous drip of gear oil, which mixed with dust to create a nice oily sludge. Fortunately I'd picked up a couple of new drive flange oil seals in Panama on a whim, so I planned to replace the leaky one and be on our way.

We drove to Quito and found an enclosed dirt parking lot in the middle of downtown where we could camp for about $3 per night. Within walking distance were a whole gaggle of restaurants serving delicious – and virtually free – meals. Middle Eastern kebabs could be had for $1.50. Indian curry with naan and rice was $4. Our favorite lunch place turned out to be a nice Italian restaurant with crisp white table cloths and well-dressed waiters. Main dishes came from the wood-fired oven in the center of the room. The standard lunch included fresh squeezed juice, an appetizer, a large bowl of soup, a well-stocked salad bar, a main course, and a dessert – all for $3. Ecuador, with its

$1.50/gallon gas and dirt cheap delicious food, was going to be a welcome relief to our budget.

I started off by repairing our propane line. As expected, none of the hardware stores carried the fitting I needed, so I improvised using things I had in the van. I ended up fixing it MacGyver style with a bolt and some plumber's tape. Next it was time to fix the transmission leak. I drained the gear oil, cut away the safety wire and removed the CV joint – laughing to myself that I had ever thought I'd be done messing with CV joints – and then removed the clips and washers that held the drive flange in. Upon removing the drive flange it was obvious that the oil seal had been pressed in crooked when it was rebuilt. I compared my new seals with the crooked one and discovered that the shop in Panama had sold me the wrong seals. What? Another inept worker in the Latin American car repair industry? Shocking!

I was unable to remove the seal without destroying it, and nothing I tried would cause it to straighten out. I cursed my luck and reassembled everything. I would have to deal with the leak, and resign myself to continually checking the oil level. It just never gets any easier!

The next day I went to several VW parts houses and found that nobody carried a tie rod for Nacho. One would have to be ordered from Guayaquil, which would take two days. It made me nervous because the parts guy never asked me what year Nacho was before placing the order over the phone, but he assured me it was the correct one. I gave it a 5% chance. In the meantime, Sheena and I decided to escape from civilization for a while, and make the trip South to go camping and hiking at Cotopaxi volcano while we waited. We'd just drive carefully so our front wheel assembly wouldn't come apart.

Getting to Cotopaxi involved traveling over several mountains at or around 14,000 feet. At this elevation, Nacho operates at about 30% power since the fuel doesn't have enough oxygen to achieve complete combustion. We repeatedly coasted down long stretches of freeway, and then chugged up long stretches in first gear. Eventually we arrived at the dirt road turnoff for Cotopaxi, which was followed by many miles of dirt road. Finally we arrived to our campsite at the base of the mountain;

the wind whipped through our the nearly-frozen tundra known as our camp, while the temperature plunged toward freezing. Our camp was at a frosty 15,000 feet in the shadow of the even frostier 20,000 foot volcano.

The following day we donned our hiking gear and set off across the treeless landscape toward the volcano. Being above the tree line allowed us to hike cross-country straight up the side of the peak. We had grandiose plans of reaching the snow line and exploring the edge of the glacier that clung to the side of the mountain, but by mid-afternoon we had only climbed a little better than half way to the snow line.

We regretfully turned around and ran down the side of the volcano in order to make it back to camp before dark. We crawled into Nacho just as the sun crested the horizon, where we cooked dinner and made tea, raising the inside temperature to sixty five degrees while outside it plunged below freezing. Sure they have mechanical problems, but you still can't beat a Vanagon for overland travel.

We opted to spend one more day at Cotopaxi, choosing this time to hike in the other direction. In a failed attempt to locate the trail on our map, we ended up hiking all day along an abandoned road bed through the mountains. This marked the second straight day of not coming across another human here in the beautiful Andes. Another comfortable night in Nacho ensued, and then we were off to collect our tie rod.

In Quito we found parking in a neighborhood close to the VW shop. I crawled under the van with two wrenches and a tie rod puller. Yes, I actually brought a tie rod puller. Five minutes later we were walking down the street with a badly worn tie rod in one hand, and virtually no chance of finding the right part in the other. As we entered the parts house, the owner reached down and grabbed the part, holding it up with a big grin on his face. I held it up to the bad tie rod and, to my disbelief, found it to be the correct part. I happily paid him and walked back to Nacho, where I crawled underneath and easily installed the new part while fútbol moms drove by and pedestrians stared.

Having had our fill of Quito, we fired up our safer and more reliable Nacho and headed West. We were ready for some surf and sun, so we bid farewell to the mountains with a smile on our faces and a drip on our transmission.

# 44

*Puerto Lopez, Ecuador — September, by Brad*

The fishing boats didn't go all that far from shore, perhaps a quarter of a mile, to a line where the sea turned from light to dark. A shelf, most likely, where the sea floor dropped off to greater depths. I sat on my knees on the paddleboard, paddling for all I was worth to get through the surf break without being toppled. In my back pocket I carried the hand line I'd rigged up; to a locking carabiner I had tied a 120 pound fishing line about twenty feet long. To the end of the leader I tied a heavy duty hook, and on it I attached the only bait I could find in the van: a hunk of Swiss-style sausage.

I wasn't interested in those hipster vegan fish. No, I was interested in the man eaters. The kind of fish that require a 120 pound fishing line and a locking carabiner; one that would be interested in eating manly nuggets of mystery meat stuffed into a piece of pig intestine. Of course a fish like this, or a shark for that matter, could easily drown me and take my paddleboard with it. For this reason I would attach the carabiner to a bungee cord, which would in turn be attached to my board. I had my dive knife at the ready for the emergency cut-and-swim.

After passing through the surf break the water became more gentle. I stood up and paddled out to sea, past the line where the water turned from light to dark. I took out my hand line, unraveled the leader and dropped the bait into the water. The line unraveled through my fingers until it was taut, and then I clipped the carabiner to my bungee cord and sat back to enjoy the warm Ecuadorian morning. For a while I sat with my legs dangling off one side of the board, and then I laid down on my back and closed my eyes. As I lay there on the board, the water gently rocking me with each passing wave, I considered the depth of the water below me. I thought about the distance these waves had traveled, and the distance we, ourselves, had traveled. Twenty feet below, the Swiss-style sausage dangled at the edge of an oceanic abyss, taunting the passing fish. A quarter mile away, life in Canoa ticked by at a relaxed pace along dirt streets. Ten thousand miles away life went on at home without us. Sheena, unable to see me lying down, wondered if I'd been pulled under by a Great White.

After nearly an hour, I figured I should come back and let Sheena know I was still alive. I rolled up my hand line, threw the sausage overboard, and headed back toward the surf. As I approached the shore I was repeatedly pummeled by set waves, which, as usual, nearly drowned me. By the time I reached shore my hand line had become unraveled and I was lucky not to have been killed by my supersized man-eater fishing hook. Sheena, content that I was still alive, went back to reading her book in her lawn chair in the sand.

The following day, while descending the coastal road through a cloud forest toward Puerto Lopez, our brakes decided they'd had it. I gently depressed the brake pedal coming around a curve, and it gently traveled all the way to the floor. The ensuing panic stomp did the trick, effectively jerking Nacho to a slower speed. I'd stumbled upon the temporary fix, allowing us to travel the rest of the way to our destination: every time I wanted to slow down, I had to do a panic stomp on the brake pedal. Failed brake master cylinder. Damn. More of that emergency roadside Volkswagen maintenance would be required.

We pulled into Puerto Lopez and drove the main road along the water until we had left downtown, jerking to an abrupt panic stop before each speed bump. A few hundred meters outside of town we found a nice spot to camp on the beach and panic-stopped into a serene location overlooking the bay. We poured rum into two glasses and topped them up with Coke that had been chilling in the freezer, and then sunk back on the couch to listen to the waves. Outside of our screen door the sailboats and fishing vessels bobbed in front of the lights from the bay while a cool sea breeze filled our small living room.

Having scored the best free beach front property in all of Ecuador, we weren't in a hurry to move on. The following morning we ignored our Vanagon maintenance woes and opted instead to go in search of boobies. It was Sheena's idea. "Let's just enjoy the beach," I'd say. "No! I want to go to the island of boobies!" She was relentless. Of course we're talking about birds here – the elusive blue-footed booby. La Isla de la Plata was only a forty five minute boat ride away and was said to be loaded with the little monsters.

At the port we found our fiberglass shell of a tour boat waiting, beached like a dead whale. Our captain played it cool and asked all of the chaps from the group to come and help him get it free. Twenty minutes and several strained backs later, we were putting northwesterly. When, halfway to the island, the engine failed, all I could do was smile. I watched as the captain and his two helpers wrenched on it for a few minutes, and then switched to watching the panic grow in the other passengers' eyes. I was just happy to see someone else behind the wrench for a change. We finally got on our way when I noticed another layer of ricketyness to our boat: one of the helpers' jobs was to steer the boat by holding his foot on the outboard motor. When the captain needed to turn, he would yell at the boy, who would push the motor a little with his bare foot.

"All right everybody, there are four hikes we can do," our guide said. We had disembarked and were gathered around the map of the hiking trails around the island. "The map, you see, is backwards. You have to flip it like this. The printer made it backwards. There are four hikes, my fraings." For some reason Latin American guides always say "my friends," but pronounce it "my fraings." Every time I hear it I think of John McCain.

"This hike is very far away, so nobody likes it." He swirled his hand over the blue line. "This one is very boring, you no see any boobies or frigates. This one boobies, but only frigates flying. This one is shortest, but has boobies and frigates, my fraings." It was clear that our guide wanted to do the shortest hike. The island was no more than a half of a square mile, so no hike was really all that long. "So my fraings, we will do the short booby and frigate hike?" We nodded.

The trail wound through a dry wash and up the side of a small mountain covered in palo santo trees, and punctuated by thickets of luffa bushes. That is luffa, as in *luffa sponge*. It turns out that luffa sponges grow on bushes inside of huge spiky seeds.

"These are luffa sponges, my fraings. They make your face so soft, my fraings." Our guide mimed washing his face with one of the sponges.

Throughout the hike we dodged blue-footed boobies and red-breasted frigates perched in the trail and all over the surrounding cliffs and trees. I kept myself entertained by proclaiming "Look! Red-breasted frigate!" using my best nerdy birder lisp every time I saw one. I'm 29, but I'm not above acting like a twelve year old. Just ask Sheena.

Back on the boat it was time to head back to the mainland, but not before partaking of the second part of our tour: snorkeling at the island.

"My fraings," our guide announced, "It is time for snorkeling." He glanced over his shoulder at the water and the white sandy beach. "You will have one hour to snorkel. There are many fishes and corals to see." We all nodded in anticipation. "But as you can see the water is very cold. It may make you sick from the cold. The wind is also blowing. So you will not have any fun. Maybe today is not the day for snorkeling. Does anyone want to snorkel?" We peered around at the group, now completely turned off by the idea of snorkeling, and fearful for their health. Not wanting to be the only ones swimming in the arctic cold water with the deadly wind making us sick, we kept quiet as the boat sputtered to life and stammered out to sea.

On the way back to Puerto Lopez our boat ran out of gas. Again we were stuck, the other passengers fretted, and I couldn't wipe the ridiculous smile off of my face. After replacing your own transmission on a high mountain Colombian farm, there's nothing more satisfying than watching it happen to someone else. It's like all of a sudden waking up and realizing that you're not alone in the world.

Eventually the helpers unearthed an extra fuel bottle from the depths of the boat's bilge, and we were on our way. A short time later, Sheena let out a joyous squeal and all at once I knew we'd be stopping again. Next to our boat a whale breached, and then her two calves followed. We spent a half an hour circling the enormous animals as they repeatedly surfaced and jumped around. I imagined one of them biting my Swiss-style sausage link and taking me into the depths of the ocean while I fidgeted for my dive knife. I really dodged a bullet there.

The following morning it was time to get down to business. By the glow of Nacho's dome light after our boat trip I had removed our brake master cylinder. I now carried it in my sweatshirt pocket as I made my way at 6:00 in the morning toward the Puerto Lopez bus station. I would go to Guayaquil, a five hour trip, and not come back until I found a replacement. By 7:00 I had found the right bus and was relaxing my way southward. Someone else drove, for a change.

As the bus passed through grasslands and canyons I listened to Radiolab and This American Life on my iPod. Ira Glass dug deep to find out what happened during the massacre at Dos Erres, Guatemala, and I thought about how long ago we had driven through that region. It seemed like an eternity. Being able to sit there and stare out the window while being entertained was a welcome luxury. By now the uncertainty of when and how our van would be fixed didn't concern me. We'd been through this before, and everything would certainly work out. How could I complain, after all, while listening to what happened at Dos Erres?

When the bus reached Guayaquil I grabbed a sandwich and walked out to the taxis. I hopped in one and directed him to a VW parts importer. When we reached the place I stepped out and passed my old master cylinder through the barred service window to the parts guy. He disappeared for a minute and emerged holding the exact part I needed. I paid him, thumbed another taxi back to the bus station, and hopped on the next bus for Puerto Lopez. The whole day was all very non–Latin

American in its efficiency and in the way everything worked on the first try. I suppose that after you've traveled across continents and smuggled really heavy car parts across international borders to fix very difficult mechanical problems, everything else just seems easy.

On the bus ride home I sat in the bulkhead seat next to a pleasant Ecuadorian woman with a lot of grocery bags. On the bulkhead there was a large picture of Jesus superimposed over a backdrop of a serene Swiss mountain lake. Jesus was made in the image of a Latin American boy, but in an effort to make him look as innocent and tranquil as possible, he had turned out looking more like a prepubescent Latin American girl wearing a satin bed sheet. He certainly looked nothing like the Middle Eastern man that he really was. I find it curious that every Christian society does this same kind of Jesus stylization. I stared at this innocent-looking bed sheet-wearing prepubescent Latin American girl for five hours, while listening to episodes of Fresh Air on my iPod.

As the sun went down and the bus descended the same road where our brakes had failed, Terri Gross interviewed Maurice Sendak, the author of *Where the Wild Things Are*. Maurice spoke about his impending death and the sadness he felt at having had to watch his friends pass away, while at the same time looking positively on the times he had.

"There's something that I'm finding out as I'm aging – that I am in love with the world. And I look right now as we speak together, out the window of my studio, and I see my trees – my beautiful, beautiful maples that are hundreds of years old, and … I can see how beautiful they are. I can take time to see how beautiful they are … It is a blessing to find the time to do the things, to read the books, to listen to the music … Live your life, live your life, live your life."

# 45

*Puerto Lopez, Ecuador — September, by Sheena*

"To *Los Frailes* Beach?"

While downshifting a gear to a stalking pace, every three-wheeled rickshaw driver asked me the same question. While taking a tour of the coast in a spectacular dual-toned rickshaw piqued my interest, what was more appealing was watching them go by. The plethora and odd arrangement of decals was mind boggling; dripping flames, cartoon characters, sports logos, marijuana leaves, Jesus heads, and batman-shaped windows, tinted in black plastic to hide the backseat passengers. A slight squint in the eyes and shake of the head was understood as a no thanks.

No, today I couldn't be distracted by water and beaches. I had my fun the day before, peering into the strange obsessive sex lives and ritualistic ways of blue footed boobies. These birds were more obsessed with mating than a class of high school boys. Wherever there was a female, a male wasn't far away, flaunting his beautiful blue feet by raising one foot and then the other. The lady birds didn't seem to pay any attention, though they would eventually and invariably choose the males whose feet had the richest azure hue. We watched duels between male birds in which they lifted their sharp pointed bills toward the sky and blew out high pitched whistles while outstretching their wings, desperately attempting to display their dominance.

I never saw a female pick a winner, but I did see many soon-to-be mothers incubating their eggs. Instead of laying her eggs in a nest, she would defecate in such extreme quantities, essentially creating a nest of guano. This protected her eggs from bugs and made her territory visible from above and identifiable as her own.

Off in the ocean waters, you could see blue footed boobies dive bombing straight into the ocean, where they would slice through the water and devour off-guard fish. As intense as they were, their lives were short lived. Dive bombing into the ocean slowly destroyed their eyesight, leading to an eventual heart-stopping suicide involving a cliff wall or tree.

Today was an unusual day. In the wee hours of the morning, Brad rolled out of bed without me, and ventured off to catch the early bus to Guayaquil in search of a brake master cylinder. For the second time since our trip started, Brad and I were separating for more than the length of an average eight to five work day. This used to be the norm five days a week, now one day apart seemed like an eternity. I was left to fend for myself on the beaches of Puerto Lopez.

I set out nervously to the market with a simple task for the day, a photographic challenge if you will. The challenge was given to me by a friend to take photos of cooks preparing their food. Easy enough, if you remove from the equation the part where I am shy and less than proficient at the Spanish language.

Like many markets, it was a few blocks away from the *restaurantes turísticos*, tour agencies and souvenir shops selling woven baskets, sarongs, and keychains. This one was a fabulous open air market, with a few messy but organized *comedores*. Under a tarp-roofed area, dozens of plastic tables and chairs were sprawled out, no clear distinction between one eatery and the next except for what kind of salsa sat on each table as the centerpiece. No chalkboards or menus identified the meal of the day; you just had to sit down and wait for the news. It didn't really matter anyway, they were all nearly identical. Women surrounded by pots and pans pushed out food in courses: a broth soup, then a typical plate of meat, rice, lentils, and plantain chips or *patacones*, and finally a cup of juice.

Around the corner, under corrugated metal roofs, produce was sprawled out in colorful piles. Chamomile flowers were stacked in bundles and women sat on buckets shelling peas, surrounded by a pyramid of color.

One young shop worker, totally blinged out in t-shirt imprinted with a faux diamond necklace, flexed his biceps at me as I bought a bundle of spinach that looked like a pile of wilted weeds. Grinning, he said, "Spinach is very good for you. I eat it every day because it makes me VERY strong." He looked like a Latin American version of Popeye.

One of the things I love most about Latin Americans is their incredible creativity. If they can't afford a fence, they'll make a wall of tumbleweeds and branches to keep the sheep in. If they don't have a car to haul things around, they chop a rusty, forty year old bicycle in half and weld a giant two wheeled cart to the front. No need for handlebars, just grab the front of your cart and start the thigh burning motion of moving the mass forward. These utilitarian bikes (or motorcycles for the high rollers) were second in popularity to the rickshaws. They were loved and used for every perceivable task: delivering propane tanks, glass bottles, moving garbage, carrying people, and selling food. Each one was customized in its layout, but the food stands were generally half tabletop and half grill, sometimes with a fancy striped patio umbrella for ambiance.

As evening approached, I left the market with a bag full of food: chorizo, coconut balls, mashed balls of cooked plantain, fry bread filled with cheese, and a few pinches more of confidence than when I started the day. Task accomplished.

A few days later, with my honey back at my side, we cruised on out of Ecuador and into Peru. As we wound through the mountains, I spotted a pig dressed as superman. He surely would have tripped on his plaid, baby blue cape if he was skipping along to a mud puddle. Instead he sat propped up on the table with his eyes closed next to a black charred wok, filled with succulent, juicy chunks of pork.

"I'll have some pig please."

The woman lifted the cape of the pig and sliced off a chunk of skin from its back, scooped a few chunks of pork from the wok, and layered the plate with corn, pork, and onion. It was heavenly.

As we descended through the desert canyon, I fed Brad like a baby, placing chunks of meat into his open mouth as he drove. As we drove, my mind drifted back home, where you'd never find the origin of food so exposed. Our meat is cut behind swinging closed doors, packaged in rectangular foam plates, wrapped in plastic wrap and marked with an expiration date. On more than one occasion in Latin America I've watched a family take the life of one of its livestock. To them, it was an occasion and a moment to celebrate their fortune, no foam rectangles or plastic wrap in sight.

# 46

*Northern Peru — September, by Brad*

## Claim to Fame

Mancora's claim to fame is that there's always *something* to surf.

In the morning I awoke early, having dreamt all night of riding the curl of Mancora's famous year-round wave, as promised in our Moon Handbook. I forced my eyes open and rolled out of bed, hopping downstairs using our portable toilet as a step, and stumbled into the morning light. It was already hot out, the desert sun baking my lily white skin as I clumsily stumbled through the sand. I walked onto the beach and stood next to a dead seagull. I squinted across the horizon, but my hopeful gaze was met by the flattest, calmest, glassy surface of an ocean I'd ever seen in my entire life.

"There's never a wave at Mancora. EVER!"

Tree was smarter than our guidebook. After all, he'd spent a considerable amount of time living the Sprinter Life and surfing the Peruvian coast. Tree would make a better life coach than a Moon Handbook.

## Born to Run

Instead of surfing, I laced up my running shoes and followed Sheena into a desert canyon leading away from the beach. I'd just finished reading *Born to Run*, and was convinced that I actually had an inner Tarahumara Indian deep in my ancestral soul waiting to run his little heart out.

We disappeared around the first bend in the canyon. On the ridge to our left, two mean looking stray dogs watched us like vultures. I could picture the face of a Tarahumara Indian in my mind telling me *you were born to run, man!* It was pretty hot out, and I can't say for sure that it wasn't James Franco saying *127 hours, man! It took 127 hours!* We continued deeper into the canyon.

I ran lightly on my toes, shuffling from rock to rock through the canyon while reminding Sheena, "This is all very easy for me. You know, since I was Born to Run." After a few miles my inner tribesman had fallen ill and shriveled pathetically into the fetal position. We regretted not having brought any water. If my arm were trapped under a boulder out here, I'd be dead in far fewer than 127 hours.

The melting rubber of our shoes flapped against the parched earth in the midday sun as we attempted to steal moments of shade under overhanging cliff walls. Lizards scurried through the dust and my mind wandered to the running book. A white man had drifted into Mexico's Copper Canyon and become one with the Tarahumara Indians. They called him *Caballo Blanco*. I wondered what they would call me if I were Born to Run. When I worked at my dad's Mexican restaurant, the cooks used to call me *Girafa*. They would make animal calls at me, and when I'd look, they would grab a handful of cilantro and try to feed me. "*Tienes hambre, Girafa?*" It wasn't my fault that I was a 6'3" high schooler. "Whoa there boys, better watch out or I'll call *La Migra*." Knowing more about Mexico and Mexicans now, I still feel badly about threatening to call Immigration on them.

"Aaaayyyaayyaya!" Sheena's shrill squeal snapped me out of my lethargic daydream, and all at once she was running a circle around me, her pigtail whipping my face. The vulture dogs had been waiting for us, and they knew we'd be out of it. It was at this moment that I realized that I was indeed Born to Run.

## The Flop

In the world of professional soccer, there's a move called The Flop. A soccer player dribbles the ball skillfully, criss-crosses his way through his opponents' defensive legwork, and suddenly the ball is stolen. At this moment, the player who had been driving the ball leaps forward, arms flailing, and lands on the ground. His face is pure agony; he's grasping at his ankle while he falls. He lands on his shoulder in just such a way that he is able to propel himself along the ground in a series of magnificent rolls and somersaults. When, at long last, he finally comes to rest, he does so with his agonized face clasped in his hands. *That guy was nearly killed! Is he okay!?* That's what he wants us to think. In reality he wasn't fouled, but rather put on this elaborate show to try to garner sympathy from the fans and referees. This is the main reason that most North Americans think that soccer players are crybabies.

Peruvian drivers have mastered The Flop. In a country with the worst drivers in all of Latin America, one would expect a certain level of defensive driving skill to be engrained in every Peruvian from birth. Since crossing the border into Mexico over ten months ago, I've become much more comfortable with common-sense driving. Passing with oncoming traffic is just fine; the other guy just moves over a little to allow three cars to pass on a two lane road. It's just the way it is. For this reason, passing on a blind corner is acceptable if the conditions are right. It may sound crazy to a member of a modern, rule-driven society like America or Europe, but it works down here. We do these things every day. It therefore came as a surprise that once we entered Peru, drivers started completely freaking out. Everywhere we went, drivers were doing The Flop.

In one instance, I followed a slow semi truck down a straight road. A Peruvian approached in the other direction, but there was plenty of room for me to pass. I pulled out and began to pass the truck. Almost immediately, the Peruvian in the oncoming lane started frantically flashing his headlights at me. My heart continued to beat at 63 beats per minute. No reason to be nervous; I'd done this a million times. As I

217

passed the semi truck I signaled and pulled in front of him. A few seconds later the Peruvian passed by, and as he did he performed the most elaborate Driver Flop I'd ever seen. Inside of his cab he created a vivid scene of total disgust. His arms whipped wildly around his cab, his eyes were wild with rage. One arm flailed wildly out the driver's window, signaling his deep repugnance at me for having nearly killed him. This pass, by the way, would have been totally acceptable even in the USA. Every day we encounter at least two or three Flopping drivers. Crybabies.

## Desert Clowns

Spending extended periods of time in the desert can make a person crazy. In Nevada, people see aliens. In Sedona, hippies seek out energy vortices and pass the day sitting naked on the red rocks, becoming severely sunburned in all the wrong places. Peru's Northern desert is as vast as any on Earth, and it has its fair share of crazy people. Here, they all wear the same uniform; they're the police who are stationed in the small pueblos that dot the immense sand wasteland.

The police are deployed in pairs. They place an orange cone in the middle of the highway and stand there going stir crazy in the sun, just waiting for a poor sucker to pass by. Our desert driving days are spent passing slow semi trucks, and then coming across police checkpoints, where all of the slow trucks pass us again. Seeing our milk faces through the windshield, the police lick their lips and flag us down.

"Hello officer, would you like to see my importation paperwork and my license?"

"Where are you from? How far have you driven today? Where are you going? Why don't you have a front license plate? What kind of van is this? Is this van from the USA or Germany? Do you like Peru? Have you tried the *caldo de gallina*?" The conversations always start the same. These people are bored, and they lean on my door with their arm perched on my windowsill as they talk. They're here for the long haul. They have no reason to pull us over other than the fact that they're bored out of their minds and just need someone to talk to. It's like being cornered by a conspiracy theorist; you can't leave until they've had enough. It would be fine if it ended here, but every time we're stopped the police go too far.

"What do you do for a living? How much money do you make?" They always want to know how much you're worth.

"I'm an engineer, but I prefer not to discuss money."

"Come on, what's your salary? You must be very rich to be driving all the way from America."

"I said I won't tell you what I earn. But in general people in America make $500 per month." If they have the right to be jackasses, then I have the right to be a liar. "We earn $500 per month, but rent is $1,000 per month. For this reason, people in America are all in debt and they're actually very poor. "Well okay, maybe not a total liar.

"You could live like a King in Peru on $500 per month. Do you guys sleep in your van?" At this, the police officer pokes his crazy head into my window and has a look around. "Wow, it's like a small apartment in there. Do you and your wife have sex in this van?"

"I'm sorry, I don't understand Spanish." Sure, the whole conversation has been played out in Spanish to this point, but to a crazy person my response may seem rational. The police officer starts motioning with his hands so that I might understand what he's saying.

"Do you," (hand gesture) "and your wife," (hand gesture) "have sex inside of your van?" (grotesque hand gestures)

"I'm sorry, I don't understand Spanish."

In Northern Peru, the police are nothing more than insane desert clowns going stir crazy in the sun.

## Kidnappers

"I'm thinking about getting a wheel alignment done. Do you know of a good place around here?" We had driven for a few weeks on a new tie rod, but hadn't had our alignment checked. James and Lauren, having temporarily settled down in Huanchaco, would be the perfect people to ask. After all, they were like us – Americans driving the Pan-American highway and dealing with similar incompetency issues.

"Don't do it, man. I brought our truck to the BFGoodrich shop a few weeks ago to get an alignment, and then I drove to Cuzco. When I got there my tires were completely bald." I looked at his tires; the tread was completely gone with the exception of a 1/2" ridge on the outside of either front tire.

"What happened?" I asked, my finger sliding over the surface of one of his new racing slicks. They were completely destroyed.

"The guy did the alignment with a broomstick. He held it between the tires, and then adjusted the alignment by eyeballing it. Obviously it didn't work. These guys have no idea what they're doing."

It sounded like I was hearing an echo. If you're driving the Pan-American highway and need auto work done that you can't do yourself, you're better off setting your vehicle on fire and flying home.

We walked inside and found Sheena and Lauren up to no good. Lauren was leaning out of their second floor window holding a piece of string. I could hear a kitten screaming. Closer inspection revealed that the string had a basket tied to the end of it, and in the basket was an open can of tuna. Lauren was trying to bait the neighbor's kitten it into her hanging basket.

Kidnapper.

Sheena offered words of advice and encouragement. "Just a little to the left. She's smelling the tuna. One more leg and she'll be all the way in…"

Accomplice.

Before long the cat had taken the bait, and Lauren reeled her away from her loving home in the tipsy basket. Brian David Mitchell celebrated his kidnapping of Elizabeth Smart by setting up camp by a river in the Wasatch Mountains and reciting a marathon of Mormon prophecies to his victim. We intimidated our victim by making popcorn and playing a game of Gin Rummy on the roof. "Squeakers" pleaded a relentless torrent of high pitched squeaks. Like Brian David Mitchell, we didn't even care.

We sat around James and Lauren's apartment, the lease for which they had recently taken over from Stevie and Tree of Sprinter Life, and talked about what had happened since our last meeting. They were with us on the morning that our transmission failed in Colombia, but they had continued on while we remained in the mountains. As we talked, someone knocked on the front door. James got it.

"Oh hi! How are you? You know, we actually have your cat!" Lauren was already fast at work stuffing Squeakers into the basket and opening the window.

"Just hold on Squeakers! Everything's going to be fine, just hold on!"

By the time James reached her to get the cat, the basket was out the window. He ran back to the front door where the neighbor waited, confused. She hadn't yet been home, and didn't know her cat had been kidnapped.

"Actually," James told her, backpedalling, "we don't have your cat. We just…uh…It was nice talking to you!" When the affair was over we all congregated on the couch. Lauren looked worried.

"I hope little Squeakers is okay," she said. "She jumped out right when I put the basket out the window."

We all migrated to the window to see if Squeakers was dead. No trace of a cat was to be seen on the pavement below. No fur, no blood, no tuna. Lauren looked at us. We looked back at her. The moral divide between us grew, as we couldn't allow ourselves to be associated with a murderer. Finally, at long last, a happy squeak emerged from the neighbor's downstairs grotto. Squeakers would live to see another day.

# 47

*Huanchaco, Peru — September, by Sheena*

With one deep exhale, I stripped the sheets off and sat up in bed. I tied my hair back, slipped on the previous day's clothes, walked into my flip flops, and slung the camera over my shoulder. I pointed my body down the stairs, turned left, and walked a block to where the street intersects Huanchaco's desolate beach. The waves crashed down in layers, validating the accuracy of the wave chart tacked up by the pier. Today would indeed be a huge day. My tired eyes scanned the waves. The rafts were nowhere to be seen.

Out of commission for the day, the reed rafts, or *caballitos de totora* leaned against the rock wall separating the promenade from the beach. Just the day before, while on my morning run, I ran by and saw a vastly different scene. It was fantastic. In the water, perched atop their Venetian-like reed rafts, fisherman floated over waves with upright postures. Maintaining their balance, they robotically dipped their long bamboo paddles into the water from side to side. Their eyes pierced through the depths of the water, in search of the fish. Once they were beyond the waves, they straddled their *caballitos* , dropped their weighted gill nets or line and hook and fished.

A short while later when I ran back down the promenade, the tired fisherman were on land, congregated along the rock wall where their rafts stood upright, drying for the remainder of the day. Lashed to their hips like sets of house keys, skinny fish hung on wire loops.

In Huanchaco, this method of fishing has been going on for centuries, with the image of reed rafts even depicted on 2,000 year old Mochica ceramics.

Far past where the sidewalk drops off into dirt, a sandy road continues to an agricultural zone. Wispy strands of reed or *wachaque*, grow in the marsh. Masterfully bound around two chunks of foam, the reed is shaped into a Venetian style boat, with one end tapering upward, just like the long sweeping curve of a handlebar mustache. On the other end, the reed is precisely cut, dipping down to form a cozy depression for the boatman to sit.

As I turned away from the rafts, a man with kind eyes, chocolate colored skin and a quick smile appeared before me. Long before the sun's warm rays had begun radiating from the sky, he had been alongside the promenade, staring out at the sea. Oblivious to the chill in the air, wearing a warm fleece and beanie, he lingered, wanting to converse.

He told me he was a fisherman, and in a matter-of-fact tone he explained that there would be no fishing today. The waves were too big and the water too turbulent for spotting the fish. He would be back out again tomorrow to fish if the sea would allow it. It was clear that while he would have liked to have been out fishing, it was just as well if he didn't. The act of catching fish didn't change what he'd be doing for the majority of the day. He'd still congregate along the wall with his buddies until the sun set, talking of wives, woes, and weather. I promised to come back the next day to buy some fish, sold either along the wall or in the market, but for the next two days the waves were harsh and the murky ocean water obscured the view of the fish.

Despite not buying any fish, I did explore the market that lay hidden between two massive garage doors. Here I tried *chicha* for the first time. The woman standing behind the pot deftly ladled the deep purple juice into a small snack-sized plastic bag, and with a few quick flicks of the wrist she inserted a straw in the top and tied a bow around it to seal it from spilling. It tasted just like fruit juice, except that it was made from cobs of dried purple corn soaked in water. I came to find out that *chicha* is so popular in Peru that it has earned its own universal identifier in the country. If you spot a long wooden branch, pole, or pipe protruding from the ground with a bag tied to the end of it, you know there is a local concoction of *chicha* for sale.

With *chicha* in hand, Brad and I wandered the streets splashed with colorful murals, enjoying the day while pondering our next move. The second highest mountain range in the world, the Peruvian Andes, was near. It was time to pull out the wool socks and hiking boots and head to higher ground.

# 48

*Cañon del Pato, Peru — September, by Brad*

A few years ago I attempted the Pines2Mines mountain bike race—an eighty mile off road jaunt from Flagstaff to Jerome—on my cyclocross bike. Everyone told me I was of unsound mind for wanting to ride this bike, which amounted to a road bike with knobby tires. "Too rough," they would say. "So-and-so tried it a few years ago and said *never again*." Naysayers. I went out there and gave it hell, and after the first fifteen miles I was in the top five and feeling pretty good. I sat in and planned where I'd break away. Maybe the final twenty mile climb to Jerome. At about this time I hit a rock and got a flat tire.

Before I even came to a stop I had my new tube out and partially inflated with my mouth, and had my pump in my hand. I hopped off my bike, pulled the old tube out, put the new one back in, and started pumping. Air sprayed out of the valve stem; my new tube was bad. I got my only other tube and put it into the tire and started pumping. Air sprayed out again. *Both* of my spare tubes were bad. I sat my ass on a rock, pulled out my patch kit, and started patching.

Fast forward to the sixty five mile mark. I've endured thirteen flat tires and a broken spoke. Yes, *thirteen* flats. At one point I had dropped a patch under the rock I was sitting on, and watched it fall down a snake hole. I sat in the dirt under the roasting sun and desperately stabbed the hole with sticks until I'd recovered my precious patch. Now I sit on the roadside wearing my spandex superhero costume with my wheel in my hand, the 105 degree sun beating down on me. There's no shade, only dust and weeds and heat waves. I'm out of water, and I am out of patches. End of the road. I look down and realize I'm covered in dozens of spiders. It's like a bad dream. Eventually I see a deer hunter driving by in his truck – the first truck I've seen in eight hours. I stand in front of him in my superhero costume so he has to stop. We drive together, a spandex-clad bike racer and Donny the deer hunter, in the cab of his beat up pickup truck. He recounts the time he hung out with two naked strippers from Flagstaff at a nearby hot spring while they worked on their stripper tans. I start to pass out from exhaustion in the passenger seat, and his story gets caught up in my delirium. Strippers are dying of heat stroke in the desert, covered in dirt and spiders.

Sometimes we go into the wild knowing good and well that we shouldn't. And sometimes we find ourselves stranded in the desert, covered in spiders, begging horny deer hunters for help. But if we always heed the warnings, what on Earth will we tell our grandchildren about?

I'm pondering this conundrum in the shower on the last night we'll spend at James and Lauren's apartment in Huanchaco before heading into the wild. It's only been a few days since we were last stranded by a mechanical problem, and they've been coming like punches ever since Costa Rica. The next day we plan to drop off the pavement and head into the Andes on a desolate dirt road climb that strings its way through dozens of hand-dug tunnels before depositing us in the *Cordillera Blanca*, Peru's most massive mountain range. This is the famous *Cañón del Pato*. But to get to the start of the canyon we think we've found a short cut. Google Maps can't make a route of it, but looking closely at the satellite imagery seems to show that the short cut goes through, and if it does, it would shave 17 miles off of the normal road that's used to access the canyon. It would be a long path through the middle of an empty desert, through some mountains, and somehow crossing a large river. *If we always heed the warnings, what on Earth will we tell our grandchildren about?*

At about this time I'm slammed in the back of the head by a Louisville Slugger and the inside of the shower flashes an electric blue. Rather than my life flashing before my eyes, all of the times I've been electrocuted in the shower on this trip flash before my eyes. I snap out

226

of it as the fireball dissipates and the shower walls return to their pale yellow hue. The echo of my yelp still echoes in my ears. Was this a sign? I chalk it up to Latin American electricians not knowing what they're doing. Just like the mechanics. These on-demand hot water shower heads consist of a rat's nest of loose, hot wires that the water runs over to heat up. If some innocent shower-taker happens to touch the shower head and create a ground for the circuit, the poor bastard gets fried. This is the 9th or 10th time it's happened to me; I feel like a prisoner in a Bush-era POW camp.

In the morning we brush aside all of the obvious warnings and head South. We still haven't decided if we'll take the ill-omened short cut when we roll up to it on the side of the highway. *What's the worst that could happen?* Before we have a chance to decide against it, a man with a clipboard approaches. He takes down our information on his page; I spy the names on his sheet and see that only a couple of vehicles per day cross his post. This seems like a bad idea. For our future grandchildren's sake, we press through. Before we know it we're bumping along a rough dirt road toward a line of ominous, sandy desert mountains. We're driving on the surface of Mars.

Driving through the desert between mountains and cliff walls, it's easy to imagine that we're in Iran or Pakistan. The road winds through sandy spires and through low passes until finally we emerge at the river. Across the canyon we can see the primary road that ultimately leads into Canyon del Pato. This is the point at which our short cut becomes ambiguous; neither Google Maps nor our GPS give a clear indication of a way across the river. The GPS shows a route, which turns out not to be real. Google had said we'd cross over a small dam, which also turns out not to be possible. We continue on for miles along the rough dirt road clinging to the canyon wall while on the other side a nice paved road shuttles cars along at high speed. Finally, at long last, we come to a guard shack next to a rickety wooden bridge. We stop to pay our toll for using the bridge, and then a man lifts a metal pole with a rope and we drive through, finally reconnecting with pavement. No spiders, no deer hunters.

By early afternoon we've reached the mouth of the canyon. Two soldiers stand guard over the entrance to the canyon. Desert clowns. We chat for a while about nothing and one of them asks me if I had taken any pictures of them. Unsure of the best response, I play the dumb tourist and tell him in broken Spanish that the canyon is pretty. Soon we're free of his boredom trap and driving through the canyon, past inhabited structures that could have been plucked straight out of a rural settlement in Afghanistan.

Given the fame of this canyon road, there are surprisingly few vehicles. It doesn't bode well for the mechanical failure that we're expecting to happen at any moment. Construction on this road was started in 1952, and a French company now operates a hydroelectric dam near the top of the canyon. We occasionally pass pickup trucks emblazoned with the company's logo, their roofs covered in elevated steel mesh to minimize the damage from rocks that fall from the sheer cliff walls. A new road has since been built farther South to access the *Cordillera Blanca*, but this one is still here for those with confidence in their vehicles and adventure in their hearts. We press on, passing through one hand dug tunnel after another, clinging to the cliff wall on the narrow dirt track. Below us, the *Río Santa* batters the sandstone cliff walls with its emerald-colored torrent.

By evening we've only made it halfway, so we look for a place to camp. We come across a bridge spanning the canyon, and on the other side there is a large open area above the river. The bridge sounds as if it'll come apart as we drive across it; the boards comprising its driving surface are held together by steel bands, and the rivets holding the steel bands on have all come apart. The steel rattles and the boards shift, my eyes intently focus on finding the best driving line, and Sheena nervously eyes the swift current passing underneath us.

In the morning the sun slowly crawls over the canyon rim, illuminating the multicolored sandstone walls across the river. The night's chill is transformed into a still heat. It's a classic desert morning; we sip our coffee and take in the smell of the desert plants and rocks as they're heated by the sun. Mornings in the desert have a distinct smell, as if the night has deposited a layer of condensation on everything. When touched by the sun, this condensation turns into an evaporating perfume that smells like shale, cactus, mesquite, and dry sticks. It reminds us of Arizona.

After crossing back over the rickety bridge we're back on the road, gaining elevation through the Canyon of the Duck. We realize that yesterday's drive was just the mundane prelude to the real show. Quickly the canyon walls close in and the road winds along one wall, ducking through tunnels, the opposing wall sometimes less than twenty feet away, while the sheer cliff faces rise upwards on either side of the river a hundred feet or more. This must have been one hell of a road construction project. We see almost nobody else on the road for hours.

I remember sitting on the couch at Sheena's parents' house watching an episode about this road on some sort of Death Road Trucker TV show. It was about six months before we left on our trip, and I told them we'd be driving that road. It seemed so far away, like it would never actually come to pass. Yet here we are, driving our Nacho, of questionable mechanical integrity, through those tunnels, along those precipices, and across those bridges. It doesn't seem as deadly in person.

The insides of the tunnels are rough. It's as if they were blasted with dynamite and carved out with picks until just passable, and then the workers moved on to the next tunnel. There are thirty five single lane tunnels in all. The actors on Death Road Truckers had scared looks on their faces as they passed through these tunnels. They crept along slowly, cameras showed their tires pushing pebbles off the edge into the rushing river below. At any moment, it seemed, their world could be turned upside down by a collapsing tunnel, a failed bridge, or a landslide.

We just thought it was fun. This is how we know that we're more hardcore than Death Road Truckers.

By day's end we emerge above the rim of *Cañón del Pato* and reconnect with pavement. Nacho has survived the trip and so have we. Our eyes are rewarded by views of the snow-capped peaks of the *Cordillera Blanca* as we sail down smooth pavement toward the mountain

Hamlet of Caraz. Warning signs be damned; our grandchildren will have plenty of stories to listen to.

# 49

*Parque Nacional Huascarán, Peru — September, by Brad*

As evening set in, I stood outside of the van loading supplies into our backpacks. I divided the tent, sleeping bags, stove, and other supplies carefully into each of our bags so as to equalize the weight. We had removed every ounce of unnecessary material, eliminated a tent stake or two, all in the interest of saving weight. Finally it was time to divvy up the food; I called to Sheena inside of the van. While I had loaded the packs, she was responsible for getting the food together. She opened the door and handed me a fifteen pound trash bag full of fruits and vegetables.

"Sheena, WTF? We're going backpacking. We have to carry this stuff for DAYS!"

"What, do you expect me to eat powdered SOUP for three days?"

"Yes, that's exactly what I expect you to do. We're going backpacking, and backpackers don't eat stir fry for dinner. They eat powdered soup. Just enough to stay alive." I wasn't getting through to her. The trash bag, bulging with beets and carrots and bell peppers hung heavily in her fatiguing hand.

"I'm not eating powdered SOUP for three days! That's not HEALTHY! We're eating VEGETABLES!" It was clear she wouldn't budge on this.

"God, you're so high maintenance!"

Her eyes opened wide and her eyebrows lifted, giving her the face of a crazy person. She spoke slowly and deliberately. "You don't even know what that *means*."

We had set up our basecamp in the dirt parking lot of Hospedaje La Casona, a block off of the main plaza in Caraz. We would leave Nacho there while we trekked the Santa Cruz circuit through Peru's *Cordillera Blanca* mountain range.

Our guidebook mentioned that hiking in the park would cost five Soles per day. We would start the trek in the pueblo of Cashapampa, which would cost twenty soles to reach in a *colectivo*. At the end of the trek we'd end up in the small village of Vaqueria, and would have to take a series of *colectivos* back home. All in all the whole trip should cost around sixty five soles, or about twenty five dollars. Just to be safe, I grabbed 150 soles out of our safe and pushed it into my pocket. It was 5:30 in the morning, and it was time to go catch our first ride.

We found the *colectivo* – a clapped out station wagon – and crammed ourselves between goat herders wearing sheepskin vests and skirts – about the only other people who have a need to go to Cashapampa. We handed the driver twenty Soles and settled in for the two hour bumpy dirt road into the foothills of the *Cordillera Blanca*.

"This trail costs 65 soles per person." We had almost slipped by the guard shack unnoticed, but we'd been caught. And the cost was much higher than our guidebook had reported.

"But señor, that's 130 soles for both of us. Our guidebook says it's only 5 soles per day."

"Do you have your guidebook with you?" Of course we didn't. We had to ditch it to make room for the fifteen pound bag of vegetables. "The ticket has the price printed right here. I don't set the prices. If you want to go in, you pay 130 soles."

"But we won't be able to get back home from Vaqueria if we give you all of our money. What do you suggest we do?" Vaqueria was a four hour drive from Caraz, mostly on rough dirt roads. Without a ride, we'd be screwed.

"Go back to Caraz and get more money," he said. With only two *colectivos* per day, this would mean waiting ten hours for the next one, and then trying again the following day. In a moment of weakness I jammed my hand into my pocket and pulled out all of our money in a big wad. I handed it to the guard, ignoring the worried look from Sheena. Walking for three days into the world's second highest mountain range without any means of getting back home seemed risky, and we had no backup plan. If I were a gambling man, my kneecaps would be shot out by loan sharks in no time.

"This pack is *sooooo* heavy," Sheena whined. We had stopped in the shade of a large granite boulder for lunch. She looked at her feet, standing there sort of pigeon-toed, knees slightly bent, stooping her shoulders to exaggerate the weight of her pack. I reminded her that I was always right, and that she should have known better than to question my all-knowing authority on packable, lightweight hiking foods.

We made lunch of fresh ciabatta bread, tuna, lemon infused mayonnaise, herbs du Provence, and sliced fresh tomatoes. I'll admit, although quietly and out of earshot of Sheena, that it was pretty damn good.

By day's end we had arrived at a lagoon. One edge of the lagoon was defined by the canyon wall, while the trail skirted the opposite edge of the water. We found a flat spot above the trail and pitched our tent for the night.

While cooking dinner, a group of hikers passed in the opposite direction. The last straggler from the group wandered up to our camp to say hello; a French woman in her forties.

"Have you come here alone, without a guide?" she asked. We told her that yes, we were hiking alone.

"The agency in Huaraz lied to me!" She had apparently asked a tour operator if she was permitted to do the hike without going through a tour operator. Textbook conflict of interest. Through her obvious anger, she was still in high spirits and very pleasant. I told her the story about how not having a guide meant that we'd been responsible for managing our own money, and how that had lead to our current predicament.

"You have no money? Well here!" she reached into her pack and gave us all of her money – precisely eight soles; the equivalent of three dollars and ten cents. It wouldn't be enough for a *colectivo*, but it was something.

"Thank you! You don't have to do this. Can we offer you some food in return?" We were communicating in Spanish, because her English was as rusty as my French. Apparently her Spanish wasn't much better; she misunderstood me, thinking that I was asking her for food.

*These Americans...*

"Si, si!" she said. I went into the tent to grab some snacks for her, and when I came out she was handing me all of her granola bars.

"No, no, I was offering *you* food," I said, "in return for your kindness."

She finally understood, but insisted that we keep her food anyway. Such benevolence! And from the French! I decided that I would never again refer to fried potato strips as "freedom fries."

On the following morning we hit the trail early. We planned to cross over the 15,610 foot *Paso Punta Union*, and would need as much daylight as we could get. The pass, although visible from our camp, turned out to be farther away than we had anticipated. The sheer size of these mountains can be deceptive, and distances are hard to gauge. By lunch time we had only reached the foot of the pass. We hunkered down behind a hill, out of the frigid wind, and made ourselves more gourmet tuna ciabattas with sliced tomato and freedom herbs, or rather, French herbs.

The trail switched back relentlessly up the side of a rocky cliff toward the pass. To our right the ridge continued around to become the canyon wall, while to our left an enormous 20,000 foot peak jutted straight up, terminating the ridge. Glaciers skirted the lower flanks of the peak, and far below a turquoise glacial lake collected the runoff from the ancient ice.

By the time we reached the pass it was late afternoon. Like climbers with minds fogged by lack of oxygen we lingered at the top. We knew that we were at the pass too late in the day, and that we should get down as quickly as possible before night fell, but the setting was too incredible to pass by. Bundled up in our down jackets and wool hats we sat there, silently admiring the extremeness of the mountain and its glaciers. Every thirty seconds the creeping ice let out a loud pop; the crack of a wooden baseball bat crossed with a head on collision and an exploding firework. It was the first time either one of us had ever heard a glacier groan. At one point a hunk of ice broke off and came crashing down the rocky face toward the lake, five hundred feet below. Never had I felt so insignificant. It was the most impressive and grandiose spectacle we'd laid eyes upon over the course of our entire trip. We regretfully pried ourselves away from the scene and started down the other side of the pass. It was nearly 5:00 and the sun was approaching the horizon. Cold was setting in.

We hurried down the back side of the ridge, but before long we lost the race to the cold and had to hunker down for the night. We left the trail and headed for a small lake just below the ridge with a skinny finger of a peninsula jutting into its center; it would be the perfect spot, albeit a little cold, for a campsite. To access the lake we had to shimmy along a ledge and then lower ourselves down a rock face. On the peninsula we found a perfect sandy spot for our tent, unloaded our gear, and set up for the night.

The water in the lake was so clear that it seemed invisible. Looking into the water from the edge of our peninsula was like looking off of a cliff; a couple of enormous boulders sat just below the surface, and beyond them the depth created blackness. Everything in this place was enormous – the boulders under the lake's surface, the depth of the water in the lake, the peak looming over our camp, and the range of glacier-covered peaks extending down the valley below us.

As we drifted off to sleep the rapidly dropping air temperature stabbed at our faces like daggers through the face holes in our down sleeping bags. The last thing we heard as we drifted off to sleep was the soft sound of snow falling on our tent.

The following day we followed the trail through a canyon along the river's edge, and by afternoon we reached the first signs of civilization. By early evening we reached Vaqueria. It could hardly be called a town, as only eight families call the high mountain village home. Walking into the village we came across two men moving a pile of rocks and we asked them where we might find a place to pitch our tent.

"There is no need to pitch a tent, you can stay in our house," one of the men said. I explained to him that we didn't have any money, and would be happy to camp.

"I won't charge you," he said, "go up to the house and tell my wife that you're our guests. I am Manuel, it's a pleasure to host you."

The man's wife showed us our room – a dirt floored tack room on the ground level. Manuel moved a few saddle blankets out of the way and spread a patchwork tarp on the floor for us, and proudly displayed that we would have electricity – a single bulb hanging from a wire in the center of the room. We fell into a deep sleep with the smell of horses and dust in our noses.

In the morning we awoke well rested but without a plan. We sat by the roadside reading our books, waiting for passing traffic. After a couple of hours we heard the rumble, and then what looked like an enormous chicken truck trundled up the road. I put my hand out and wiggled my fingers in the way that we'd seen Peruvian hitchhikers do, and the truck stopped in front of us. From the cab three men peered down at us.

"We're trying to get to Yungay," I told them.

Blank stares.

"We have eight soles."

The men talked amongst themselves, and then one man spoke. "Climb up," he said, motioning to the roof above the cab.

Almost immediately the truck began chugging uphill. Sheena and I shared the open, wooden toolbox on top of the cab with an old Peruvian man. The chilly morning air stung our lungs and we bundled up in our jackets. Being so high up in the air and traveling through such a surreal setting brought smiles to our faces that we couldn't shake. Sheena sat crumpled in a little ball, her rosy cheeks and wide smile shining from beneath her hood. After a half an hour of climbing we crawled into the back and nestled ourselves amongst the stacks of empty crates where the sun could warm us and we were protected from the cold breeze.

I looked up from my book to see the canyon walls closing in more tightly around us. The fantastic white peaks that were previously hidden came into view, towering overhead. We stood and propped ourselves up by holding onto the sides of the truck. By stacking three crates on top of one another we created viewing platforms, and from our new vantage point we discovered that we were preparing to cross over a pass. This pass, however, was no ordinary pass. Mount Whitney is the tallest peak in the lower 48 states, and stands at 14,505 feet. Our chicken truck clambered ever higher until we finally passed through a small gap in the rocks, marking the highest point of the road. We were at 15,636 feet; 1,131 feet higher than Mount Whitney! Still, Peru's highest peaks loomed thousands of feet above us. Words like *surreal* and *awe inspiring* do nothing to describe these mountains. There aren't words for it.

Our awe quickly turned to terror as the truck pitched its nose downward and we saw what lie before us: the single lane dirt road dropped straight down a vertical mountain face, losing over 3,000 feet of elevation all in one go, over the course of thirty four consecutive switchbacks. From our perch, ten feet above the surface of the road atop the old chicken truck, we could see the first fifteen switchbacks, stacked one on top of the other down the cliff face, but the road beyond was obscured by the steepness of the face we'd be driving down.

At the sight of the switchbacks, Sheena turned to me, her red cheeks poking out from her black jacket. "Bradley," she said, "if we die in this truck today, I just wanted to let you know that I had a really nice time." Her face was still splashed with that ear to ear smile, her eyes glassy from the wind.

The driver picked up speed as he approached the first switchback. Sheena and I looked at each other, fear in our eyes. I swallowed hard. I knew, deep down, that we were going to die. I slunk down into the crates and buried my face in my jacket. If I couldn't see what was happening, then maybe I would be less scared. Oh hell, who was I kidding? I'd already seen the road, I knew we were dead meat. I came to terms with the fact that our trip down the cliff would go however it would go, regardless of whether or not I watched. I slowly stood and peered over the top of the truck. My fingers gripped the wood. My knuckles turned white. My butt puckered so much that my pants nearly fell off.

After the first couple of switchbacks, I realized that we were in more danger than I had originally thought. At the apex of each switchback, the tracks of the other trucks ended at the cliff's drop off, meaning that they had pulled up to the edge, and then reversed before finishing the turn. The curves were too tight to do in one fluid motion. However, here we were, driving just a little too fast, making the entire turn in one go. I craned my neck out the side of the truck to watch our tires, and to my terror, found them inches from the edge on every turn. Besides the obvious danger of falling off the edge, I couldn't stop thinking about the inept local mechanic who would have last worked on the truck's brakes.

I turned to our Peruvian hitchhiking companion and asked the obvious question: "So, do lots of people die on this road?"

"Oh, not so many," he said. "The last time was a couple of years ago. A bus fell off the side. Everyone onboard was killed." He didn't need to add that last part – no, that part was obvious. It didn't matter, I had already made my own escape plan in the event that the truck went over: I would hold onto the truck's sideboards until I felt the ground, and then I'd grasp like hell for anything I could grab onto, letting the truck fall away without me.

Later on I told Sheena of my escape plan. "Oh, I was thinking about it too," she said, "but I couldn't think of anything. I figured I'd just have to go down with the truck."

By the time we neared the bottom of the switchbacks, my intense fear had transformed into complete elation. Now that I thought about it, this was turning out to be the most fun I could remember having —*ever*. You can't even pay for fun like this. This was more exhilarating than any roller coaster; it gave the same feeling in my stomach, but it lasted for *hours*. And when you look off of a roller coaster, you see a city. I was seeing 22,000 foot peaks covered in snow, draining into turquoise lagoons, and I didn't have to sit in one of those plastic seats with the safety bar. In fact it was quite the opposite; near the end of the trip I noticed that the two metal flanges holding the tool/hitchhiker box to the roof were both broken. Further inspection revealed that in fact a single bolt through a wooden plank was holding the whole thing on. Guessing the worst, I checked the nut and, yes, found it to be only finger tight.

After four hours the chicken truck dropped us off on a curb in Yungay. Sheena and I were covered from head to toe in dirt, our faces crisscrossed with smile lines in dust. I had learned something on this trip: if you want to have an adventure, a good place to start is to throw caution to the wind and leave with only enough money to get you as far from home as possible. The trip back will surely be a memorable one.

# 50

*Hatun Machay, Peru — September, by Sheena*

An Austrian with crisp blue eyes and a full red beard chopped firewood outside in his lederhosen and flip flops. Cold air cut through us. It was close to freezing and the sun still hadn't set. Questioning where we were, Brad glanced at the GPS. No wonder Nacho was misbehaving, we were almost at 14,000 feet.

Hundreds of sheep swarmed the hillside like ants. They moved in unison except for the chaos arising from the pack of baby sheep among them. Oblivious to the world around them, they were lost in a game of sprinting in circles, karate chopping the air, and vertical bouncing like frightened cats.

When the sun began to set, I bundled up, ready for a quick evening hike.

Hatun Machay sits on the hillside opposite the *refugio*. It is a stone forest considered to be South America´s best rock climbing destination, and the area was unbelievable. As I approached the edge of the outcropping, overhanging rock formed caves. Dirt like finely sifted flour covered the earth and overhanging rocks were littered with 10,000 year old petroglyphs and cave paintings. The walls were like a sketchbook of doodles; stick figures, snakes, geometric carvings, ancient happy faces, deer and hunters.

As I entered the heart of the rock outcroppings, smoke wafted in the air. Sheep skin dried on a string and small rocks were stacked purposefully, forming rock barriers between the boulders. Someone lived here. Like chameleons, dome shaped huts made of straw were almost invisible in their surroundings. An older woman in brightly colored clothing sat in the doorway of her home. Antonio, her husband, appeared like a ghost. In his hands, he cupped a bowl of ramen soup, vegetables floating on the surface. He offered me dinner. The wife retreated into the environment, shy, and perhaps tired from the day. Antonio showed me his home, comprising three huts; one for cooking and the others for living. They raised sheep and lived simply. They had lived within the rocks for decades and would continue until death.

I continued onward, exploring the granite rocks. Sheets of razor sharp rock jutted up into the sky, like artisan chocolate melted on tinfoil, cooled, and placed upright on a fat slice of cake. Other sections of the rock were pockmarked and dimpled from the ancient water that perhaps once ran over them. As the sun began to set, the sky turned bright pink and blue. Unfathomable beauty.

The sheep that ran earlier were now corralled in for the evening, pinched between the boulders and peering out at me in boredom.

A fire crackled in the morning and the *refugio* was suddenly packed with climbers. While Brad roasted the last of our raw coffee beans from Colombia, a beautiful dreadlocked Argentine girl pulled an oversized apple pie from the oven. Between bites of the apple pie, a pot of hot water and a tin of coca leaves circled the communal table. Wildly popular, coca tea is drunk by hikers for elevation sickness and chewed by truck drivers to increase alertness. Coca leaves, as harmless as poppy seeds in a lemon muffin, yet illegal in the United States.

Once our bellies were full of pie, we took off into the rocks for a short exploration. As we wandered up the hillsides, we crossed a small trickling spring. A tin pitcher sat next to it, used by the natives for a quick drink of water while herding the sheep. We retraced my steps from the previous night, exploring everything all over again. The local women were out of their huts, gathered on the hillside, shearing sheep.

It was nice to be roaming the hillsides. Just the previous day we were passing through town after town. Skirting the Cordillera Blanca, we again went through Yungay, a town with a horrific past. Nearly the whole village disappeared in 1970 when an earthquake dislodged a massive chunk of ice and mud from Peru´s tallest mountain, Huascaran. 18,000 dead in just a few minutes. Yungay also happened to be the hometown of the older man who had ridden down through the mountains with us on our wild ride.

After seeing Yungay we stopped in Huaraz, a city of cement and ramshackle buildings. It was an intense mess of fast taxis, European trekkers, and entrepreneurial spirits along the sidewalks selling all things growing from the ground. Peruvian snack food – puffed corn glazed in sugar – was sold in bags the size of small children. In the market, distant relatives of my pet guinea pig were gutted, raw, and hairless. We had seen the living ones in the countryside, nestled in a bed of hay, plump and pregnant. In honor of my sweet Punkie, whom I lowered into the ground in my neon pink lunchbox in the 4th grade, I just couldn't eat them.

Word on the street was that there was a brewery in town that couldn't be missed. With Brad on a seemingly never ending mission to seek out good beer, this would be the mission for the day. We had been tricked in the past so we both remained leery; most bars tended to have European beer bottles on display, yet the reality was they were merely decorative, like antique relics in a museum.

Two Tasmanians joined us for drinks at the brewery. Earlier in the day they had attempted to recruit us on a 10 day circuit hike through the Huayhuash mountains. They needed fellow hikers to divvy up the mass quantities of food required for the long haul. I had flashbacks from our hike and knew I was not the person for the job. As the designated walking pantry on our last hike, my feet had suffered. My baby toenails were near extinction, black with massive gaps behind each nail.

We spent the evening sampling the beers, eating popcorn, and throwing darts. Ana and I competed viscously for who would finish last place in the game.

As soon as we left Huaraz, rural life picked up again. Local women carried bundles of wild plants in their shawls and entire families worked in the fields. Livestock roamed the streets and distant peaks jutted up into the heavens, like an erratic lifeline on a hospital monitor. Twenty two of those peaks towered over 19,850 feet, views I promise cannot be done justice by photography.

Back at Hatun Machay, it was time to get Nacho back on the road. First we'd have to climb back up the rough road to the 14,000 foot pass we'd driven over the previous day. Nacho despised the altitude and I couldn't quite grasp how we were going to get back out. I jumped in the passenger seat as Brad held onto the reins of our drunken, bucking horse. Brad slipped the clutch all the way up the hill as Nacho clung on to dear life. We bounced around in our seats like a set of dice. Books exploded off of our library shelf. I screamed. Brad tried to look brave [ed. note: Brad *was* brave]. Yet, we made it.

We floated out of the Cordillera Blanca mountain range, from 14,000 feet to sea level in the span of only 100 miles. We stopped only when we ran into the sea.

# 51

*Near Lima, Peru — September, by Brad*

The moment the man spoke, I knew we were in for a ride. He had been standing there harassing another vehicle, and was just finishing up when he saw us coming slowly up the hill toward him. Immediately he snapped to attention, dollar signs in his eyes, and frantically waved us over.

As the police officer approached our window he straightened his back to give the illusion of professionalism. He looked at me and inhaled, pulling the corners of his mouth back to reveal his teeth, raising his eyebrows, and telling us with his grimace that we had really screwed up.

"I pulled you over because you have committed a serious infraction," he said. He didn't tell us what we'd supposedly done wrong until he'd planted the fear in our hearts and given it enough time to take root. He slowly swept his gaze over his boots, down the road behind us, along the side of our van, and then stopped at my face, staring, trying to be intimidating.

The moment he spoke I figured him out. His predictability was pathetic. In northern Peru all of the cops we'd come across had been nothing more than clowns in uniform, and he was no different.

"You, unfortunately, were speeding. What is the reason that you were speeding so fast? This is a serious infraction." He paristaltically barfed the words up from his gut and spewed them out for me to look at, as if to let me figure out what to do with them.

"I was speeding? That's strange. When you pointed at me I was being overtaken by three vehicles in a row. Why didn't you pull the overtaking vehicles over instead?"

"Those other vehicles have already been stopped up ahead. I radioed them in." He pointed to his cell phone, which was clipped to his shirt near his shoulder. It wasn't a radio, but he grabbed it and tilted it toward his mouth to show me that he could magically use it as a radio.

"How do you know I was speeding? I don't see a radar gun."

"My colleague at the bottom of the hill has the radar. He radioed you in and I stopped you." We were in the middle of the desert, and he had no colleague at the bottom of the hill. In a desert devoid of all life, you notice when there are other living things around. Still, he wanted me to believe that we had been caught up in the middle of their sophisticated web of radios and radar guns.

I was visibly getting ticked off by his pack of lies. After having been pulled over by numerous ill-intentioned, corrupt police officers every day since entering Peru, I no longer viewed them as being in a position of authority. I found myself addressing them informally, as if dealing with a pest. They were sloppy, inappropriate, and impossible to respect.

"You committed a serious infraction. The ticket is 300 US dollars." He threw that out there and let it fester for a while before continuing. "What are you going to do about this problem?"

"I'm not going to do anything about this, because there isn't a problem. I wasn't speeding, so there is no problem."

The back and forth continued this way for 10 more minutes. He repeatedly told me about the infraction, I denied all wrongdoing, and he asked what I was going to do to remedy the problem. He was tireless. Finally he got the hint that he wasn't getting anywhere.

"Does she understand what we're saying?" he asked, pointing with his chin toward Sheena.

"*Yo no entiendo nada!*" Sheena said, clearly indicating that, yes, she did speak enough Spanish to understand what we were saying.

245

"Please get out of the vehicle." At this, the clown walked behind Nacho and waited for me. I let out a stream of profanities and felt barely able to keep myself from throwing it in reverse and gunning it. I cooled off, got out, and met him behind the van.

When I met him, he was no longer speaking formally, now choosing to speak to me in a quicker, familiar tone. Sort of what you'd expect when being shaken down by a criminal.

"Look, just give me something material. If you give me something – a gift – I will let you go. What do you have in the van?"

"Tell you what," I said, "I will give you a snack. You can either have a granola bar or a banana." He had gone over the line, and I decided that I'd rather pay for a ticket than give this d-bag a bribe. We hadn't paid any bribes yet, and I wasn't about to start. I wouldn't be able to look myself in the mirror if I knowingly let this scumbag walk away with anything of value.

"A snack is not enough. Give me your watch or your wedding ring. Are these surfboards? I would take a surfboard too."

Who did this comedian think he was? "I'm sorry *hombre*, but I'm not giving you anything." I decided to level with him – put all of my cards on the table. "When we left home, my wife and I agreed that we'd never pay a bribe to a police officer. Therefore, it's impossible for me to give you anything. If you're hungry I can give you a snack, but I'm not giving you my watch or my wedding ring or my surfboard. I'm happy to take the ticket."

I knew I was putting him in an impossible situation. To give up now would be shameful. He would have lost to a gringo tourist.

"Just give me something material," he repeated. His tone had changed; he was feebly grabbing at the fading chance of a successful shakedown.

"Are we done? I'd like to go now," I told him. My internal filter was full and I no longer cared about the outcome. He stood there looking at my vehicular paperwork in his hands. After a few seconds he folded them slowly and handed them back.

"You can go."

And so there in the desert we left him, the uniformed Peruvian *bandito*. The saddest of all of the desert clowns.

# 52

*Lima, Peru — September, by Brad*

## Elderly Woman Behind a Counter in a Small Town

There are many interesting things about Alex.

Jeff and Amy had given us his phone number in an email, told us we should look him up. As a gift for finishing his Master's degree in mathematics, Jeff and Amy – both math professors at NAU – brought Alex to Mexico City, and in doing so planted a travel bug that would refuse to die. A few years later he picked up and moved to Lima. Didn't speak Spanish, no job, no plan, just wanted to do something different.

This is an interesting thing about Alex, but it isn't the *most* interesting thing.

Sheena and I were in the process of giving Nacho a deep clean – scrubbing chunks of mystery substance off of the stove, wiping strange and smelly juices from the fridge – when we heard a creak from the front gate of the hostel. Someone entered and we followed the sound of boots on pavement to our sliding door.

"You must be Brad and Sheena. Hi, I'm Alex." He bore a vague resemblance to Eddie Vedder, but the words poured out of his mouth like smooth molasses, each calming utterance having the bass of distant thunder and the haunting resonance of a well worn vinyl record.

He is a man with the voice of Eddie Vedder; *this* is the most interesting thing about Alex.

From our hostel we walked the two blocks to the Miraflores waterfront and turned left. Along the boardwalk high above the ocean people zipped around on bikes and rollerblades wearing tights and elbow pads, while youth couples necked on park benches against the ocean backdrop far below. Alex talked about life in Lima, but all I heard was the soothing sound of Pearl Jam.

*I wonder if he sings in the shower. If I sounded like Eddie Vedder I'd shower thrice daily just to hear myself sing.*

Alex brought us to a nice restaurant nestled in the cliff face, and we found seats on the outdoor patio overlooking the ocean. Portable gas heaters competed with the cool sea breeze wafting up the cliff face as we ate dinner and Alex talked about Peru using his Eddie Vedder voice. After dinner we ambled along the boardwalk.

"If you're interested," he said, "I was headed to a friend's apartment for horror movie night. You guys are welcome to tag along." Our plans consisted of sitting around in our van and then going to sleep, so this seemed like a great idea by comparison. A few minutes later we were in an elevator climbing to the 16th floor of a waterfront apartment building.

When we arrived, *Nightmare on Elm Street* was paused onscreen; a sweaty man stared crazy-eyed at a woman, his mouth agape. We chatted with Alex's friends — all expats from one place or another — and ate microwaveable *chicharrón*. I frequently wandered into the kitchen where, from high above the city, the lights of Lima spread out like a sparkling carpet all the way to the horizon.

Hours later, in the wee hours of the morning, Sheena and I strolled along the boardwalk back to our van. When we had left the apartment, *Nightmare on Elm Street* was still onscreen, still paused on the scene with the crazy-eyed man. I tried to imagine what it would be like to expatriate to Lima, but my mind was haunted by a voice, like smooth molasses.

## In Hippie Bus We trust

As Sheena and I strolled the sidewalk toward the hostel where we were camping in Lima, someone yelled at us.

"Hey!"

To our left a 1985 VW Vanagon with a pop top slowly lurked by, the driver leaning out the window. "Are you guys Brad and Sheena?"

We looked at each other, surprised. Last time we checked... "Yes!"

The man with the van turned out to be Miguel, a reader of our blog. He'd first written to us at the start of our trip asking if we'd be passing through Lima.

"I'm on my way to the monthly Westfalia club meeting. Want to follow me over in Nacho?" It was nearly 10PM and we were tired, but when propositioned by a charming stranger in an old van, how could we say no?

We hurried back and got Nacho ready, and then followed Miguel through Lima traffic for 40 minutes to a Burger King parking lot.

After weeks in the mountains among shepherds and small town folk, hanging out with a bunch of Westy fanatics made us feel right at home. We opened up the sliding door and had a Nacho open house. People cycled through, sitting on the couch, taking photos of various things, and asking questions. After a while families coming out of the Burger King started looking at the vans, and a new wave of couch sitters cycled through Nacho.

While Sheena held down the fort I walked around and checked out the other vans. I found myself standing next to a freshly painted 1970's camper van, listening to the owner recount his recent trip to the mountains.

"I was going up a hill and I noticed some smoke in my side mirror. By the time I pulled over there were big flames coming from here." He pointed to the lower corner of the rear engine hatch. "I used the fire extinguisher, but it didn't work. Too small. Someone else came by and put the fire out with their extinguisher. He showed me how to do it – you have to point the extinguisher like this..." he pretended to hold a fire extinguisher and aimed it at the engine bay. "Psshhht! Psshhht! Psssshhhhhht! See? Just like that." Everyone looked at their shoes and solemnly shook their heads. It was as if one of the man's own beloved children had spontaneously combusted during the road trip.

Westfalia people everywhere, it seems, share a common weak spot for these cars. We give them names, we decorate them, and we spend far too much money on them. We lower our heads when they eventually go up in flames, but then we fix them and give them a fresh coat of paint.

# 53

*Reserva Nacional de Paracas, Peru — September, by Sheena*

Desert coastlines have always intrigued me. Two seemingly different environments, yet they make an appearance together on occasion. They are an odd couple. They are no peanut butter and jelly or tea and scones, but they work.

Once we left Lima's city limits, where green lawns, bushes of flowers and palm trees were on sprinkler system life support, the frigid air of the Humboldt Current made itself known, sucking the landscape dry. The Pan American cut alongside mountains of jagged rock. Chipped away from cliff faces, broken boulders lay scattered, some caught in place during their spiraling descent through loose gravel, others making it to the Pacific Ocean where they sat in piles. Where the mountain was too immense, the road tunneled its way through the innards of the beast.

Brad could hardly focus on driving, his eyes darting from the road to the waters below. "Oh I bet there are so many fish down there." And yes there were. Small villages hung off the edge of the mountain, seemingly selling only seafood.

We had come down with a bad case of seafood obsession after our arrival in Lima, with ceviche and fillets of grilled fish as our lunchtime staples. The most mind boggling experience was in the Lima market at the intersection of two walkways. The past has shown that in Latin markets, vendors group together by product type. The fruit stands in one walkway, the flower arrangers in another, and *comedores* in a cluster, vying for your dollars. Yet, as we rounded the corner, unexpectedly there sat a *cevicheria* in a maze of smoothie stands. It was bustling. Elbows pinned to our sides, we shimmied into the seats of two barstools and ordered the standard bowl. What came out, however, was nothing near standard. Two bowls overflowed with chunks of fish, clams, and vegetables marinated in lime juice. *Cancha,* popped maize kernels, fresh herbs, and a brothy spicy *aji* sauce transformed the dish into a hot steaming stew. I'd go back in time for this meal.

Back on the coast, we chose a random seafood joint and filled up on more ceviche.

With our tummies full, we drove on. Just as the highway began to stray from the coast, we veered off to Paracas National Park, stationed on a hammerhead shaped peninsula. In all directions, valleys of hard packed sand unrolled before us. Sand dunes freckled the landscape, windswept and dusted on one side with a spattering of white shimmering salt. The road disappeared and the desert appeared before us like a skateboard park. With no dotted lines to steer in between, donuts formed in the sand and tracks crept up the side of steep dunes. Brad, like a kid with his favorite Matchbox car, took Nacho to his limits.

Yet, Nacho was no Matchbox car, which, with the flick of a wrist could jump rivers and fly through the air. Nacho was a different breed; more of a house on wheels than a sports car, sputtering to a stop before ever mounting a sand dune.

"Quick Sheena! Take a picture. I can't hold Nacho here much longer." Poor Nacho would lose traction and Brad would gently reverse him back down to safe ground.

Our campsite was spectacular. The valley of desert broke off at the coast, exposing sediment that had formed in flaky sheets of rock. The rocks ended abruptly and a sweeping coastline of red beach took its place, teeming with birds and the occasional seal. Like a rice cracker, salt formations pockmarked the ground and gaping crevices fell down to the red sand.

Without reference points, the landscape was deceptive. Everything looked close. Nothing looked steep. We spent a morning, out of control and laughing, running down the sides of the sand dunes, nearly front flipping with every leap.

To the East of Paracas, we continued on down the freeway through the Ica desert, a land of more sand dunes and dirt formations. Just as our throats became parched from the heat, we were granted with fields of grape vines. A checkerboard of vineyards began popping up, leaving the sheets of sand behind, until they were eventually overtaken by the town of Ica. Shipped all throughout the world and to every nearby village and city, they are the world's best producer of pisco, a white grape brandy, produced since the 16th century with the arrival of the Spaniards. Pisco, while commonly drunk alone, has also been the main ingredient in a variety of mixed drinks, with the most common easily being the Pisco Sour. Here is the traditional recipe: blend 3 oz pisco, 1 oz lime juice, ½ oz sugarcane, 1 egg white, and 4 ice cubes.

While in Ica, we stopped at a small bodega called El Catador. We were shown the pisco making process which, in one long run on sentence goes like this: grapes are crushed under a huge adobe platform with a 150-year old *huarango* trunk (here our guide *insisted* he take our photo), the juice is poured into clay containers called *botijas de barro*, and then distilled in boilers of copper basins.

While eating handfuls of purple speckled corn, we sampled all the varieties of pisco. We left with a bottle of "love potion" pisco, which our guide insisted was so smooth and sweet, and that we'd drink the whole bottle before realizing it, resulting in the inevitable.

Our drive continued on. Farther South, we entered the flat *pampas* of the San Jose desert , an ancient sketchbook containing 70 pages of plant and animal figures, all within a range of 1000 square kilometers. The media used: scraping of dirt. Sometime in the past (no one knows exactly when), canals 20 centimeters deep were scraped into the manganese and iron rich surface. What gave way below was a layer of lighter colored rock. In the 1970s, when Peru discovered these drawings, the Pan American highway already ran straight through one of the figures. For travelers, this made for a very quick sightseeing adventure. We veered off the highway and travelled up a set of rickety set of stairs to a lookout tower. From above, we could see three sets of Nasca lines: a set of hands, a lizard, and a tree.

Pretty cool. All in a day's drive.

# 54

*Machu Picchu, Peru — October, by Brad*

When I was in sixth grade I went on a school field trip to Peru. When I say it out loud it sounds like I was one of those kids that everyone loves to hate; some spoiled brat who went to a high dollar institution with tasteful school uniforms. In reality I lived in the quaint meth lab town of Chino Valley, Arizona, and went to school in a converted mini-mart. It really all came down to my mom being totally rad.

See, in sixth grade my mom was my teacher. And my mom, being a totally rad teacher, marches to the beat of a different drummer. She figured our class ought to have a theme for the year. Our math would be themed, our science would be themed, et cetera, and she decided that the theme of every subject would be the rainforest. It's kind of like that Our Lady Peace album on which every song is written about the novel *The Age of Spiritual Machines*. And what better way to keep a bunch of hyper kids focused on learning about the rainforest than by giving them an incentive to actually learn something? Our incentive was that we would actually go to the rainforest at the end of the year to experience what we'd been learning about.

But how do you send a bunch of sixth graders to the rainforest when they don't have parents with the income to even send them to a high dollar institution with tasteful school uniforms? Two words: child exploitation. As a part of our math and physical education classes, we spent the year organizing bake sales, bike-a-thons, silent auctions, and other fund raisers with the goal of raising $1,800 each. At the end of the year we held a benefit dinner at John McCain's house and auctioned off a Jaguar automobile to finish off our fundraising. We earned every penny without parental funding.

When school ended, we all flew Iquitos, Peru, and took a long boat trip down a tributary of the Amazon until we reached a lodge, where we would spend a week hanging out with scientists, fishing for piranhas, learning from indigenous people, and meeting with jungle tribes. And who said teachers can't make a difference?

Years later my mom told me that for $800 more we could have stayed another week and gone to Machu Picchu. "Eight hundred dollars!?" I exclaimed, "Why didn't we do it?" She explained that she didn't want to dishearten us with such a big number. Twelve year olds are fickle, after all, so she just let it be. Now, seventeen years later, it was time to make things right.

Unfortunately, over the last seventeen years something happened: seventeen years of inflation. Now $800 will merely earn you the privilege of walking the Inca Trail to the ruins. The tourist train from Cuzco to the town of Aguas Calientes at the base of the mountain on which Machu Picchu sits would run us close to $400. We would clearly have to find a better way, and this time child exploitation wasn't an option.

We decided we would go to Machu Picchu, but we would forego the welcome mat and enter through the lesser known broken screen door behind the grease pit in the alley. Machu Picchu, deep down, has all of the ingredients of a great adventure, and we were ready to stumble face first into it with our eyes closed and our hands tightly clasped behind our backs.

Following our idealistic vision of Andean adventure, we found ourselves sitting on the sidewalk under the excruciating sun waiting for an unlikely bus during a surprise bus strike. The few *colectivos* that passed by our roadside outpost in the town of Ollantaytambo were covered in the splatter of used motor oil, thrown by the striking transport workers as the minibuses charged through the picket line in Cuzco.

"Your bus will never come! HA HA HA!" The taxi driver across the plaza had tried to convince us that we should pay him $100 for a ride to the next town, and seemed to think that laughing at us would convince us that it was a good deal. I scowled at him like a mean high school girl, and swore to Sheena that we'd skip going to Machu Picchu before we'd pay him for a ride.

A small indigenous woman with droopy shoulders and a funny Yosemite Sam hat sat on a log, waiting for the same bus.

"Will the bus come?" I repeatedly asked as the hours ticked by. She shrugged her shoulders each time. We were waiting for the one local bus that went to Santa Maria each day, but were unsure if it had made it out of Cuzco. It was already two hours late. This was the first step in getting to Machu Picchu without using the tourist train.

The ruins at Machu Picchu are located at quite an inconvenient location for tourism. No roads go there, and the train is a relatively recent addition. It used to be that the only option was to hike for five days to get there. Given the agonizing price of the hike, we decided to take a medley of local transportation routes to get us close, and then walk the rest of the way. The transport strike was putting unneeded strain on our already shoddy travel plans.

All at once the Yosemite Sam lady jumped up and sprinted into the street, her plastic shopping bag flailing behind her. "This is the bus! Run!" Two ladies from a shop were yelling at us, not wanting us to miss the only bus of the day, which, as we found out, only slows down in Ollantaytambo long enough for those at the ready to jump aboard.

Inside the bus we found every seat full, with a few unfortunate latecomers sprawled out in the aisle. The bus driver's assistant snagged Sheena as she went by and told her she could sit in the front with them, while I clambered into the back and found an open place in the aisle for the four hour ride. The bus was too short for me to stand comfortably, so I crouched down and jammed my elbows into the seats on either side, giving me a somewhat sturdy restraint for the winding mountain road ahead.

Scouring the bus, I realized that we were off to a good start in eschewing the tourist trail; on a bus of fifty passengers, we were the only milk faces. Indigenous women sat with bags full of sheep's wool and vegetables, while men stared blank-eyed at the seat in front of them. A small yellow sign on the front wall of the bus read *"Viajar como rico, pagar como pobre"*: *Travel like you're rich, pay like you're poor.*

I made friends with Ricardo, the man to my left, who ran a small kiosk that sold things made of plastic. "All types of things," he told me, "as long as they're made of plastic." We chatted as the bus wound upward into the mountains, but after a half an hour the bus driver's assistant came to find me.

"You can come sit in the front," he told me, and then turned around and walked back up the aisle. I saw that the people sitting around me were excited for my good fortune. I'd been cherry picked out of the group for the privilege of a front row seat. The driver, it seemed, was proud to have tourists on his bus, and wanted to show us a good time.

The front of the bus was separated from the rear by a wall and a door. The driver and two assistants were visibly excited to be able to entertain us for the trip over the mountains. The driver pointed to the landmarks and archeological sites that dotted the roadside as we ascended the mountain. "See that rock? It is shaped like the Virgin Mary. See that one? It's shaped like a condor!" He told us that he used to be a tour guide. "On the right you see agricultural terraces from the Inca!" He pulled a USB drive from his pocket and plugged it into his stereo deck. The vivacious pulse of Andean polka filled the small compartment as we wound up the switchbacks into the clouds.

At first the music was normal enough. I imagined the band as a group of Peruvian men wearing matching white suits, stepping in time to a simple dance while they sang and played their xylophones and accordions. And then the eagle squawking started and I broke into an uncontrollable laughing fit. These things happen at the most inopportune times. The music was just too gosh damned hilarious.

*Amor....mi amor....*

*(simple tinkle of xylophone)*

*Yo quiero que me quieres, y te quiero sí te quiero*

*Tu me quieres? Tu me quieres? Mi amoooooooooorrrrrr!*

*(eagle squaaaaaaawk—simple tinkle of xylophone—accordion jam)*

*Tu me quieres mi amoooooooooorrrrrr?*

*(majestic echoing eagle squaaaaaaaaaawk)*

At the most dramatic xylophone riffs and eagle squawks the young assistant would pound his fist on the railing while bobbing his head to the beat. It took great effort to mask my uncontrollable laughter.

After a couple of hours the bus ascended into the clouds and finally pulled over at the top of the mountain pass. A cold wind drove rain pellets into the passengers as everyone disembarked for a leg stretch. The driver motioned for me to follow him, so I walked with him away from the group and toward a small chapel next to the road. As we entered the chapel, he turned to me and whispered the exact phrase that every unseatbelted bus passenger fears most:

"I must pray so that we make it down the other side."

My body spasmed in fear, but a quick response from my lower abdominal muscles somehow kept me from soiling myself. I managed to enter the church without spontaneously combusting or being struck by lightning, which put me in an awkward situation; I wasn't sure what to do. Did he expect me to pray with him? Our safe passage down the mountain was really none of my business, and I wasn't interested in dabbling in the world of the superstitious. I stood there awkwardly in the middle of the church as our driver lowered his head in front of the flickering candles of the shrine. He whispered in Quechua for a minute while I shifted my eyes between him and the door, still not sure what to do. As he finished I coolly swiveled on my heels and joined him in stride.

"So, we safe now?" I said, only half joking. Before boarding the bus I bought some wafer cookies from a lady at a kiosk to share with Sheena, the driver, and his assistants. A hastily chosen last meal.

The prayer must have worked, as the trip down the mountain went off without a hitch. The bus careened around switchback after switchback to the soundtrack of xylophones, accordions, and majestic squawking eagles. We ate wafer cookies and nuggets of puffed corn while the terrain transitioned from treeless high Andean mountaintops, to high elevation forest, and finally to semitropical jungle. When the bus stopped at the muddy roadside in the tiny Quechua village of Santa Maria the bus driver flashed a huge grin and shook our hands. We said goodbye to the assistants and thanked them for their kindness. I ran quickly into the back of the bus and said goodbye to Ricardo, who beamed a giant smile when he saw me coming, and gripped my hand firmly as he wished me good luck.

We had gone into this ordeal as anyone should enter any kind of adventure: without all of the necessary information. We only knew that we needed to find a ride from the tiny village of Santa Maria to the even tinier village of Santa Teresa, an hour and a half away by dilapidated dirt road.

"Santa Teresa?" The toothless man looked homeless, and his battered minivan looked like the minivan of a homeless person. "I'll take you there. Get in!" He seemed eager for us to get in his van, already full with indigenous people and workers from the hydroelectric dam. After a three minute rest from the last leg, we tossed our backpacks aboard and squeezed in between the indigenous ladies in the back. The clapped out minivan whimpered to life and we lurched forward, along with our dozen fellow passengers, onto the rocky dirt road.

From the back of the jankety minivan we watched helplessly as the sides of the road dropped away into escarpments, terminating in the river far below. The indigenous lady's goat hide jacket tickled my ear. I longingly considered the comfort and luxury in which our fellow visitors traveled the primary route in their tourist train. The men with their trimmed and coiffed moustaches and double breasted suits, custom tailored and freshly starched. The women in their silk gowns and tightly strung girdles; their clean, curly locks whimsically brushing their powdered faces as they laughed at all of the dapper men's funniest jokes. They would just now be ordering their second round of Scotch, sagaciously disputing investment strategy while occasionally pestering the peasant help for an extra napkin, or a fresh cube of ice for their drink. Or perhaps my discomfort and the smell of rank goat made me imagine that the tourist train was some kind of luxurious flashback to the roaring 20's.

Without incident the jalopy van dropped us in the middle of Santa Teresa – a tiny village perched on a crumbling geographical shelf with a commanding view of the river below. At this point we slid into the back of the death taxi; a tiny white hatchback piloted by a teenage Peruvian kid, all jacked up on coca leaves. And why take just two measly tourists when the car can legally seat four? After the seventh passenger was crammed aboard we were thudding and slamming our way out of town, the suspension completely bottomed out, the gears grinding, the driver continuously fiddling with the stereo in his jacked up state. From here it would be a forty five minute ride to the hydroelectric dam, and would be as far as we could go by car. From there we would walk, if we ever made it that far.

Not long after leaving town I realized that we had made a grave mistake. Coca Boy liked to drive his car fast like it was a video game. And to make matters worse, the road was a one lane, rocky as hell, level 9 death road. After a short but very fast section of forest, we emerged from the trees and clung to the edge of a sheer cliff face in a full-on Tokyo drift. I began to wonder how we had come to find ourselves in another death road situation in the span of only a few short weeks, but fear kept me from thinking about much other than our impending demise and how much it would hurt.

The road had been carved into an impossibly steep and inaccessible rock face, and as such the single lane was tight and narrow. Its outside edge terminated at the cliff; there was no shoulder or berm, and there was certainly no room for a guard rail. There were no straight sections, most corners were blind, and the road's surface was rough and littered with marble-sized gravel. My pesky engineering degree keeps me thinking of silly things like coefficients of static and kinetic friction on roads like these, and I subconsciously choose a safe speed so as not to cause my tires to switch from one to the other. On this road, a safe speed would have been around 20 or 25 miles per hour, but even then it would have been quite scary due to the exposure. If I were driving Nacho, we would stay in second gear and under 20 miles per hour. Clearly our coca-jacked teenage driver knew nothing of coefficients of friction, as evidenced by his exceedingly fast video game driving speed.

Coca Boy approached every blind corner with the driver's side tires only inches from the cliff edge, driving on the wrong side of the road. This, we assumed, would allow him to see ever so slightly farther around each blind corner to increase his reaction time to oncoming traffic. Before long my whole body felt fatigued and realized that every one of my muscles was flexed; my fingers were like pencils, digging into the armrest on the door, my teeth were grinding, and my abdominal muscles were constricted like someone with terminal constipation. Each time we drifted into a corner I involuntarily swallowed hard, as if constricting my airway could somehow help to reduce the severity of my injuries in the impending car crash. I reached back and zipped my rear pants pocket shut so my identification wouldn't be separated from my remains during the accident. I forced myself to look at the speedometer: it read 60kph. We were traveling around these tight corners, on this single lane rocky road, along this cliff, hundreds of feet in the air, at 45 miles per hour. I swallowed hard.

Just then, we flew around a blind corner and found ourselves staring into the grill of an oncoming *colectivo* van at full speed. I watched our driver hesitate, not knowing whether to put it into the cliff wall or take the head-on collision. The whole world became silent as he slammed his foot to the floor, sending the car into a skid. Rocks and dust enveloped us and I could see baseball-sized stones flipping into the air all around us. I stopped breathing and my throat started clicking, as if trying unsuccessfully to utter the word *uh*. In the dust we could no longer see, but we knew that we had come to a stop. When the dust cleared we were staring at the van's grill, only a couple of inches from our hood.

"Slow down, *pendejo!*," the other driver yelled as he pulled around us.

Coca boy, embarrassed by his near "Game Over," tried to save face by fiddling with the radio and driving even faster. When we were deposited at the hydroelectric dam we knew we'd cheated fate. We also agreed that a long trip across the continent, such as the one in which we were engaged, would never be survived on public transportation. We slung our backpacks across our backs, found the railroad tracks, and walked into the jungle.

Some time ago, a hydroelectric plant was built into the side of the mountain adjacent to the one on which Machu Picchu was built. By chance, the train tracks going to Aguas Calientes – the tourist town built to serve the ruins – pass right by the hydroelectric plant. By walking into the jungle and finding the tracks, we were able to walk like a couple of hobos toward the village – the final step in creating our own Huckleberry Finn style adventure. Without the floating down a river. Or the racism.

Two hours after putting on our hobo hats we emerged at Aguas Calientes. The sun had set and darkness was settling in. As we entered town I grabbed the business card from a fast talking hotelier and continued walking. It would be my silver bullet in winning us a cheap hotel room. As we entered the town plaza we identified a nice hotel and waited for the hotel shark to latch onto us; every business in Aguas Calientes comes with its very own hawker out front, who tries anything to get you inside.

"Hotel? You want hotel? 100 Soles!" With dozens of hotels to choose from, these people will get desperate, and I knew that. I pulled the business card from my pocket.

"Actually we've already chosen a hotel. Here's where we're staying, and it's only 30 soles per night. You said yours was 100?" It was a white lie, and the place on the business card was actually 75 soles per night.

"They told you 30 soles? It's all the way down by the river. There's nothing to do down there. For you, I can do 35 soles. But don't tell anybody, okay?" My scam had worked! We were shown to our private room with three beds – clean, nice smelling, hot shower, and on the town plaza – for which we would pay $17.

Next it was time to eat dinner, and I was beginning to have fun. Most of the restaurants in town had been empty at dinner time. We'd heard many a story of people paying $100 in Aguas Calientes for crappy pizza and beer, and we, being in the middle of Operation Cheapskate, weren't ready to submit. I decided a bidding war was the best approach. I approached the hawker in front of a nice restaurant.

"How much for the set dinner?" I asked. Each place had a set meal price with various options for main dishes, and they were all exorbitantly priced.

"Dinner menu for 75 soles each. Free pisco sour!" At this point she did what every food hawker does, and spouted the contents of her menu at lightning speed. "Hay alpaca, hay cuyes, hay gallina, hay bisteck, hay trucha!"

I thanked her and walked two steps across the walkway to the closest restaurant and asked the same question.

"Dinner for two 75 soles each! Free pisco sour! Hay alpaca, hay cuyes…"

"Wait!" I said, interrupting her. That lady says she has the best food, but you're the same price. Can you go lower?

"For you, 65 soles, come inside! Table waiting! Free pisco sour!" I thanked her and walked the two steps back to the other lady.

"She says 65 soles. Can you go lower?" It was a dirty trick, but knowing that these meals could be had in any other place in Peru for a few soles made it feel all right. In the end we managed to get our $75 dinner down to $28. It was still double what it should have been by Peruvian standards, but good for this place.

At the end of the meal our sneaky waiter tried to tack on a 20% "fork tax," which I outright refused to pay. Not knowing what to do with me, he relented.

*KerCHUNK…tick…tick…CLUNK…kerCHUNK*

Five o'clock in the morning was announced by the metallic clunking of the amusement park turnstile at the park entrance, clunking away like a time clock admitting hordes of people into the ruins like the dull minutes of a workday. We had woken up before dawn in hopes of beating the first tourist train and salvaging a bit of peace and quiet for ourselves within the ruins. Several hundred others had the same idea, and the turnstiles admitted us one by one like United Auto Workers clocking in to build Cadillacs.

The ruins at Machu Picchu are impressive, but not because of the ruins themselves. When compared to those at Palenque or Tikal, they pale in comparison. They aren't grandiose or awe inspiring in their size, scope, or detail. What makes them interesting is the setting in which they were built. They are perched atop a mountain ridge, surrounded by sheer peaks on all sides. Looking out at the ruins is awe inspiring not because the ruins are amazing, but because the mountains are amazing. And because there happen to be ruins in such unlikely and awe inspiring mountains, and because of the photo. You know the one – the signature photo of Machu Picchu taken from above the ruins that shows up just about everywhere.

For me, the best part of the ruins was the Inca Drawbridge. This bridge is accessed by a long cliff side trail that terminates at an overlook of a wooden bridge built over a crevasse, clinging precariously to the side of a thousand foot vertical rock face. It had Indiana Jones written all over it, but more importantly it was far away from the rest of the ruins, by now already crawling like a human ant farm. We stared at the bridge for a few minutes, and then decided we'd better rejoin the hordes.

While we were away the ruins had become a zoo. Park officials walked the grounds holding traffic whistles. Whenever someone touched the wrong thing, they blew their whistles, giving the place the feel of Picadilly Circus at rush hour. On the path through the ruins, tourists are only allowed to walk in one direction. At one point we decided to go back and look at something a second time, but were scolded by a park official and told only to walk forward.

"But we wanted to see…"

"NO! ONE WAY ONLY!"

We invariably found ourselves sandwiched between tour groups led by Peruvian guides, who, by my best estimation, were making up most of the information that they fed to their groups. After a while I became more entertained by the tour groups than by the ruins, and my focus shifted to a Machu Picchu study in sociology.

"My fraings," one guide said using his best enchanted forest voice, "you are standing…in the most majestic place… on earth…(*wait for it*)…*Machu Picchuuuuuu* (*fade to whispering silence.*)"

We rounded a corner and found a group huddled in a circle, the guide getting ready to speak.

"My fraings, have a look at that mountaing…what do you see?" The tourists looked at the mountain. A young brunette looked intently, perhaps hoping to unlock the secret before being told by the guide.

"My fraings, this mountain is a *condooooor*…" His enchanted forest voice was quite, well, enchanting, especially when saying things like *condor*, or *Machu Picchu*.

"Oh yeah! I see it! See, Hank? That hump there is a wing, and I think that other one could be the head!"

"Yeah, a condor!"

"My fraings," the guide was just buttering them up for the grand finale. "Who has a map?" Someone provided a map. "Please, my fraings, gather around. Yes, gather around. Do you see this map? It is a map of *Machu Picchuuuuu*. What do you see? (*silence/confusion*) These ruins are shaped like a *condoooor!*" I swear, to this man everything looked like a damn condor.

"Oh yeah, Hank, see? If you twist the map like this it kind of does, right? I could see that. Yeah, like a condor!"

Next we followed the group to a big rock sitting on the ground.

"My fraings, this is a rock. But it is not just a regular rock. This rock is an *energy rooooccccckkkk*. Please, my fraings, let me explain. From this rock the Inca got *eeennnnneeerrrgyyyyy*. If you rub your hands together very fast and then place your hands near the rock you can feel the *eeennnnneeerrrggyyyyy!*"

At this point the tourists rubbed their hands together and got serious with the rock. One tourist forgot to rub her hands together, but was still able to feel the energy.

"Oh yeah, I can totally feel it, right? This is, like, so awesome." At this the guide interrupted her.

"My fraing, it only works if you rub your hands together first!" He pantomimed what to do, at which she tried it and continued to feel the placebo. Doh! I mean the energy.

We continued walking and found another tour group in a regular looking room with blocked out windows around its perimeter. Each window, it seemed, may have been a place to put something on display. The tour guide had made up his own story though, one that would make the place seem much more enchanted.

"My fraings, please, do you see these holes? Please, place your heads inside." At this the tourists seemed to think the guide was out of his damn mind. He persisted.

"Now, please, my fraings, place one of your heads inside each hole. Yes you, and you. Head in the hole. All right, everyone ready?" The tourists stood there like ostriches with their heads inside of the display cases. "Now everybody at the same time, say *'ommmmmmmm...ommmmmmmm.'*" He made a sound like a stereotypical Buddhist monk meditating. The tourists all made this noise in unison.

"You see my fraings? This room is very *maaaagicaaaallll*. When everybody meditates at the same time, the whole room hums. This is the meditation room, my fraings."

To leave the ruins we pushed our way through the entry/exit tunnel against the flow of hundreds of new tourists streaming out of fresh buses from Aguas Calientes. We had found our Andean adventure all right. And for that I owe Coca Boy a thank you letter. Oh, and thanks for the motivation Mom; as twenty nine year olds we're still fickle.

# 55

*Las Salinas de Maras, Peru — October, by Sheena*

"When I was a kid living in Chino Valley," Brad told me, "I used to duck fences so that I could go and lick the salt blocks that the farmers set out for the cows." Brad wasn't ashamed. He loved salt. "Once you lick through the outer layer of dried cow saliva, it's like sitting down to a nice bag of salty potato chips."

In Nacho we have a cylindrical stainless steel salt and pepper mill. It is our most used kitchen utensil containing our most important food additive. We use it every day with every meal. No traveler sets up camp without it. Our German cyclist friends carry their salt in a small canvas satchel, carefully stored in one of their waterproof pannier bike bags. With every meal, they loosen the hemp cord and take a few pinches out, sprinkling its sparkling granules on their food.

It is a magical and powerful mineral. For thousands of years humans have extracted it from the sea and searched for it on land. Wars have been fought over it and taxes on it have increased the wealth of nations. It runs through our bodies. We *crave* it, yet it so often goes unnoticed, always in the shadows. It never takes credit for why something is so delicious; it always hears the applause from backstage.

Like so many trades, the art of salt harvesting has sadly been demoted, dying in the modern global economy where standardized processes rule all. Now, our option in the standard grocery store is a blue box of Morton salt, made by a company whose primary production of salt is not even for consumption, but rather for industry. Fortunately, there are still regions in the world that have held onto their traditions. In the Sacred Valley of Peru, one of these rare birds still exists.

A salt harvesting demonstration was just finishing up for a camera crew. Two women with crisp white blouses and exuberant smiles stomped their bare feet in a salt pool. They scraped the pool with their wooden boards, forming a mound of salt which they scooped up with their woven baskets. Their pool shimmered in the sunlight. And behind them, a couple thousand more pools brilliantly shimmered. We squinted, the sun's rays ricocheting off of every particle of evaporating salt.

It was an unexpectedly beautiful sight: ponds terracing down the hillsides like puzzle pieces, separated by salt covered borders and trenched canals. Main arteries of salt-laden water ran alongside the walkways, splitting off into capillaries which reached each and every excavating pond. There was no organization to the mess, just a helter-skelter collage of salt pools, all in different stages of the evaporation process.

The pools varied in readiness from simple puddles of water, to clumping blossoms of salt formation, to ripe and ready for the scraping. Salt mounds were sculpted like miniature pyramids, letting the sun's rays suck them dry one last time. There were also walking arteries along the salt pool borders, made for traversing down into no man's land. They were almost indistinguishable from the other ridges, yet the locals knew them by heart as well-traveled walking routes. Some were steep like climbing walls, some were precariously narrow, requiring arms to be outstretched for balance, while others would allow the harvester to cover distance quickly.

A few hundred meters down the valley, an older man and wife with tired faces harvested from their pool. Why the camera crew had chosen not to record the actual workers, but instead two costumed actors, was beyond me. With a trowel in hand, the man patted the top of his salt mound flat. They loaded their riches into canvas bags and secured them onto their backs with a long piece of fabric. They scrambled their way through the maze of salt pools, rubber sandals gripping the shimmering white surfaces of the paths. This couple owned one salt pool out of the thousands; Salinas de Maras was owned by hundreds of families, and plots which had been passed on through the generations were sometimes sectioned off to other family members.

But why salt pools here? It seemed so random, and its location was rather difficult to access. A dry desolate mountaintop landscape and then voila! As it turns out, it isn't so random after all. Salt has been cultivated in the Peruvian Andes since well before the arrival of the Incas. Higher up in the mountains, off of a tributary on the Urubamba river, rain and snowmelt makes its way through subterranean streams, passing through a deposit of salt dating back tens of millions of years, creating water saltier than the sea. After being diverted from the river, the water meets its resting place at 10,000 feet in elevation, trapped in place, left to slowly evaporate in thousands of terraced ponds along the valley's narrow canyon slopes.

With a few packs of mixed salt rubs in hand, we were on our way. Like all days in the week, the Quechua people were out and about. Young girls walked their sheep home and women herded pigs, sheep, and cows, controlling the herds with their tree branch whips. They always stood out against the rocks and grass in their skirts radiating in a rainbow of hues while they worked the land or their animals.

Life in rural Peru is one defined by hard work. Working and living overlap to such an degree that the two are nearly indistinguishable. They never seem to rest, always working the fields, transporting or selling livestock, buying, growing, or cooking food. The children grow up in the fields, and are fully involved in the economic and household tasks. They swing their picks high, tilling the land alongside their parents, breaking for lunch, and when the sun goes down.

# 56

*San Pedro de Atacama, Chile — October, by Brad*

Nacho rests serenely at the *mirador* above the Valley of the Moon, the shadows from the jagged cliffs spilling like water into the dry valley as the sun begins its slow slide below the horizon. Inside, Brad and Sheena sit on the couch, Shakira is on the stereo. They both gyrate their hips to the music. It's not a tasteful gyration either – it borders on crass. They each hold their t-shirts up to reveal their skinny bellies moving in and out like the pulsating chest of a dying fish to the snappy Latin pop music. Brad has always been the better Shakira gyrator, and Sheena knows it. His hips don't lie. Sheena pours Brad another glass of pisco, and he drinks it. Suddenly, she slams his head into the plastic shoe bin. Blindsided. Sheena flashes the lights on and off like a strobe light, making scary faces at Brad. All at once they both stop, look at each other, and one of them says it: "What would people think if they actually saw this?"

It's hard to believe, I know. *Shakira? You guys listen to Shakira?* To understand this, we need to go way back.

In 2002 I found myself in the back seat of my friend Scott's pickup truck, headed south. A mountain bike racing team from Mexico had scored some cash from the Mexican government, and had used it to bring some American riders down to compete in their racing scene. The local media was informed, and in true Mexico fashion they created a fictitious rivalry between one of our guys and their National Champion, Ziranda Madrigal. Interviews were held, and the radio blared promos about the clash between their national hero and the invader from the North as if it were some kind of *lucha libre* match. The stage was set – all we had to do was get there. And to do so, we did what any self respecting adventure seekers would do: we loaded a bunch of sweaty, totally macho dudes into a couple of pickup trucks and headed for the border.

Before we reached the border, the mood inside the truck was calm. We were composed. Conversations were had, speculations were made, and stories were told.

After we crossed the border, Scott did something risky. While surrounded by a bunch of sweaty, totally macho dudes, he slid a Shakira CD into the CD player. I waited for the side punch to land on Scott's cheekbone, but it never came. Instead of filling our hearts with pain and our heads with feelings of killing Scott – the pansy – something else happened. Actually, it kind of worked. Shakira's spicy accent narrated our journey southward, forever linking her voice to the barren landscapes, dry arroyos, cinder block towns, and highway taco stands in our subconscious minds. Her voice sneaked through our open windows and into the passing desert like a nimble cat. And only *dios* knows how much I like cats.

That's right, I'm a cat man, and I'm not ashamed to admit it. And I'm also a Shakira man.

The Atacama desert in Northern Chile is a vast and expansive place. We drove for three days across lands where, throughout all of recorded history, rain has never fallen. The only substances in all directions for as far as the eye could see were sand, pebbles, and heat waves. With nothing to do except watch the hours turn into days and stare at the skinny dotted line from steering wheel to horizon, we had to find a way to pass the time. And what better way than to wriggle our hips to the sweet meowing voice of Shakira.

# 57

*Paso de Jama, Chile/Argentina — October, by Brad*

It's late morning and the desert sun is already high overhead. The dirt crunches under our tires and swirls up behind the van as we head out of town to the East, leaving the desert outpost of San Pedro de Atacama behind. We stop on the outskirts of town to surrender our importation paperwork to the customs office. It's 165 kilometers to the Argentine border, but nobody's out there. This is the last sign of civilization for a very long time.

Once on the highway, I start to feel anxious. We're already a smidge under 8,000 feet, but the pavement unfolds before us in an arrow-straight line up a mountain and out of sight. The lack of switchbacks means the road is steep. We're in the middle of nowhere, in the driest desert on Earth, driving into no-man's land. There is virtually no traffic. The combination makes me feel a little uneasy, but I don't know why. We're driving a twenty eight year old hippie bus with almost 300,000 miles under its wheels. Why worry?

To our left, Bolivia rises into the sky in a fantastic display of snow-capped volcanoes. It's as if someone has placed the Andes on top of a Georgia O'Keefe painting. The volcanoes ring the northern edge of the Atacama desert, and beyond them is *altiplano* — the high plains from which the Andes grow — all the way to Colombia. As we climb eastward on the highway, it appears as though our trajectory will intersect the rim of volcanoes. Our GPS shows that we're within a few kilometers of Bolivia.

It's desolate, barren, stark land. Tufts of low grass start to show through the crushed pumice at the roadside; we're back in the *altiplano*, and Nacho is feeling the elevation. As we plod slowly upward, our speed plunges slowly downward. Every mile robs our engine of precious oxygen, and soon we're traveling at a walking pace in first gear. I glance at the GPS: we're over 15,000 feet.

We catch a semi truck carrying a load of cars to Argentina. The elevation turns this into a slow motion race – the truck is driving as fast as an elderly person shuffling with a walker. We're moving along somewhat faster; whereas he may be traveling at four miles per hour, we're doing at least six. In slow motion, we pull out beside him for the long, slow pass.

A minute later, we've become level with his window when all of a sudden Nacho dies. We've found the elevation at which our engine can no longer pull enough oxygen from the intake air to cause gasoline to combust. The truck driver shoots us a confused look, but all we can do is wave and shrug our shoulders as he slowly pulls away from us. We sit in the oncoming lane with the flashers on until, a lifetime later, the truck finally passes us. We coast backward and off the side of the road.

Over the next few miles we develop a process for driving in the death zone: when Nacho dies, we pull over and let the engine rest for 10 minutes or so. Then we fire it up and ease back onto the road while slipping the clutch to get up to speed – about five miles per hour. We do this process repeatedly for the next several miles until we top out at 15,748 feet. After that the road drops down and levels out around 14,500 and we're back in business.

Once on the *altiplano*, things get surreal. We pass orange sand dunes and salty, deep blue lagoons. Llamas monitor our slow but steady progress from nearby hillsides. We pass between dunes and our eyes come to rest on stone megaliths jutting out of the hard earth and into the sky. We find a dirt track heading toward the megaliths, so we take it. We're driving in a bizarre, psychedelic Beatles song.

Just before reaching the first of the stone towers, we stop. We have a problem. The stone towers, as it turns out, are on the other side of a fairly vast wash, which sits at the bottom of a fairly vast hill. To get to the megaliths for the compulsory Nacho-in-action photos, we'll have to descend the vast hill, cross the vast wash, and climb the other side – a vast embankment. Given our luck at climbing the mild paved hill earlier in the day, we're not convinced that we'll ever make it out alive if we drive down the hill.

I get out of Nacho and set out on foot toward another vehicle, far out on the horizon. They'll be able to tell me what to do. Sheena hangs back to read her coming of age princess novel.

Fifteen minutes of walking brings me down the vast hill, across the vast wash, up the vast embankment, and then across a vast plain to where a 4×4 van sits. I find its driver fiddling with his radio. His t-shirt has a picture of a handgun, with the English words "point blank" emblazoned across the chest.

I introduce myself to the man and ask him, *que tal?* He wastes no time in telling me that I'll never get out of this place if I go down the vast hill. I ask him if he thinks I can drive along the vast wash until it crosses the main road, and he wastes no time telling me that I'd be a fool to believe that *that's* a good idea. I thank him and set out across the plain, down the vast embankment, across the vast wash, and back up the vast hill to where Sheena is still reading her coming of age princess novel.

"We're good, I think. You know, I think we'll be fine. What's the worst that could happen, right? I think we'll make it. It's supposed to be an adventure, isn't it?" Sheena's face is the word *unamused*, personified. She makes it clear that this is a stupid idea, and that she totally disagrees with this decision.

I pop it in gear and drive down the vast hill. We cross the vast wash, and then I gun it. We barely make it up the vast embankment.

For the next hour we explore the stone monuments, taking numerous Nacho-in-action shots. The rocks are amazing; some force of nature has caused the skin of the rocks to have formed into elevated scales. While we snap photos and eat a picnic lunch, the 4×4 van leaves, making quick work of the vast hill, and leaving with our hopes of a courtesy tow.

It's time. We buckle up and Nacho roars to life with the ferociousness of a lethargic houseplant. As we approach the vast hill I feel sickly. The beginning of the hill is uneven and rutted, so we can't carry much speed into it. I realize, only now, that this was a stupid idea. As we start to climb, Sheena unconsciously starts quietly squealing under her breath. She sounds like the soundtrack to a horror film.

We start out looking good, but halfway up the vast hill it becomes clear that we won't make it. Five miles per hour...four...three...two...almost stalling now...

"TURN LEFT!" Sheena shrieks.

"OKAY!" I yank on the steering wheel without thinking, leaving the track behind. Cutting across the sandy hill, tilted at thirty degrees, we start to pick up speed. Three miles per hour...four...five...

"TURN RIGHT!" Sheena squeals. I yank the steering wheel to the right, carving out a switchback in the rocks. It's working! To an experienced off-road driver the sight of our hippie bus slowly slinking through the rocks up this mild hill might be enough to evoke a belly laugh. A couple more cranks on the wheel and we're slowly putting away from the vast hill, safe. I look at the hill in the rearview mirror and think to myself, *boo ya, biatch!*

I only think it, because to say such things out loud would reveal how childish and pop-culturally outdated my train of thought can be.

For the next hour we glide past more lagoons studded with pink flamingoes and hills dotted with llamas. The whole thing is all very surreal. And then out of nowhere, we see it: a sign declaring *Limite Internacional Chile/Argentina*.

We made it! Arizona to Argentina! At the time we don't consider the fact that the end of the continent is still as far away as the distance from Arizona to Nova Scotia.

On the Argentine side of the border we continue to be stricken dumb by the landscape. We pass more lagoons, flamingoes, and llamas.

278

We drop into a valley and immediately the landscape turns pancake flat and white. Beyond us to either side there is nothing but salt for as far as the eye can see. We can hardly contain Nacho; he bolts off of the road and onto the salt plain for some roadless exploration.

By day's end the landscape has shifted again. We descend from the *altiplano* and into a desert reminiscent of Tucson, Arizona. How strange it is to find this landscape, so similar to our home state, in Argentina.

We coast into the town of Purmamarca for the evening. Tourists stroll the streets of what seems like an old Western town in the shadow of colored sandstone hills. We could just as easily be in Sedona as in northern Argentina. From the driest place on Earth, to one of the highest passes in South America; salt flats, flamingoes, towering rocks, and desert. Today the sky was as blue as any sky I've ever seen. It was a perfect road tripping day. It was a truly epic day.

# 58

*Uspallata, Argentina — October, by Brad*

It was a blustery day in 1997. Brad Pitt plodded through the mountains in tattered footwear, his worn out jacket proving no match for the icy wind sweeping down from the slopes of Aconcagua – South America's highest peak. While the film he was making was called *Seven Years in Tibet*, he was actually in Argentina, just a few miles outside of the small town of Uspallata. In 1997, actors staged a conflict between peaceful Tibetans and fierce Chinese soldiers bent on taking their land. Little known to Brad Pitt at the time, a similar conflict would take place 15 years later, not far from where the icy Aconcagua winds chilled him to the bone, between peaceful Americans and fierce Chilean border agents bent on taking their food.

**Three days before the conflict...**

We leave Mendoza and hook West toward the Andes. Scenes of vineyards and cottonwood trees soon give way to low shrubs and dry arroyos. On both sides of the road the hills grow into craggy peaks. An old railroad bed parallels the road, as does the *Rio Mendoza*, a wide river carrying glacial runoff to the fertile wine region below.

On the roadside we spot a shrine amid a sea of trash. Legend has it that a woman traveling with her infant child died of thirst in the desert, but her child survived by suckling the milk from her dead mother's breast. In remembrance of the story, travelers are given free rein to throw their plastic bottles on the roadside, where the occasional whipping wind scatters them into the countryside and the *Rio Mendoza*.

Nine miles later, we coast into the village of Uspallata in a valley surrounded by towering peaks. We find a place near a stream and set up our home. Straight in front of Nacho, high in the towering mountains, forever roams the collective memory of Brad Pitt in his tattered jacket.

**Two days before the conflict...**

We explore the town – little more than a highway with a few unpaved offshoots that lead to *estancias* and the surrounding canyons. To protect the village from the harsh winds that come down like frozen avalanches from the Andes, extensive groves of deciduous trees have been planted around the town. The trees make the place seem *tranquilo*.

References to Tibet are all over the place. The *Tibet bar* punctuates one corner, while Tibet tours and Tibet markets abound. To someone unaware of the town's famous recent past, the references would be very confusing indeed.

We hike to the top of a low hill outside of town where we find another shrine, this one devoid of any plastic trash.

In the evening we make a lasagna from scratch in our Dutch oven, watch a local teen flyfishing in our stream, and then retire to bed.

**The day before the conflict...**

I am awoken in the morning by a *gaucho* leading a herd of horses across the stream right in front of our camp. Throughout the day, more horses cross the stream. I am again awoken in the night by yet more horses crossing the stream, en masse. I start to wonder what's up with all of the horses crossing the stream.

**The day of the conflict...**

We wake up early, have coffee and pancakes, and then tear down camp. We head west and climb farther into the Andes. The terrain looks remarkably similar to the Himalayas. I guess that explains why they chose this place to film Brad Pitt pretending to be a Himalayan mountaineer.

We eventually arrive at Aconcagua and pull over. Our plan is to hike up to the base of the mountain, but one step out the door puts those plans on the backburner; the wind is howling and it's absolutely freezing. Springtime in the shadow of a 22,841 foot peak isn't as balmy as we'd thought it would be. A quick walk around a field, a few minutes looking at a natural bridge and we duck inside of a *tienda* for some hot chocolate while sitting around a wood stove.

Back on the road we approach the Chilean border. With any luck, by nightfall we'll be wearing fancy turtlenecks and quaffing expensive wine in a seaside restaurant in Viña del Mar. The abandoned train tracks paralleling the road are enclosed in a manmade tunnel of plate steel to protect it from the deep winter snows. The plate steel is rusty, dilapidated and sagging, giving the tracks an unreal scariness. They're like Marilyn Manson reincarnated as train tracks.

The road approaches an unbelievably steep and towering triumvirate of mountains, seemingly impassible, and I wonder how we'll get over them. My question is answered when the road dives into a tunnel straight through the biggest mountain. We drive for a few miles in the subterranean tunnel, icicles hanging from the roof, and then we see a sign hanging from the tunnel wall: *Bienvenidos a la Republica de Chile*. We've crossed the Chilean border underground.

Sheena ducks into the back of the van to do our routine of hiding all of the food before getting to the border guard shack. She's getting pretty good at it by now. She tucks our meat, fruits and vegetables into every nook and cranny, while leaving a few straggling pieces of wilted vegetables in our fruit bowl as decoys for Customs to find and confiscate.

We emerge from the tunnel into an unreal scene of snow-covered mountains sweeping down to the valley where the road and the abandoned train tracks are. A few kilometers more and we arrive at the Chilean border control building. It's a busy day, so we sit in line for close to an hour before it's our turn to enter the enormous A-frame drive-through building.

## The conflict

We're waved into vehicle control and find a place to park. We enter the building to get our passports stamped, our importation paperwork taken care of, and we sign an affidavit stating that, under penalty of a $1,000 fine, we aren't transporting any food. It's time for our Customs inspection.

Outside in the freezing air I scour the parking area for an inspector. I'm looking for the most relaxed and unintimidating one, so that if things start going wrong, they might be more easily distracted by shiny objects or random questions. I start going for the young girl whose inspector jacket is slightly too big, but she dodges me at the last minute, leaving me staring at a strict, intimidating-looking man in his thirties. Bollocks! Looks like he works out too.

"Ready for your inspection?" he asks. I take a deep breath and invite him over to Nacho, handing him my signed affidavit. After a cursory walk around the exterior, he asks Sheena to open the sliding door. He steps in and gets to work.

"Do you have any food in here?"

"Food? No sir, we don't have any food in here," I respond. I'm trying to look a little surprised by his question, as though the thought of having food inside of a car is completely stupid. My acting does nothing to convince him, so he starts opening things.

Drawer one: no food. Drawer two: no food. Drawer three: no food. Cabinet: completely stuffed with dry food. He slowly turns his head at me and shoots me a disbelieving look. The proverbial Nazi soldier has just found the proverbial stash of hidden Jews under the floorboards.

"I thought you said you didn't have any food." This must be very rewarding for him, watching liars like me squirm.

283

"Oh, right, sure that's food. But I thought you were talking about things like fruits and vegetables. Is it illegal to cross the border with oatmeal and stuff?"

He slowly turns back and starts emptying the cabinet until every last crumb is out on the counter, and then he goes through it piece by piece.

"You signed the affidavit, right? Did you even read it?" he asks in a slightly insulting tone.

Not knowing how to break it to him that nobody ever reads anything that they sign at a border, I try to be vague." Not very well, no."

He begins throwing our food in a pile on the floor. Once he's created a nice mound he moves on to Sheena's clothing storage area under the couch. He withdraws her clothing piece by piece until, halfway through, he pulls out a bag of apples. He holds it up, turns to look at me, shakes his head, and throws the apples in the pile. A few shirts later he removes our cucumbers, cilantro, tomatoes, and bell peppers.

The inspector leans back and stretches his shoulders, and then turns his head to look at me. He's done messing around.

"I will give you one more chance. Just tell me where all of your food is."

I confidently explain to him that he's found everything – that we keep all of our food up here in the front area. He definitely doesn't believe me, and positions himself on the couch, ready to tear our whole world apart. He reaches his arm into Sheena's sleeping bag and slowly withdraws a huge head of cabbage, and then gives me the stink eye.

"Do you always keep your cabbage in your sleeping bag?" he hisses. He lets out a disappointing sigh and starts getting rough. He claws at our belongings and throws them at me, and tells me he will remove everything from the van.

Within a few minutes, most of our belongings are on the ground in the parking lot and the pile of food on the floor has grown to include all of our meats, cheeses, fruits, vegetables, dried fruit, backpacking food, honey, and anything not in its original packaging. There's over $200 worth of food on the ground, and he's spilling it everywhere. Finally he looks behind a curtain and finds the carton of eggs.

"Are these eggs hard boiled or raw?" he asks.

"Raw," Sheena says. We're done lying; we've lost the battle.

Not satisfied with our too-little-too-late honesty, the inspector removes two eggs from the carton, holds them over Sheena's pillow, and smashes them against each other. The eggs explode all over her pillow and the inspector's hands. He wipes his hands on her pillow and hands it to me. Classy.

Sheena shoots me a furious glance. By now we're all feeling a bit pissed off. Just like every traveler we've met, we always have food in our car. This is our home, after all. And just like every traveler, we always deny having food for the purpose of crossing borders. It's a formality that no border agent has ever really cared about. This guy, however, deeply cares.

"Wait, stop. Just stop touching our stuff. We don't want to go to Chile any more. We're going back to Argentina."

The inspector looks at me, eyebrows raised. "Are you sure?"

"Yes, just get out of our car."

He jumps out of the van and asks me to follow him. I follow him to his group of inspector friends, where he informs them that we will be going back to Argentina. One of the women looks surprised and asks why we're going back.

"We're going back because you're stealing all of our food," I say. I'm still pissed about the eggs, and I'm not doing much to mask my anger. At this, our inspector's eyes nearly pop out of his head and he charges at me, stopping an inch from my face.

"Did you say STEALING!? You signed the affidavit, right!?"

At this, I realize that in fact he's right, and that we're really the bad guys. In our minds we think he's a jerk because he's the first border Customs agent we've ever met who actually cares about people smuggling food over international lines. We later find out that Chile in general is very serious about crossing borders with food because of their lack of invasive insect species, and their desire to keep it that way.

Still fuming, I tell the agent that my Spanish vocabulary is lacking, and that "stealing" is the only word I know to describe the act of taking away someone else's property. The agent scribbles "VOID" across my completed importation paperwork, and shoves it in my hand. We retrace our steps through all of the border control processes and get stamped out of Chile.

Once we arrive back at the Argentine side, we have to explain why we're back so soon from Chile, and why we don't have properly discharged Chilean import paperwork. When asked whether we're carrying any food, we look a little surprised and say no. We're casually waved through, back into good old Argentina.

When evening rolls around, we camp in the same place by the river outside of Uspallata. I drift off to sleep thinking about Tibet and Brad Pitt. It's almost as if today never happened. A horse crosses the stream outside of our window, and I fall asleep wondering, *what's up with all of these horses?*

# 59

*Roads of Argentina — November, by Sheena*

In Ecuador I bought a painting. It was a messy chaotic scene of people, animals, mountains and plains.

In Argentina, a similar style painting would go something like this: a flat sheet of desert surrounded by snowcapped peaks. Grapes droop from a tangle of vines in one corner. Stray dogs happily run in packs down the street. In the hills gauchos ride their horses, checking the fence lines and rounding up sheep.

In another corner of the painting, siesta time is taking place. The streets are desolate and the stores are closed, with the exception of ice cream shops. People wander, licking their *dulce de leche* ice cream. Acquaintances meet in the street, greeting each other with a kiss on the cheek. The women all have long beautiful hair, reaching all the way to the small of their backs. Men fashion long hair as well, pulling the tangle of hair high in a bun on top of their heads. In a grassy field, families cluster around an *asado*. The grill is stacked to capacity with ribs, *bife de lomo*, legs of lamb, and links of blood sausage. Bottles of Merlot sit like table centerpieces. Long after the families are gone, smoke rings linger in the air.

Alongside the grassy fields, bushes of orange flowers and stalks of purple dragonflies border the road. In a tree, red flags and ribbon hang, symbolizing yet another *Gauchito Gil* shrine. Down by the river, flyfishermen's rods drip with trout. *Mate* gourds are cupped in every set of hands. Staying high on life, they sip their bitter tea from sun up to sun down.

Argentina: it really is all rainbows and unicorns. Culturally, it is vastly different from its neighboring countries. The metamorphosis of culture, facial features, and cuisines that consistently took place from one neighboring country to the next ended abruptly here. Goodbye rice and potatoes. Hello wine and meat.

Argentina's cultural uniqueness is hard to reduce down to bullet points, but it's worth a try.

## Gauchito Gil, the cowboy saint

I met the most famous saint in all of Argentina for the first time in the desert along the Ruta 40. The landscape was bare all around, but under a mature tree, red flags, strips of fabric, and artificial flowers were strewn throughout the branches, announcing his presence. He sat under an arch painted in a matching red. He wore his hair long, slightly wavy with a wispy mustache. His blue long sleeve was pushed up to his elbows and a red scarf tied around his neck. He was five inches tall and made of a hard plastic.

While the real Gauchito Gil, a.k.a. Antonio Mamerto Gil Núñez, died in 1878, shrines of him number in the thousands. As the story goes, he was an outlaw who became a symbol of bravery, stealing from the rich and giving to the poor. Today, many people stop at the roadside shrines, giving thanks to Gauchito and asking for safe passage by leaving offerings such as water bottles, jewelry, car bumpers, and scraps of clothing. We on the other hand stopped at his shrines, using them as an excuse to stretch our legs and explore the offerings. Always colorful, always unique and intriguing.

While most shrines were dedicated to Gauchito Gil, there were others. Deolinda Correa set out into the desert with her infant baby in the 1940's in search of her husband who was forcibly taken to join the military. She died in the desert, but as she lay down, dying of thirst, she set her baby to her nipple, who survived until her body was found by gauchos. The gauchos took the child in, raising him on the plains driving cattle. Now, Argentineans leave bottles of water at her altars to calm her eternal thirst.

## Siesta

Argentineans are serious about siesta time. Beginning at 1:00 PM all businesses shut down. Grocery stores. Banks. Retail shops. All closed until 5:00 PM, Monday through Friday. The only exceptions that I noticed were ice cream shops. Always open. Always there to serve. You can only imagine how serious Argentineans are about their time off on the weekends and holidays.

And what is it like in a city where everyone is on siesta? Runners take over the sidewalks and friends ride down the street on their bikes. Young crowds sit in the town square and drink *mate*, and older couples rest on park benches, watching the day go by. As much as the siesta frustrated us as travelers, we could see its benefits, forcing people to focus on themselves and their relationships; a generous break from the commercial aspects of the everyday world.

## Late night dinners

Many restaurants don't open their doors until 8:30, and an early dinner typically *starts* at 9:30. It is not uncommon to finish dinner in the early morning hours. I wondered for quite some time if it meant that Argentineans woke up late, but they do not. They are at work by 8:00, with little breakfast and littler sleep.

## Desert oases: where wine really flows like water

Argentina's wine regions are located within the broad valleys and sloping plains of the desert, where ideal conditions exist for grape cultivation. Our first wine destination was in Cafayate, known for its dry white *Torrontes*. Day one was a success, checking off five of the six estancias that offered tastings within walking distance from the town square. As we continued south through Mendoza, the most important wine region in Argentina, vineyards and estancias flooded the outskirts of the city. The wine was cheap, plentiful, and most importantly, delicious. Between touring wineries, we stopped in at other establishments, like Simone's Olive Oil where the owner indulged us in his creations, soaking cubes of bread in bowls of olive oil, tasting the varieties and their different qualities.

## Gauchos, Asados and 55 million cattle

In the 1500's, Spain drastically influenced Argentina's culture with the importation of cows. Today, Argentine beef is world famous. All we ever heard from every traveler who had made it to Argentina before us was "Oh just wait until you get to Argentina — you can get a steak the size of your plate and 4 inches thick!" Was it really true? Could it be?

Just a few blocks down from the main square in Cafayate, under the tall trees shading the walkway and beside the red umbrellas, a chalkboard advertised *parrilla completa* for two. Inside the focal point of the restaurant was the massive grill stretched across the length of the restaurant. Atop were chunks of steak, chicken, chorizo, sausage, and ribs that could bring a tear to your eye. We enjoyed a very meaty meal, with coals under our table top grill to keep the food warm and tender. Argentine meat was as good as advertised, and for the next week we ate at a *parrilla* every day, attempting to satisfy our incessant craving after such a long hiatus from quality beef.

## More food culture

At a roadside stand a family worked together in an assembly line, scooping seasoned meat filling into the center of sheets of dough, folding them over, and pinching them closed. In wood fired ovens, dozens of raw dumplings went in, and what came out was Argentina's most famous street food: the empanada, golden brown and perfectly puffy. This became Brad's favorite food, and it was ubiquitous in every town. Every bakery, restaurant, and gas station offered their own version. My favorite? Locro soup. A warm and creamy concoction of hominy, squash, spices, and chunks of stewed beef shoulder.

## Smitten for yerba mate

Everywhere we went, people drank yerba mate. In the park, groups of friends sat in circles sharing a single vessel of the bitter tea. In stores, employees sipped their mate as shoppers browsed their merchandise. On the bus, commuters poured water from their thermoses into their gourds. Over and over again. Argentineans only carry on their daily business *if* a mate is in hand.

The drinking of yerba mate involves a host and one or more people, beginning with the preparation of the drink. The host packs the yerba (the herb) into the mate (the vessel used for holding the tea – usually a hollow gourd) and once tightly packed, the bombilla (metal filtered straw) is arranged to sit firmly upright in the tea. Lastly, warm water is poured into the mate and passed to the first participating drinker. The custom as a participating drinker is never to touch the bombilla with your fingers and to drink all of the tea from the mate before passing it back to the host. And it must always go back to the host. 'Thank you' is only whispered when you've had enough and are bowing out of the tea time rotation.

Interestingly, while yerba mate is an essential part of Argentine daily life, it isn't typically a part of the tourist experience. And despite it being the most popular drink in Argentina, it isn't served in restaurants due to its tedious preparation process and the fact that every single Argentinean person carries his own mate with him everywhere anyway.

What does it taste like? Just try to imagine the intense tart and bitterness of a liquid produced by stuffing 10 tea bags into a single serving cup. This stuff is strong, and not for the faint of heart. We wanted to love it, but I think you have to have a little bit of Argentina in your blood.

# 60

*Junin de los Andes, Argentina — November, by Brad*

We've been burglarized. We started this trip fully expecting not to be robbed; in fact our motto about our fellow man is, *in general, people are good*. We especially didn't think we'd be robbed in the relatively well off country of Argentina, and even less so in the Swiss Alps–esque Lakes District with its flyfishing, chocolate shops, tea houses, and general affluence. But we've been robbed, and in the Argentine Lake District of all places. It only takes one bad banana to make you want to bludgeon the whole group of bananas with a sock full of hot nickels.

We had just passed through the "trout capital of Argentina," the small mountain village of Junin de los Andes. Following the advice from my well-researched map of awesome fishing spots, we traveled five kilometers past Junin to the place where the *Rio Quilquihue* crosses under the road. On one side of the road we found a parking area, and in the back corner we found a fairly secluded, flat place to park. It would be the perfect place to camp before wrangling some fish in the morning. We parked Nacho, locked the doors, and walked the 100 yards to the bridge to look at the water.

Arriving at the bridge we spotted a small trail leading down to the bank. It seemed to afford a better view of the water, so we walked down it. At our farthest point, we were 200 yards from Nacho, and almost able to see where we were parked. No matter, we were in the middle of nowhere and there wasn't a soul around. We sat by the water for about five minutes, and then decided that we'd caught enough fish over the course of the last week. It wouldn't hurt to eat a few more meals and clear some fish out of the fridge before catching more. We headed back to the car to travel a bit farther South.

When we arrived at Nacho, I unlocked the sliding door and got in so I could wash my hands. Nothing seemed out of the ordinary, except that the new walking stick that Sheena found was broken in half on the floor.

"Hey Sheena, it seems your walking stick is broken," I said.

"You BASTARD! You broke my walking stick!" She was clearly pissed. She'd dragged me around the shore of *Lago Tromen* all morning to find this stupid thing.

"I didn't break it, I swear! You must have stepped on it!"

Sheena gave me the stink eye and we had a laugh, and then I got out and walked around the side of the car. At first my mind didn't know what to do with what I saw.

Broken glass. Window gone. big dent in the door frame. Door unlocked.

I opened the door and looked inside. My seat was covered in glass shards, and there was a dusty footprint on Sheena's seat. The glove box was open, the center console was open. Sheena's beloved walking stick was broken like the very core of her little heart.

Nobody has ever broken into our car before. But this is more than a car, it's our home. Some dirty rat bastard had broken our protective shell and had gone inside of our home without our permission.

We took a quick inventory of what was missing. The first discovery was the hardest to accept: he'd made off with our entire camera bag. It contained our digital SLR camera, all three of our nice lenses, and all of our lens filters. The contents of the camera bag alone were worth more than $2,000. He also got my Kindle e-book, my iPod with all of our pictures backed up on it, onboard air compressor, tent and sleeping pads, tow rope, dry bag, and our beloved GPS, *Shackleton*. Camera, music, navigation, air, camping, towing, books. In total, over $3,000.

"Did he get the computers!?" I said, nauseous with shock.

Sheena checked the secret computer spot and a relieved look came over her face. We would get to keep our photos and the rest of our digital lives, but it was only a small consolation. We felt absolutely violated. We got in the van and headed back to Junin, feeling like we wanted to curl up and die.

Our first stop was the police department, where a very unenthusiastic officer halfheartedly filled out a police report after making me wait outside for a half an hour. "Has this happened to anyone else in this spot?" I asked. "Oh yes," he responded, "It happens all the time. The *campesinos* are very fast. They rob all of the tourists who park in this spot." This angered me even more. If the police knew that someone was robbing all of the tourists who park in a certain spot, why not set up a decoy car and put the culprit in a "don't drop the soap" situation?

We felt horrible and wanted to go home. Our faith in humanity had been shaken. We decided to hole up in a campground for a couple of days to recover our wits.

By the second night of our stay at the campground we'd made friends with Matthias and Andrea, two Germans exploring South America by bike. Furthermore, our other new German friends Achim and Ute pulled into the campground in their overlanding truck. We all gathered under our awning for the evening, barbequed steaks, shared a few beers, and tried to forget about our bad luck.

In the morning, Sheena and I stood at the sink washing dishes from the previous night. The sun was out, we could hear the river rushing by, and birds were chirping overhead.

"You know, I don't know why, but I actually feel pretty good right now," I said to Sheena.

"Yeah," she responded, "that's because we're surrounded by love."

At the end of the day, our motto still holds true. In general, people are good.

# 61

*Bariloche, Patagonia, Argentina — November, by Brad*

We sat in hypnotized silence, swaying back and forth as we glided along the curvy shoreline of *Lago Nahuel Huapi*, the rain saturating our windshield just as fast as the wipers could clear it away. To our right, the dark water was made even more ominous by the jagged rain-pocked waves, purposefully marching in rows across the lake's surface, a deep opaque blue hinting at the extent of the water's depth. The side of the road was lined with flowers waist high and three feet deep, vibrant yellows and blues and purples. We were surrounded on all sides by jagged Andean peaks bearing crowns of ice, and wearing streaks of iron ore and pumice and evergreen.

"Oh wow," Sheena said, as if awoken from a trance. "Tomorrow is Thanksgiving."

We'd had no use of knowing dates for so long, and often had to strain our minds to remember what month it was. Whenever I had to remember the date, I would start by trying to remember what season it was. From there I could work out the month, and then try to recall recent milestones that could give me some hint as to the day. Sitting in the passenger seat, being rocked back and forth along the winding lakeside road, Sheena must have been working it out in her head.

"What are we going to do? We haven't even prepared?" It was true, a couple of months prior we had talked about doing a big Thanksgiving blowout. We had imagined cooking turkeys and sausage and stuffing, mashed potatoes, the whole bit, and all outdoors over a campfire. We would invite anyone we knew and have a great feast. But now we were a day away, the weather was cold and wet, and we had nobody to invite. It was looking like we'd spend the holiday alone, bundled up against the cold, eating whatever we happened to have in the van. Thanksgiving in Patagonia.

We drove on in silence, swaying with the curves as the rain battered the windshield.

An hour later the road had veered away from the lakeside, climbing and descending between mountains, crossing over rivers, and after a while the rain disappeared and was replaced by a strong wind pushing down on the road from the ridges above. We sailed out of the mountains and into the foothills, pushed along by a powerful tailwind. Up ahead we caught sight of what seemed to be several motorcycles cruising in the same direction as us. After a few minutes we had gotten close enough to realize that in fact they were bicycles. Four cyclists, bundled in their jackets, easily pedaled along at 45 miles per hour, helped along by the powerful tailwind. As we reached them, we realized that two of them were Matthias and Andrea, the Germans we'd met in Junin de los Andes after Nacho was burglarized.

We gunned the engine and pulled around them, Sheena waving frantically out the window. After we'd put a safe distance between us and them we pulled over and waited. Andrea arrived first, grinning wildly.

"Brad and Sheena! Hello! I can't believe it!"

"Look who it is!" Matthias said, coming to rest in front of Nacho, out of the wind. "We have just ridden the fastest that we have ridden on our entire trip – 70 kilometers per hour! This wind is great! Meet our new friends, Wiebke and Axel."

Wiebke was athletic and tall – perhaps six feet – and had wisps of blonde hair hanging down from her helmet. Axel had a nice smile and an athletic build. On the front of Wiebke's bike sat her young daughter, Smilla, while Axel pulled a trailer carrying their other youngest girl, Selma, a three year old.

"Nice to meet you," they said, shaking our hands, "these are our children." Wiebke smiled at Smilla, who responded with a sweet, "hellooo!"

We exchanged greetings and talked for a while before we remembered Thanksgiving.

"As it turns out," I said, "Thanksgiving is tomorrow—it's the time of year when we North Americans celebrate the final meal that we shared with the Native Americans before driving them off their land. Basically a really big feast. Will you guys be around Bariloche tomorrow?"

"Ah yes, I saw it on an episode of *Friends* once," Matthias said. "We will be in Bariloche, but we have been invited to stay at the house of a fellow cyclist who lives here." He explained how this man, who has come to be known as "Pelado"—literally "Baldy," on account of the fact that he has very little hair on his head—once tried riding his bicycle from Argentina to Alaska, but didn't quite make it. Since returning home, he has opened his home to all cyclists who pass through. No reservations required, just show up and have free reign of the house, a bed to sleep in, a kitchen to use, and an instant friend. Only one catch: we were driving a car.

"Maybe if you get a cabin for the day we can come meet you for dinner." They seemed sorry, but were already expected at Pelado's house.

We loaded up and continued on toward Bariloche, sandwiched between *Lago Nahuel Huapi* and the towering snow-capped peaks of the Patagonian Andes. When we arrived it was late afternoon and cold. Rain fell in intervals and a freezing wind whipped up off of the southern shore of the lake, giving the town the feel of Zurich in the winter. We parked downtown and made our way to the office of tourism to find out about cabin rentals.

The woman at the tourism office showed us listings for several cabins, most of which were well out of our price range. We armed ourselves with the names of a few of the cheaper ones and hit the streets. For the remainder of the day we went from cabin to cabin, checking each one off of the list. Most were the size of small walk-in closets, which explained the low cost. Defeated, and with the sun gone over the horizon, we rolled out of town to the campground.

By the time we found the campground it was dark. We drove in and negotiated our way through the thick tangle of trees until the small dirt road ended. I would have to back up and turn around. Sheena got out and went to scour for possible camping spots on foot. Unable to see, I decided to back up blindly, aiming for what appeared to be a blank spot between enormous trees. Everything was looking good...looking fine...a little faster now...and CRACK! Nacho came to an immediate stop. I had slammed into a tree.

For a minute I just sat there, contemplating. Thanksgiving was a bust. I was cold. We had so looked forward to Bariloche, "The Gateway to Patagonia," but it would more than likely be remembered at the freezing cold windy city where we crashed into a tree and ate Thanksgiving spaghetti.

"Brad!" Sheena said, running up to my window, "you've just run into a tree!"

In the morning our windows bore a thin skin of ice and we shivered in our down jackets as we brushed our teeth outside, trying in vain to capture a few stray rays of sunlight through the thick evergreen canopy. We loaded up our things and headed into town where we would check our email and then go to the grocery store to try to put together some kind of sad Thanksgiving dinner for two.

On the way to the store we swung by the Berlina microbrewery and hopped on their free Wi-Fi. The first message in my inbox was from Matthias, and had come the previous evening, right around the time I was slamming Nacho into a tree.

*We finally found the "free house for cyclists." Here is a very, very friendly family and we do feel a little bit like home. I think all the Germans gonna stay here a few days. But also we wanted to have a Thanksgiving dinner with our friends from Arizona. So I asked the guy if it would be ok to have*

*a dinner all together in his house. He just says "Sí, Sí, Sí, no problem!"*
*Here is a place of big hospitality and it's no problem to find a place for*
*Nacho (and for you to sleep)... there is a farmer in the neighborhood that*
*sells meat and he was recommended by the people here. Should I ask for*
*special meat?*

We excitedly wrote back to Matthias and proceeded to drive to
the grocery store, where we spent at least a week's budget on all of the
fixings for the best Thanksgiving blowout we could concoct.

"Bacon! Sheena, they have bacon! Can we do something with
bacon?"

"Buy it!" Sheena wailed.

"I have some sausages here, how many sausages?"

"All of them!"

"Baguettes?"

"Is this Bastille Day? No! Put those down and find some dinner
rolls!"

When we pulled into Pelado's driveway on the shore of *Nahuel*
*Huapi*, Nacho was full up with bags and bags of American soul food.
Matthias met us at the gate.

"They didn't have any turkeys," he said, "but they have some
chickens bigger than I have ever seen. The farmer is preparing them for
us now, we must pick them up at 2:00."

Inside Pelado's house we were introduced to his wife, Felicidad,
who was hanging out with Axel, Wiebke, and their children. After a tour
of the property and Pelado's backyard bakery, we got under way.

Pelado made two loaves of fresh-baked braided bread. Andrea
and Matthias made a radish salad, procured two turkey-sized chickens,
and provided copious amounts of beer and wine. Felicidad made a
second salad, composed entirely of edible plants from the yard. Sheena
and I commandeered the kitchen and proceeded to season and roast the
chickens and made garlic mashed potatoes, sausage stuffing (with
bacon), green beans (with bacon), and fried potatoes and peppers (with

bacon). For dessert, Andrea made apple pie from scratch, but without bacon.

"This is great," Pelado said as we filled the table with food, "I once saw Thanksgiving on an episode of *Friends*!"

Just as dinner was served, two more cyclists arrived; Renata and Arturo from Brazil. They had heard through the grapevine that there was to be an American holiday celebration, popularized by the TV show *Friends*, and they wanted to see what it was all about.

The food was incredible, and our international group of friends took to the gluttonous tradition like David Schwimmer to paleontology. As we ate, Pelado recounted for us his experience during his attempted bicycle trip to Alaska.

"I left this house in 2001," he began, "with the goal of riding all the way to Alaska. I just decided to drop everything and go. I was going to ride until I got there, it didn't matter how long it took.

"Everything went fine until I got to the border of the United States. I spent all of my Mexican pesos before I left Mexico, and then crossed the border. The first thing I did was go to the ATM machine to get US dollars. But when I tried, it said I had no money left. I immediately called home to see what was happening, and I was told that our economy had collapsed overnight and that the banks had no more money. Everything we had was gone!

"So now I was in America with no money. I asked the border guard what I should do, and he didn't know. He said I should try the Red Cross. I had never heard of this 'Red Cross' before, but I rode there. When I arrived I told them that I had no money and no food. They took me in and gave me a place to sleep, and then they opened their cabinets and told me to take all the food I wanted. They filled my bike trailer with canned food! I couldn't believe it!

"I continued riding through America, going from Red Cross to Red Cross, and every time they gave me a place to sleep and food to eat. After this I love the Red Cross. I am a big fan now, and I tell everyone how much I love them!

"When I arrived in San Francisco it was September, and the Saudis attacked the Twin Towers. This was a very sad time and everybody got closer to one another. I felt so much love, and I started wearing a banner in support of the victims. People would clap when they saw me ride by because I was riding in honor of them.

"But then," he continued, "I ran into trouble. My visa in the United States was for three months, but because of my troubles I had only made it as far as Seattle when my visa ran out. I was so close to the border! But I was stopped by the police, and they realized that my visa had expired. They arrested me and deported me back to Argentina. I had ridden my bicycle half way across the world, and they sent me home when I was so close to the border! I was heartbroken. I have been here ever since. When I got back here I built an oven and started baking bread, and selling it in Bariloche."

Pelado's story saddened us. To have been treated with such hospitality in so many places ourselves, and to have felt warmth from strangers, the thought of our country deporting Pelado and putting an end to his dream, gave us something to contemplate. But after all of it, he still loved the United States, and above all he loved the Red Cross mission.

As night closed in around Pelado's house we looked around the table. We were Americans and Germans, Brazilians and Argentineans. Through serendipity and great fortune we had all ended up in the same home to break bread together, and in doing so we had enjoyed our best Thanksgiving to date. It's funny how things work out sometimes.

# 62

*Chiloe, Chile — December, by Brad*

*"When you get to the top of a wall, there's nothing up there…the end result is absolutely useless. But every time I travel I learn something new, and hopefully I get to be a better person."*
— *Yvon Chouinard, 180° South*

We slept very little on account of the wind, tossing Nacho about like Shackleton's rowboat. I drank my coffee, finished my oatmeal, and then emerged from the sliding door into the eerie, gray morning. Something was different. Alarmingly different. The sand dunes that had surrounded Nacho the previous evening were all gone. Smooth, wet ground was all that remained. The windshield and front grill were coated with sand, and a tide pool stood like a partial moat around Nacho.

While we slept, the waves had crept inward and engulfed our camp site. They were frightening waves, breaking in sets twelve at a time, white caps stripping off into the air like the licking flames of a fire by the terrorizing wind. These waves had crossed the sandy wasteland that had separated us from the ocean while we slept. While I danced with lollipops and wagons in my dream world, Nacho braved the high seas, just like Shackleton's rowboat, in the real world. *Pacific Ocean*: a misnomer if there ever was one.

I paced back and forth, circling Nacho in disbelief. While I did, a couple of jacketed figures made their way up the otherwise abandoned, remote beach, fighting the oppressive wind. Inspecting the wheels and undercarriage it was impossible to tell how high the water had come. Spitting rain and ocean spray had coated everything in a fine, salty mist.

The figures approached so I put up a confident façade, as if we hadn't nearly been swept away into southern Chile's penguin and shark infested waters in our hippie bus.

Retired German tourists. *Pretty far from civilization*, I thought. The whole situation had a Tim Burton air about it.

"Looks like it's going to be a balmy day," I said, trying to lighten the mood. The man tightened the hood of his rain jacket around his face against the wind. The woman opened her mouth to speak, and as she did I recoiled in fear. Her thin face was gray and sunken, and when she spoke, her lips parted to reveal teeth smeared with thick trails of blood.

*Sweet baby Jesus H. Christ!*

She said something, but the little attention I was able to spare was not enough to make heads or tails of it. It was a heinously botched flossing job, complete with swollen gums and squirting blood. I hadn't seen anything so grotesque since the last time I tried flossing.

In the adventure documentary 180° South, a young man follows in the footsteps of Yvon Chouinard on a southbound journey into Chile's Patagonia region. The culmination of the voyage puts the traveler in Chile's *Parque Nacional Pumalín*, a large swath of land put into conservation by North Face founder Doug Tompkins and his wife Kris. In the film, Chouinard accompanies the young adventurer in an attempt to ascend *Cerro Corcovado* – a peak which has only been summited once, by Tompkins.

Were the sky not so heavily cloaked by thick gray clouds, Corcovado would have been visible from Chiloe, the small island off the Pacific coast of southern Chile where we were camped. The park that Doug Tompkins helped create is visible from the island, only a few miles to the East. We later realized that our camp site on the windy beach, where we were nearly swept away by the tide, and where we were exposed to the gruesome floss bloodbath, was a filming location in 180° South.

*Parque Nacional Pumalín*, while an important conservation project, caused some navigational issues for us in our attempt to reach the island of Chiloe. When Tompkins started buying land – around two million acres in all – he raised the suspicions of the Chilean people. Upon consolidating all of his purchases into one account, it became evident that he'd acquired a tract of land stretching from sea to border – a strip that split the country in two. And by placing it into conservation, no roads would be built to connect one side to the other, effectively cutting southern Chile off from the North. In order to reach southern Chile, one would have to cross into Argentina, adding five hundred miles to the trip, or else take a pretty expensive ride on a ship.

A week earlier we had made it as far South as the small Welsh town of Trevelin, in Argentina, approximately level with the bottom of Chiloe. Our plan was to cross the Andes and take the ship to the island, which would allow us to circumvent the national park. The day before we intended to sail, we were informed that the ship was down for maintenance for at least a week. Unable to drive through Pumalín, we would have to retrace our steps five hundred miles through Argentina and part of Chile to reach it from the North.

The last time we were in Chile, we crossed the driest place on Earth – the Atacama desert. The first thing that we noticed upon crossing into southern Chile was the ample orographic precipitation. As soon as we crossed the border it began to rain, and it would not stop for twenty days.

The rain became the soundtrack to our drive through the Andes. The repetitive whooshing of our windshield wipers announced our arrival in Puerto Montt after the one day, five hundred mile jaunt, placing us near the northern end of Chiloe. The bulbous drops battered the roof of the corrugated parking shelter where we camped for four days in the city, and the downpour continued while we explored the fish market and the water front. It rained on the drive to the ferry port, and it rained on us while we camped at the penguin colony on the northern end of the island. In the end we were sure of two things: I can't remember what the first thing was, but the second is that it rains a lot in Chile.

The day before arriving at our windy beach outpost, we had attempted to reach the Pacific Ocean via a route that we had scoped out on our map. The map's key described it as a secondary dirt road for the first half, turning into "*huella*" for the second half, indicated by a thin dashed line. The route looked tortuous, and seemed to guarantee adventure. *Huella?* Something less good than a secondary dirt road? "Let's do it!" I told Sheena.

Two hours later, after leaving Sheena and Nacho near a mud bog and walking through the forest to a deep water crossing, I learned that *huella* is Spanish for *hiking trail*. Trial and error, I'm finding, is a highly effective method of burning new Spanish vocabulary into my brain. Thus, the night before sleeping in the shallows of the Pacific Ocean, we slept near a crystal clear stream surrounded by green grass and big trees at the end of a secondary road, just where the *huella* to the ocean begins.

We eventually left the barren and windy beach, making our way through colorful villages and striking landscapes on our northward trajectory. An official at the ferry port informed us that the southbound ship was still down for maintenance. With *Parque Pumalín* in our way, we were left with no other choice than to drive the five hundred miles through Argentina, back to where we had started.

This whole thing will eventually come to an end, and perhaps it will be utterly useless. But after all is said and done we may learn something new, and maybe even emerge better people.

*"The best journeys answer questions that in the beginning, you didn't even think to ask."*
— *Jeff Johnson, 180° South*

# 63

*Coyhaique, Chile — December, by Brad*

My trembling hands did their best to keep my pint of ale from spilling across the rough hewn wooden table. The day was cold, but despite being indoors I couldn't warm up. The exhilaration followed by such tragedy had sapped my body of its ability to regulate blood flow to my chilly extremities, but it wasn't the cold that caused me to tremble. The body that I had held in my hands only hours before had slipped away, never to be recovered, and was now replaced by this lifeless substitute; a cold golden ale, which I now clenched in my fingers, quivering from a deep, soul-shattering anguish. My heart became a lead weight behind my sternum. I was inconsolable. Patrons came and went through the screen door, their jackets pulled tight against the cold.

And that damned song. Was this some kind of cruel torture?

*Maybe I didn't love you*

*Quite as often as I could have*

*And maybe I didn't treat you*

*Quite as good as I should have*

I tried to block it out by gazing into my beer, concentrating on the bubbles. How they formed at the bottom of the glass like baby tadpoles. How they floated – the epitome of freedom – through the golden ether. And then how they bobbed to the surface, died, and were gone forever.

*You were always on my mind*

*You were always on my mind*

I tried to forget. I *needed* to forget. I took a deep, medicinal swig of ale and retreated into happier memories.

While driving along a stream in Patagonia's northern Lake District, we'd spotted a tiny track leading into the trees. Pushing our way through overhanging bamboo beneath lush oak trees, we came into a clearing. We situated ourselves so that Nacho's sliding door would open up to the sand bank and the crystal clear trout stream. I fished all day, up and down the banks, reeling in a dozen or more rainbow and Patagonian brown trout, all too small to keep. I showed Sheena how to fish where the creek hooked to the right, creating a perfect eddy in front of our camp. Times were good. Scratch that. Times were great.

My lip began to tremble, and I noticed that my glass was empty. Why wouldn't my hands warm up? I was losing control. I couldn't let myself lose composure. What would the others think? Would they stare, or would they be kind and pretend not to see? I tipped a finger to the waiter and pointed to my glass.

And that damned song. It would be the death of me. It was on repeat, midway through its third revolution. Was a grand puppeteer watching me, pulling these strings that caused me to teeter on the edge of sanity? Damn you puppeteer! And damn your song!

*And maybe I didn't hold you*
*All those lonely, lonely times*
*And I guess I never told you*
*I'm so happy that you're mine*

He pulled my empty glass away and set down a fresh one. I held the glass in my hands, just as I would have held her had she not slipped away into the darkness, never to be seen again. No parting glance, no chance to say goodbye. I again retreated into my mind, where better times awaited. Better times, like when we camped on the *Rio Quillen*.

In the morning we had turned onto a dirt road that skirted the river. Sheena and I had smiled at each other across the front seats while we bumped along, looking for a good fishing hole. Spotting a rock outcropping in the middle of the strong, crystal clear water held promise of rising trout. Sheena sat on a warm rock in the Patagonia sun while I let out line and set the fly just upstream of the outcropping. My fly bobbed in the current, sweeping around the rock, and was quickly taken by a beautiful rainbow trout. Eighteen inches! Boy, it was a beauty, strong and shiny and perfect.

Throughout that day and the next I landed three eighteen inch rainbows. We found a campsite under a weeping willow tree next to the river, built a fire, and ate like a king and queen. Those were the good times. I wondered if I would ever again know good times. My heart ached and it felt as if I'd never recover. I had lost my *joie de vivre*.

Just then a couple entered the establishment. The woman's shiny brown hair nearly reached her waist, and she brushed it off of her shoulder as she entered. The man unbuttoned his overcoat and smiled at his wife. Their happiness reminded me of my sorrow and I took another drink. The song played on.

*Little things I should have said and done*
*I just never took the time*
*But you were always on my mind*
*You were always on my mind*

By now my heart was numb, and I was able to reenact the day's events. I slowly relived each moment, wishing that I could go back, just for one second, to make things better. To somehow change the way things ended.

After several days of driving along Chile's Carretera Austral, we had arrived at the town of Coyhaique. We had passed through town and found a camp site at the edge of a bend in the *Rio Coyhaique*. We were surrounded by green hills where the river passed under a bridge. From our bed we could hear the water bubbling over rocks at the edges of the river. My fly rod waited patiently for the morning, and I kissed Sheena good night.

In the morning I said a quick goodbye and set out to the north, along the banks of the river. It was a cold day and the black rocks along the bank became slick with the spray of misty rain. I navigated my way down a slanted rock face to the base of an imposing stone wall where the strong current churned and dove to untold depths. I pulled out several arm lengths of line and whipped it in a cyclical motion over the surface of the water until my neon yellow leader reached the base of the wall. I set my fly down and let the current grab it, sinking my line in front of the wall, and watched the neon yellow disappear into the darkness below the rocks.

A minute passed, and then I started retrieving the line. Pull, relax, pull, relax. I imagined the fly pulsing through the water like a little fish.

Pull, relax, pull, relax, pull – KABOOM! Something hit my fly with the force of a freight train, pulling ten feet of line out of my hands before I knew what had happened.

"FUH-FUH-FUH...!" I couldn't get the expletive out – there was no time! I squeezed the line to add some resistance. This thing was huge! I had caught a salmon on the *Rio Futaleufu* a couple of days earlier, but this was far bigger. It pulled more line out; fifteen feet, twenty, twenty five. I guessed how far she had gone and figured she was just about to reach the point where the current funneled into a raging jet between two rocks. She would surely break my eight pound tippet if I let her get into that current. I eased back on the line and started making some progress in pulling her in.

I fought, pulling some line in and then letting her take it back, for ten or fifteen minutes. Whatever this was, I needed to wear it out before I would have a chance to pull it in.

My hands trembled, my heart pounded out of my chest. The mist beaded up on my jacket and tumbled onto the rocks, and I shuffled my feet to position myself near the water's edge without slipping in and being carried away. I looked to see if Sheena was around. She was nowhere to be seen.

Soon, my line was taut, and pointed straight into the dark water at my feet. I still couldn't see the fish, but I could tell that it was right in front of me. Suddenly she twisted, revealing the side of her body. A blaze of silver the size of a toddler flashed from beneath, and again the expletive stuttered on my tongue.

"FUH-FUH-FUH...!"

I positioned my net, but it was awkward. The rocks under the water were like the Alps in miniature, surrounding the fish. I managed to situate the net directly above the fish, and brought it down. It all happened so fast.

As the net came down, it became clear that she was too big to fit through the opening. The net's metal frame bisected her, but she would not go in. The fish – the most enormous rainbow trout I've ever laid eyes on – gathered her strength. While I tried to capture her in the net, my heart pounded the back of my sternum. I wasn't breathing any more, I was wheezing. And then, in the struggle to get her in the net, she gave one final, violent kick, and my line went slack.

I stood up, line in hand, and looked at the end hanging limply where my fly used to be.

"FUUUUUUU*$@#^&K!" I evacuated my lungs, funneling all of the power from my adrenaline-filled muscles, into one long, drawn out, echoing expletive. Somewhere deep in that river, through the tumultuous current, over the noise of clanging rocks and rushing water, that fish heard my heart breaking through the vibration of my vocal cords.

"If only I would have...positioned the net...like this," I slurred, holding my frigid fingers out over the wooden table, "I woulda had her. I woulda...*had* her."

"Snap out of it, my love," Sheena urged, "it was just a silly fish. Life will go on."

But to me she wasn't just a fish. She was Homeric siren, as big as a tiny human, and she was beautiful. I raised my glass as a tear collected in the corner of my eye, and the puppeteer played that incessant song.

*You were always on my mind*
*You were always on my mind.*

# 64

*Perito Moreno Glacier, Argentina — December, by Sheena*

Brad and I had waited a long time to see this place, and now, as we sipped our more than slightly unfulfilling cups of instant coffee, we peered into the distance in awe. Butterflies raced in my stomach and my mind was overflowing with anticipation. The feeling wasn't so much caused by the view, but by the set of vocal pipes on this thing. It creaked and moaned, yearning for our attention, attempting to resist the pressure of the ice pushing its massive body forward. Creak, pop, crash! We were teased to come closer.

We followed the raised walkway through the forest until we broke through the barrier of green and were left with an open and unimpeded view of the glacier. We were dumbstruck. It was truly like *nothing* I had ever seen in my life. As far as the eye could see, it stretched back into the nethermost regions of the mountains, eventually coming to a standstill before us, bold and beautiful above the surface of the shimmering gray-teal waters of *Lago Argentino*. It was hard to grasp its immensity; it seemed impossibly gargantuan. My central and peripheral vision were at capacity. Yet, from a bird's eye view, we were only seeing the very tip of this glacier.

This massive tongue of ice stretched eighteen miles into the mountains, having a width of three miles, and it towered into the sky like a solid row of twenty two story buildings. Its average height is 240 feet. I felt like an ant on a sidewalk before this monster, small and insignificant, in an instant I could be swallowed whole in one minor crevasse of its massive body. And the colors! The glacier was a swirl of white and blue; the blue formed from densely compact ice, and the white from trapped air bubbles after numerous melting and freezing cycles. If the glacier hadn't stolen the view, surely the milky grayish teal water of *Lago Argentino* would have. The strange color was the result of the sun's rays diffracting against unsettled sediment of "glacial flour" in the water. Simply spectacular.

Perito Moreno is famous in the world of glaciers. It is a fighter and one of the few glaciers in existence that is still advancing; stretching forward an average of seven feet a day. However, while it is advancing, building-sized chunks of ice are simultaneously breaking away from its face. Its growth, counteracted by the ice sloughing off of its face, make this one of the few stable glaciers in a time of global warming.

We watched for hours, unable to pull away. We listened to the creaks and pops while we waited, frozen in place, for the glacier to calve off 240 foot high chunks into the water, releasing an instant rippling tidal wave. Like lightning and thunder, there was always a split second between the belly flopping of a hunk of ice and the explosion of sound in our ear drums.

Patagonia's amazing scenery was not exclusive to Perito Moreno; it seemed to exist in all directions. In the South, on the Chilean side of the Andes we visited *Lago Grey*, where chunks of pockmarked icebergs floated in the water, and where Torres del Paine's 3000 foot tall vertical shafts of basalt jut up into the sky. At its base, shiny rock faces stream with water, draining into a crisp blue glacial lake below.

Farther North we visited the other half of *Parque Nacional Los Glaciares*, with Mount Fitz Roy stealing the show. We met up with friends, hiked in the mountains, camped, and explored the many eating and drinking establishments in the tiny town of El Chalten, which serves as a basecamp for Fitz Roy. And finally, after having our fill of glaciers and National Parks, it was time to finish this thing off. We boarded Nacho and pointed his big white nose southward.

# 65

*Ushuaia, Argentina — January, by Brad*

The air smelled of salt and the wind whipped my hair into a blazing Jerry curl as I stood at the bow of the ferry. The low moan of the engines rose and fell with each passing wave. It had been forty two months since I stood at my desk at work and sporadically blurted out the suggestion that would change the course of our lives:

"Hey Steve, let's drive your hippie bus to Tierra del Fuego."

and Steve's curt answer:

"I don't think so."

In the months that followed we would buy our own bus, start saving our money, quit our jobs, and then set off to the South. Life is short, we figured. Might as well do something interesting.

And now here we were. Behind us, the South American continent shrunk to a thin line on the horizon, while before us the island of Tierra del Fuego rose up from the ocean like an ominous rogue wave.

For the last year of driving I had imagined what it would be like when we arrived in Tierra del Fuego. I had envisioned a place from a Tolkien novel; a land carved by volcanic eruptions, where craggy old trees dripped with moss and clear streams cascaded off of shelves of hardened magma. It would be an otherworldly, nearly impenetrable place.

When the ferry landed in Tierra del Fuego, we disembarked not into a mysterious forest of eerie, moss-laden trees, but onto a flat plain with nothing but grass and wind for as far as the eye could see. *Could this be right?* we wondered. After driving up the ramp and onto the main

313

road, our doubts were put to rest. A large sign declared, *Welcome to Tierra del Fuego*. We had made it to the Land of Fire, and the Land of Fire looked just like Nebraska.

For the first mile of Tierra del Fuego, we thought we'd really scored. The road was nicely paved, straight, and smooth. We sailed along at Nebraska speeds, all the while checking out the grass and the wind. After that mile, things took a turn for the worst. The pavement abruptly ended and we bumped onto the dirt road which, over the course of the next one hundred miles, we would get to know all too well.

The other passengers on the car ferry were mostly big rigs, carrying food and supplies to the towns on Tierra del Fuego. In this place, with its blasting wind, cold climate, and permanent chill, food had to be brought in from the warmer and more fertile North. As we bumped along the potholed, washboard road, I kept asking myself, *where are these trucks going? How can Argentina justify sending supplies all this way?* And it really is a long way.

Southern Patagonia – and I'm talking the lower 1,500 miles of it, is so sparsely populated that many primary "highways" are still dirt. We frequently came close to running out of gas due to the long distances between the tiny towns. It was like driving from Phoenix to New Orleans on Jeep roads. Since there was usually no place to pull off of the road, we slept several nights adjacent to the dirt track, rocking to sleep in the fierce winds.

After one hundred miles of the bone-jarring dirt road through Chile's portion of Tierra del Fuego, we crossed the Argentine border at around 11:00 in the evening, just as the sun was setting. Where the road met the Atlantic Coast we found a construction site, and retreated from the wind behind a towering pile of dirt. As we drifted off to sleep, sometime around midnight, twilight still waned above our campsite on one of the Earth's southernmost fingers of land.

The next day we rose early and hit the road. Argentina took better care of its portion of the island, paving the last two hundred miles of Ruta 3 to ease the burden on the supply truckers. About a hundred miles into the day, the landscape started to shift. It began with the appearance of trees; moss-laden ones, no less. Next, streams began to crisscross the landscape, and the plains turned into bumpy, low hills. Soon we were driving through a full-fledged forest dotted with lakes, and the low hills sprang up from the roadsides into towering mountains.

We had reconnected with the Andes as they swept down to terminate at the southern tip of the continent. The fact that we had reached the Andes by traveling directly south meant that we were virtually there – at the place where South America narrows to a sweeping arrow tip.

We passed a lake, and began to climb. We switched back and crossed along the exposed face of a rocky peak, and then we were there: at the top of our very last Andean pass. From here, it would be all downhill to the end of the world.

The rain began to batter our windshield as we descended the windward side of the mountains, and our hearts began to race.

Six months ago, while stranded on a farm in Colombia with a failed transmission, Sheena and I had a serious talk. Nacho had had his first mechanical failure in Mexico, only a month after leaving home. From there, the failures rained down in a steady stream. Greasy hands smashed, battered, and wrenched on Nacho in Guatemala, Costa Rica, Panama, and now Colombia. After the first seven months of our trip, we had spent an average of $662 per month on car repairs. Sheena and I had to answer the question: at what point do we say enough is enough? Would it realistically be possible to make it to Ushuaia?

It took a transmission failure and a month of being stranded to possess us to ask that question, but once we had asked it, the weight of our situation dawned on us. Everything that we had worked for was in jeopardy if we kept rolling with the status quo. There was only one thing to do: whatever it was going to take. We weren't abandoning ship, and that was final.

315

We descended from the Andes before an unforgettable backdrop; Tierra del Fuego suddenly terminated into the chilly waters of the Beagle Channel. On the horizon, Navarino Island lurked under cover of an ominous rain cloud. Beyond it lay Cape Horn, and then nothing until Antarctica. This was the end of the road.

It was New Year's Eve. One year ago we were parked in the driveway of Sheena's parents' house, nervously packing the last of our belongings into Nacho. A year used to flash by in the blink of an eye, but the last twelve months had delivered more than enough experiences to fill a lifetime.

We emerged from a canyon, hooking to the right, and then we saw it. Homes clung to the sides of the mountains encircling the bay, and the port sprawled out into the channel at the center of town. The *National Geographic Explorer* sat moored in the bay, ready to leave for Antarctica. Craggy peaks capped with snow cast their shadows over mossy forests and eerie canyons of hardened magma. It was an otherworldly, nearly impenetrable place, straight out of a Tolkien novel. It was Ushuaia, the southernmost town in the world. And we had driven there.

# 66

*Punta Tombo, Argentina — January, by Sheena*

It was after hours and the sun was beginning to set. The park hours at the entrance clearly stated they were closed, yet no gate had stopped us from continuing onward. We wound down the dirt road through the rolling desert brush. Along the twenty mile stretch, signs were posted at every curve in the road: "Do not stop or get out of your vehicle." I felt like I was on a safari adventure.

We pulled into the parking lot and peered around. So this is where they lived? The water was supposed to be near but we couldn't see it. In the distance, I spotted a few motionless figures. Could it really be?

"Brad! I see penguins!"

He stared in their direction and let out a mocking laugh. "Sheena, those aren't penguins. Those are just *statues.*"

Oh silly me. And then they moved.

Curious by this strange new environment, I cracked open Nacho's passenger door. Instantly the interior of our small home was filled with crazy bellowing penguin hoots and hollers. Surely the park wouldn't allow us to spend the night here, yet no one appeared to tell us otherwise. We started cooking dinner, and just as Nacho became a sauna inside with mysteriously fogged windows, there was a tap on the window. Damn.

The man outside introduced himself as the park ranger. "What are you doing? Have you gotten out of your vehicle? Have you paid the park entrance fee? Are you sure you have not gotten out of your vehicle?"

317

With the promise that we would not exit our vehicle, we were granted permission to stay in the park for the evening. He then pointed to his house and said "If you want to watch television you are welcome to come by my house." I guess they would bend their own rules in the name of entertainment.

For over a year, our goal had been to proceed South until we could not go any farther. We made it to Ushuaia but our drive in the Americas was far from over. Our final destination was Buenos Aires, 1,500 miles to the Northeast. As we drove up the Atlantic coast, we finally hung up our jackets and pulled back out our tank tops and shorts.

In the morning it felt like Christmas as a child. I could hardly contain myself. In the most unlikely of climates, we found ourselves at Punta Tombo, the largest Magellanic penguin rookery outside of Antarctica. All around us, a quarter of a million breeding pairs of penguins were waddling in the brush and skinny dipping at the beach.

"You are the first ones in the park this morning, so it's just you and the penguins! The penguins here have had a long journey and are very hungry. If they cross your path, please, don't block them," the ranger said as we walked past his post.

Everything I know about penguins was learned from the movie *March of the Penguins*. They march for months through the cold frigid winds, hungry and tired, only to find another cold torturous place to lay their eggs. Then, due to the frigid cold temperatures, they sit on their eggs for months, balanced between their pouch and feet. They sit and wait for as long as it takes for their partner to return back with food, and then they repeat the cycle all over again.

Perhaps the penguins here hadn't seen the film. They had discovered a much warmer place to enjoy their winter. Dugout burrows covered the hillsides and penguins were scattered everywhere we looked. The landscape was low lying desert brush and hamster-like mice scurried across the ground. Guanacos grazed. Everything was in harmony.

It was baby season when we arrived and all the baby penguins were two to three months old, losing their fluffy down, and only a few weeks away from learning how to fish. In a few short months they'd begin their annual southern migration, which would last five to six months. On this particular morning, various activities were going on. Penguins carried sticks across fields, families nestled under the brush, and some male penguins attempted to show their dominance, sword fighting with their beaks. Female penguins basked in the sun, grooming their babies while slowly getting ready for the day. Babies stood motionless, whining constantly, hungry and needy. And then like clockwork, the parents would head out in parties to the sea, ready to fish.

Indifferent to humans, they were easy to watch. They had no personal bubble and loved examining us as much as we loved examining them. We crouched down low, looked at them eye to eye and said goodbye.

# 67

*Villa Gesell, Argentina — January, by Brad*

"Just a little farther, I think I'm getting something." Sheena sat in the passenger seat, laptop open, as I slowly cruised down the main thoroughfare in a nondescript beach community on Argentina's Atlantic coast looking for an open Wi-Fi signal. "Here! Stop here!"

I broke out my laptop and we sat there in the front seats quickly catching up on emails before skipping town, when all of a sudden we heard thumping. We both stopped and listened, and as the seconds ticked past the thumping grew into a ground-shaking tremor of bass, and it was moving closer. *Kids these days, they call that music?* we thought. We saw the truck getting closer in the side mirrors. *They'll give driving licenses to just about anyone these days.*

As the truck passed its driver acted out a wild dance in time with the music, his entire body surging with the beat. One arm flailed out the window, alternating between raising the roof and air-spanking his imaginary dirty-dancing girlfriend. The truck passed, and as it did we couldn't help but notice the word emblazoned across the side: POLICE.

The officer slowed and made a turn into the dirt parking lot right in front of us, coming to rest in front of a police checkpoint. He swung his door open and remained seated. His speakers filled the dry air:

*Walkin' down the street in my new lafreak*

*Yeah*

*This is how I roll*

*Animal print pants, out of control*

*It's Redfoo with the big afro*

*And like Bruce Lee, I rock the club, yo!*

Soon, the entire police squad had emptied from the checkpoint building and were holding their bellies, laughing uncontrollably. The driver sat there, half of his body hanging out of his open door, his face hidden by a pair of aviator sunglasses. He had a comedic smirk on his face and his hand pumped up and down, patting the air while he bobbed his head.

*Ah girl look at that body*
*I work out!*
*Ah girl look at that body*
*I work out!*

The plates and cups on our shelf vibrated from the bass. The driver took it to a whole new level as he turned up the volume to 11 and got out of the truck, shaking his booty and air-spanking. A female cop joined him, dirty dancing there in the parking lot, shaking what her mother gave her. The two of them were going insane as the others' faces turned red from laughter.

*I got passion in my pants,*
*And I ain't afraid to show it (show it, show it, show it!)*
*I'm sexy and I know it...*
*I'm sexy and I know it.*

Finally the song ended and a new song came on. Like a cue to exit the stage the hip hop cop danced his way back to his truck, closed the door, bobbed his head a little. All of the other cops waved goodbye and bobbed their heads in unison. The officer then threw it in reverse, stepped on it, and proceeded to slam right into a big pine tree.

He fumbled with the radio knob, turned it off, and got out of his truck. The police all gathered around the back of the truck, shaking their heads. He may have destroyed the back of his Police-issue truck, but he was sexy. And he knew it.

By early afternoon we had arrived at the town of Villa Gesell, where we had decided to stop for some beach time and a little R&R

before delving too far into the hustle and bustle of Buenos Aires. We found a suitable parking spot in town and took to the streets. With an impending opportunity to send her souvenirs home, Sheena had one mission: to buy as many trinkets as possible, as quickly as possible.

We walked along the main street, admiring trinkets, walking through stores, and stopping for the occasional empanada from one of the ubiquitous street food vendors. As I devoured my empanada, I took note of Argentina's openness about the human body; as we passed a tattoo and piercing shop, I couldn't help but notice a sandwich board as tall as an eight year old right in the middle of the sidewalk, on which dozens of photographs depicted the various types of female nipple piercings that they offered. I inspected the sign as we passed, assuring Sheena that my interest was purely scientific, and noted that the male youth of Argentina lived a much more auspicious childhood than I had.

Before long I was exhausted with trinket shopping and longed for the wide open beach and the open water. "Sheeeeena," I whined, "can we go now?" She told me to stop acting like a baby, and then disappeared into a shop that sold baskets and other woven wicker items. I opted to wait outside where I could perform more science. After fifteen minutes I started to wonder what my wife was doing so I entered the basket shop.

Inside, Sheena chatted with the owner, a woman about my mother's age. She recounted to the woman the details of our trip and excitedly told her where we were off to next. The woman listened intently, smiling.

"This is great," she said. "I really wish I could do something like this. And one day I will!" She told us that she'd been in contact with lots of people who do things like us. After a while Sheena went back to looking at baskets, and the woman came over to help.

"I get these baskets in Panama," she said. "I buy them from the indigenous people and bring them back here to sell. My daughter lives in Panama, so it gives me a chance to visit her." We told her about our time in Panama, and mentioned that we had shipped from Panama to Colombia.

"Yes, I know that process well," she said. "Sometimes I help people who want to cross the Darien Gap. I help coordinate the logistical parts of it." She excitedly opened her computer and showed us her website. I felt like I'd seen it before. I watched from behind as she clicked on pictures of people standing next to shipping containers, all the while trying to place where I'd seen this site.

An idea crossed my mind, but I quickly threw it out. No possible way. I listened for a while longer as Sheena told her about our process and the lady nodded along. Could it be?

"Wait a minute," I interjected. The woman stopped and looked at me. I felt a little bit sheepish. "This is a really long shot, but...is your name Tea?"

She looked confused, like I was some kind of stalker. "Um...yes."

"Uh...Tea Kalmbach!?"

"Yes. I am Tea Kalmbach. How did you know?"

"Oh my god! You were our shipping agent!" Sheena looked at me, wide eyed, and then looked at Tea. We all looked at each other for several seconds trying to wrap our heads around the enormity of the coincidence. It had been seven months since we had shipped Nacho from Panama to Colombia, and we talked to Tea dozens of times over the phone and through email. We had thought that she lived in Buenos Aires. Her daughter was the one who had led us through traffic and accompanied us to the vehicle inspection yard in Panama City. She told us that she had been doing shipping logistics for seven or eight months, and that she had been disheartened early on because one of her early experiences had gone very badly. We kept quiet about it, because we assumed that she was talking about us, although she didn't know it. We bought some baskets, gave Tea another big hug, and left her store in a fit of laughter and waving.

Argentina, with its dirty dancing police officers, to die for grilled meats, spectacular wines and cheeses, perfectly flaky empanadas, its attractive men and women, and its carefree attitude, has proven to be the best capstone to our southerly drive that we could have hoped for. And if there were a grand wizard behind the curtain calling the shots, he couldn't have planned a more appropriate coincidental meeting to celebrate the fast approaching end to our drive through the Americas.

We walked back to Nacho, checked for any unexpected pine trees around the van, and made our way to the beach to celebrate our last stop before Buenos Aires.

# 68

*Buenos Aires, Argentina — February, by Brad*

It shouldn't have taken me as long as it did to realize that I was not sitting face to face with a stock broker, as I had been told, but with a boss in a money laundering ring. After five months of selling illegal currency on Argentina's black market I should have been less naïve, but clearly I was no more than a stable boy in this rodeo.

The building was nondescript, sandwiched between skyscrapers in downtown Buenos Aires, its windows mirrored and unmarked. The blank hallway on the fourth floor was punctuated by nothing more than a green button on one wall. The heavy deadbolt let out a metallic clunk, and we entered the office.

A deflated-looking receptionist sat on a flimsy chair behind a bare desk. The meeting room where we waited for the money launderer contained a cheap desk, four chairs, and a telephone. There wasn't a computer in the whole building and what furniture there was seemed rented and cheap; the place could be evacuated in no time flat if the cops showed up.

We handed the man our stack of US dollars, and he handed us a bigger stack of Argentine pesos. And just like that we saved $1,411, or 35%, on the price of the shipping container in which Nacho and two motorcycles would set off from Buenos Aires to travel across the high seas.

When it comes to beauty, Argentina comes up aces. We are envious of its mountains. We are envious of its rivers, streams, and its lakes. We are envious of its gorgeous women and its handsome men with their slender bodies, perfect faces, olive skin, and long, dark, voluminous hair. But when it comes to its economy, Argentina is in shambles, swirling faster and faster into an uncontrollable toilet dive. For this, we are not envious.

A few years ago, Argentina enjoyed a prosperous economy. Its currency was tied to the US dollar, trading one to one. The Argentine people vacationed to "cheap" places like Europe and the USA. Then, in a series of botched economic moves, Argentina devalued its currency, inflation became rampant, the government went through a bond default, and the people's bank accounts instantly vaporized. With unbridled inflation, the people began rebuilding their savings in US dollars; by keeping their savings in pesos, they would effectively lose ten, twenty, thirty percent per year due to inflation.

Then, in 2011, the government made it illegal to obtain US dollars in Argentina. This, of course, gave rise to a black market for US currency. When we arrived in Argentina five months prior, the official exchange rate between the peso and dollar was 4.7 to one. Since we had US dollars with us, we were in a position to sell our dollars on the black market to Argentine people who needed them. We made our first sale at 5.875 pesos to one dollar, effectively reducing the price of everything we would buy in Argentina by 25%. We would make a sale every week to keep up with inflation.

Sitting in the money launderer's bleak office in Buenos Aires five months later, we would make our last trade at 7.5 pesos to one dollar, while the official rate had only risen to 4.9. In five months, the peso had inflated 28%.

Over the course of our stay in Argentina, we would save over $2,000 by selling our dollars to ice cream shop owners, parking lot attendants, auto parts dealers, and money launderers. To use an ATM was to throw perfectly good money in the trash. The rivers and streams are pristine, the lakes and mountains are awe inspiring, the women and men are steamy hot, but there is no hope for Argentina's economy.

A few weeks prior to arriving in Buenos Aires, we had been in El Chalten, the town at the base of Mount Fitz Roy. While eating breakfast one morning, someone knocked on our door. It was Kevin, a Canadian motorcyclist who reads our blog; he had recognized Nacho and came over to say hello. We got to talking, and learned that he and his riding partner, Jan, were also nearing the end of their trip south.

"So what are you doing next?," he asked.

"Once we get to Buenos Aires we'll put Nacho on a ship to another continent and keep going," I said. He considered it for a moment, and then threw out an idea.

"Mind if we put our motorcycles in the container too?"

When we reached Buenos Aires, the four of us rented an apartment in the San Telmo neighborhood. It would serve as our basecamp while we drove around town for shipping broker meetings, customs visits, container loading, and meeting with money launderers. While we were at it, we decided we might as well see what the city had to offer, and to our delight Buenos Aires turned out to be totally excellent.

Day after day we explored the city. In La Boca we admired the urban art and street performers, in San Telmo we explored the antique market and sampled restaurants, we found an extensive beer cave in Microcentro, and explored the most elaborate graveyard on the planet in Recoleta.

On the very last day before loading our shipping container, I decided that Nacho needed some tender loving care. I cleaned our air filter and swapped out our water pump, which was on its last legs. Last, I wanted to give Nacho a bath so that he would be shiny for the new continent. First impressions are the key to long term success, right?. I filled a couple of buckets with water, grabbed some dish soap, and went down to the street, where Nacho awaited.

I cleaned up the front, side, and back of the van, and then moved to the last side, which faced the street. I set the bottle of soap on our folding chairs and went to work. A few seconds later I came back around, and found my soap in the planter, and our folding chairs missing.

Some rat bastard had stolen our weather-beaten, dry-rotted, faded, rickety folding chairs right in front of my eyes! He would have had to lug them a half a block before he'd be out of my sight, but I never saw a thing. I asked the bystanders at the bus stop, but they didn't see anything either. All I could do was shake my head. Why couldn't people just earn money the honest way, like the money launderer?

Finally, after 24,000 miles of driving through fourteen countries over the course of thirteen months, we drove Nacho one final time to the port. As we came to a stop inside of the shipping container, I glanced at the odometer; it read 299,999 miles. The very first order of business when we open the shipping container in a new land will be to roll this puppy over to 300k. Sounds like a good omen to the start of a new adventure.

# Part 6

# East or West

After about a week of sitting in our little cabin in Colombia, shielded from the outside world and hiding from the fact that our transmission had failed, Sheena confided in me, in no uncertain terms, that she was feeling defeated.

"Bradley," she had said, "I'm feeling defeated."

A moment's thought revealed that I, too, was feeling defeated. Our original harebrained plan had been to drive our 29 year old van all the way around the world, yet after having driven a smidgeon more than the length of Central America, we had destroyed our wheel bearings, brakes, axles, transmission, and our morale. On average, we were spending over $600 per month to keep Nacho on the road, and I was literally under the van every 200 miles fixing some major problem. Could we endure this for three years?

That day in the safety and seclusion of our little cabin we sketched out a new plan. Originally we had decided to drive to Argentina, and then ship to Asia, where we would continue driving around to Europe. We had assumed that the Americas would be an easy shakedown, and that when we hit Asia the real adventure would begin. This was supposed to be a warm up. We clearly knew nothing.

Our initial gut reaction was to drive back to Cartagena, put Nacho back on a ship, and go home. This made the most financial sense and would allow us to regain our sanity, which we had lost the moment Nacho voided his bowels on that Colombian mountain road. But what of the Andes? Patagonia? Tierra del Fuego? Could we leave all of that on the table?

We most decidedly could not.

Instead, we committed to finishing South America. We would do our best to patch Nacho up and limp along until we reached Ushuaia, at which point we would discuss our options. We would either ship Nacho home, or we would ship to Europe.

We had already lived in Europe, and knew it well. Going there would be easy, and we wanted something easy for a change. From

Europe we could start driving east, and the moment it got too difficult
— due to impermeable borders in the Middle East, the excessive cost of
driving a private car through China, spontaneously erupting civil war, or
a spontaneously combusting Nacho — we could always turn around and
come back to the comfort of Europe and then return home.

Asia seemed too big a commitment. Once we arrived there, we
figured we would pretty much have to keep going until we hit Europe.
No way. We needed an option with a bailout plan, so that day in
Colombia we decided that our choices would be to go home, or to go to
Europe.

But then a funny thing happened. After leaving Colombia our
mechanical problems pretty much disappeared. I later came to the
realization that most of our problems had occurred due to my allowing
inept Latin American mechanics to place their ravishing hands on our
poor Nacho. Once I committed to doing all of my own mechanical
work, and could ensure that everything was done correctly using the
proper tools, the world was good again.

By the time we hit Argentina, we had pretty much forgotten
about problems of all sorts. I was fluently speaking the local language,
the months passed while being punctuated only by mild and infrequent
mechanical hiccups, the food was good, there were shopping malls and
movie theaters and good roads and nice people. Sheena wondered aloud,
in no uncertain terms, if we really needed a break any more.

"Bradley," Sheena said one night in Argentina's Lakes District, "I
wonder if we really need a break any more."

She had a point: we'd had our break and we were over it. We
spent the last few months in South America living the easy life. Like a
couple of fools who fail to learn the lessons of history, we decided that
we were ready for a challenge.

On one hand there was Europe: modern, familiar, good food,
smooth roads, expensive.

On the other hand there was Asia: Exotic, restricted, the Middle East, Kalashnikovs, the Himalayas, sherpas, yaks, chanting, Iran, burkas, camels, elephants. We knew that once we got to Southeast Asia we would be trapped there by restricted land borders. And we knew that if somehow we made it to India we'd likely be stuck there by virtue of the fact that we're American, and getting across the Middle East would be no easy task. It was a disaster waiting to happen. Or it was the greatest adventure we could ever imagine. Could we afford to risk taking a route whose bailout plan would cause us to miss out on all of this?

The real adventure begins when we willingly go in without having any idea how we'll get back out.

The heat was stifling and my shirt clung to my skin like a wet blanket as I shuffled sideways in the dark. A stream of sweat stung my eyes as I located the lock, fumbled the key into it, and then opened the door. Stale heat oozed slowly out of the opening as I squeezed myself into the driver's seat. After thirty six days at sea the battery was nearly dead, but somehow the starter reached deep down and found the energy to turn over the reluctant engine, coaxing Nacho to life. The alternator belt squealed like a bloodthirsty banshee as I eased the transmission into reverse and slowly emerged from the shipping container into the humid air. The smell of palm trees and warm sea mixed together to create a perfume that hung in the air.

We had arrived in Malaysia.

Sheena smiled and pinched her fists against her sides to contain her excitement. A dark-skinned man directed me to a parking spot next to a dilapidated building, a bead of sweat formed on my brow, and as I came to rest the odometer turned over 300,000 miles.

*Continue the adventure at drivenachodrive.com*

*View a photo album from the journey at drivenachodrive.com/panamerican*

Made in the USA
San Bernardino, CA
28 July 2014